Rainbows, Bluebirds
and Buffleheads

RAINBOWS, BLUEBIRDS AND BUFFLEHEADS

DISCOVERING LIFE THROUGH BIRDS

BILL BEATTY

quarrier press

Charleston, WV

Quarrier Press
Charleston, WV

Cover and book design by Mark S. Phillips
Front and back cover photographs by Bill Beatty

10 9 8 7 6 5 4 3 2 1

Library of Congress Control Number: 2016-936910
ISBN 13: 978-1-942294-07-8
ISBN 10: 1-942294-07-7

Printed in USA

Distributed by:
West Virginia Book Company
1125 Central Avenue
Charleston, WV 25302
www.wvbookco.com

Dedicated to:
Greg Eddy, Dot Broemsen, and Glen Phillips
They helped, guided, and gently pushed me to be a better birder,
naturalist and person.

TABLE OF CONTENTS

PREFACE

All my life I have enjoyed wild things. As a boy I never stopped long enough to think about it. I just lived it...things just happened. As an adult I often reminisce about past times. I have a good memory and delight in thinking about the outdoor things I did as a boy; dissecting each activity in detail. The second chapter I write about killing a bird, and though it was an important and telling aspect of my young life, I thought it may not fit with everything else I wrote. It is graphic and sad. The rest of the book is happy and uplifting. I am the sum total of all my experiences so the story stayed. Then I didn't understand the feelings that erupted from killing that bird. Now I understand. The jigsaw puzzle I was, is being put together in the present.

During my childhood my friends and I had a freedom rarely found in today's children. We explored nearby meadows, woodlands and streams. We did good and bad things, often not able to sit still long enough to realize the difference. Most weekends during warm weather my Dad took me to wild and remote places where he and my uncles would fish and I would explore.

All the time out in the wild I was learning, but not

understanding. The ability to grasp all that I had done as a boy began during college in Plant Taxonomy class. I began to put names to things I remembered from my childhood. Also, the tough-guy exterior was giving in to my marshmallow heart. Seeing the bluebirds on the sumac berries shook me to the core and I had to deal with feelings that I always had, but kept hidden away from everyone including myself. The world around me appeared to be changing, but it hadn't. It was me that was changing.

I've heard it said that every seven years we are new… biologically, that all the cells present seven years ago have been replaced. Butterflies transform from caterpillars and frogs from tadpoles. I too have changed physically, spiritually and soulfully. Hiking up hills to ridge tops and down again carrying binoculars, tripod and camera has kept me fit. Standing atop Dolly Sods and looking into the starry sky, hearing the sacred song of the hermit thrush, or perhaps watching a screech-owl hatch from its egg I am overcome with the "feeling." All goes blank as I contemplate age old questions: who am I and why am I here. I am the sum total of all my experiences and I am here to share them with those who want to know about wild things and wild places. I feel obligated to relate what has been related to me, to pay it forward.

I have learned much; not only about birds, but other nature topics as well. My time alone in wild places is abundant. I feel very fortunate for the opportunities. But I am most fortunate for those who were kind to me and helped and guided me in different ways. Greg Eddy, my Geology professor at West Liberty State College, had probably the greatest impact due to his persistence in urging me to continue with birds by going with him and his wife Ann on early morning bird walks, introducing me to the Brooks Bird Club, and being instrumental in me obtaining the naturalist job at Oglebay Institute's Brooks Nature Center in Oglebay Park. Dorothy (Dot) Broemsen encouraged me and introduced me to mnemonics. She and I worked together, encouraged each other and laughed together for 18 years...and we continue to do so today. She is a wonderful friend and special person. Glen Phillips, birder extraordinaire, introduced me to Christmas Bird Counts, Breeding Bird Surveys, Point Counts and insisted on me chasing birds with him. I learned so much from him.

I have been fortunate to work my entire adult life in nature-related careers: as a naturalist, teacher, writer and photographer, thanks in great part to these three people. The best way to learn about birds is to go out with others who know. The Brooks Bird Club and its many members, past and present, were also instrumental in my learning, interests, and successes. I am not just the culmination of my own experiences, but also the experiences and mentors of others who helped me along the way. They led, they taught, they shared and influenced me in ways I could never have dreamed of. Today they live in me as I share and teach. Everyone should be so fortunate. Thanks to you all.

A special thanks to Jan Runyan and Bev Beatty for editing my written thoughts into proper grammar and structure.

When I think about all the birding experiences throughout my life I realize that most have taken place in West Virginia, the Mountain State and am reminded of a poem:

HILL HUNGER
by Lillian Mayfield Roberts

I think that something in the hill child dies when he is
    taken to the level lands;

A man bred by the ocean understands, and he will tell you
    that his sick heart sighs

For hiss of surf and all his being cries for roar of waves and
    spray upon his hands.

Ever beneath his weary feet the sands, ever a sail before his
    searching eyes.

And so, I think the hill child always sees that broken line
    inked in against the skies,

Where saffron sunset drops to meet the trees upon the
    hilltop and the nighthawk flies,

And when his mind cannot recapture these I think that
    something in the hill child dies.

RAINBOW BIRDS

The rows of houses where I grew up formed a maze. It was what some people called "the Projects" and others referred to as "Defense Homes". Streets looped around long rows of attached white houses. They were built for the Westinghouse workers during World War II. With 500 families in the Projects, there were lots of people...lots of kids. We never had problems having too few kids when we played baseball or football. I had lots of "best" friends.

When I was about six, birds suddenly became a focal point for a few of us. I think it initially had to do with dead birds we occasionally found.

We devised methods to get as close as possible to different kinds of wild creatures. We may have learned our techniques from older boys in the neighborhood or perhaps from a parent or neighbor. Starlings and pigeons were the most conspicuous birds, but we also knew robins, redbirds, wild canaries and crows. Decorating the peaks of most row house roofs were long lines of pigeons and starlings. They adorned electric lines and telephone poles. Enormous flocks appeared, disappeared, and then reappeared in courtyards feeding in a frenzy between the row houses. Each bird's movements were deliberate yet mechanical in appearance. Both the starlings and pigeons seemed like toys when they walked, as if someone had wound them up with a special key and, when released, the inner spring caused them to walk in a jerking motion with their heads out of sync with their feet.

"Look at the rainbow on that bird!" I yelled.

Dead on the sidewalk was a starling. As we moved, or when we moved it, the colors we saw would change. The feathers were all black. But these black feathers also glowed with different shades of green and purple.

"How can there be a rainbow on a bird?" Jerry asked.

"God made it that way," Ed remarked.

"That's true," I added, "the Bible says so."

"Do you read the Bible?" Ed asked.

"Not really. My grandmother told me about it," I answered.

We questioned everything that amazed us and shared our explanations for the wonders we encountered. Arguments frequently arose over the varied interpretations. But when God was reasoned to be the answer, no argument ensued.

We had incredible patience when it came to trapping birds. With a cardboard box, roll of kite string and stick in hand, Ed and I went about our business of setting the trap. One end of the box was propped high off the ground with the stick. Securing the string to the bottom of the stick, we carefully unrolled the ball across the lawn and around the corner of the building. A crust of bread was torn into small pieces as bait and placed beneath the box.

"Pigeons must really be dumb," I said. "They sit up there watching us and looking at the trap. They even watch us bait the trap."

Ed responded, "They're either really dumb or really hungry."

For a time the pigeons were content to stay on the rooftop watching the bread crumbs far below. Frequently peeking around the corner, Ed and I watched as two pigeons finally flew down.

"You know they can see us," Ed said. He continued, "Even when they aren't looking at us, they can see us."

We knew that sneaking up on a pigeon was impossible. Trying to hit one with a rock was just as fruitless. Still we tried. From far behind we had waited until the bird wasn't looking and quickly raised a hand to throw, but always, in the blink of an eye, the pigeon was airborne and gone.

"Shhh! Look, one's heading into the trap. Don't pull until it's all the way in."

Ed whispered, "Okay, okay, be quiet," and then yelled, "IT'S IN. WE GOT IT!"

We ran to the box as fast as we could. Past experiences had taught us that a pigeon thrashing in the box could raise it just enough to escape.

Holding the box tightly to the ground, I asked, "Do you want to do it or do you want me to?"

One of us would push down on the top of the box, while the other would go after the pigeon. Being the first to touch the bird was highly desired. Being able to get a good strong grip on it and successfully remove the bird from under the box conveyed hero-like status. The downside was that if the bird escaped, you became the scapegoat for days to come.

This day we both would share in the victory or the defeat. Like surgeons brandishing scalpels, we methodically began extricating the pigeon from under the box. If we raised the box too high, the pigeon would squeeze out the bottom. My arm slithered in from one end; Ed's arm from the other. Holding our captive firmly against the ground, we tossed aside the box and our two remaining hands surrounded the trembling bird.

"Look at the rainbows!"

Rainbows glistening from the feathers never ceased to fascinate us. We touched them, blew on them, and made the colors shift and change with each minor movement. Other wonders of the pigeon world were also discovered. They rarely bite and, when they do, it doesn't hurt. Boy and girl pigeons hide their parts in secret places—we never found them. Pigeons have incredible dandruff. And they're a lot warmer than we are.

On hot summer days, when the heavens opened and rain poured down, my friends and I raced through the neighborhood like water sprites, dancing through every puddle, heads tilted back, mouths agape. Raindrop after raindrop rolled down our throats. Running across a lawn we slid and fell, splashing water everywhere. Rivulets of water swelled with each added raindrop. We raced leaf boats, built dams, and gloried in the magic of water. Soaked and muddied, we were true to our passion: to experience life and delight in one another.

Then suddenly someone would shout, "The sun!"

Savoring the moment, almost too excited to breathe, we turned our backs to the advancing specter of heat and light to survey the sky.

"I see it, there it is!" "I see it, too!"

Each of us found it necessary to verify the presence of the rainbow as its color exploded across the sky. We felt privileged to witness this marvel of the ages. Our shouts became mere whispers as we leaned towards a nearby ear to speak. Outstretched arms with pointed fingers shrunk back in recognition of this holy moment. All too soon the magic of the moment faded from the sky, signaling the beginning of another round of *the Great Rainbow Debate*.

Mystery cloaked our interpretation of the significance of rainbows.

"Do you think there's really a pot of gold at the end of every rainbow?" Mike asked.

"Sure there is, but I'd never go look for it," I answered.

"Why not?" Ed responded.

I explained, "My grandmother says that if you find the gold and the rainbow disappears while you're there, you disappear with it."

"My Uncle Ken says that it's not gold. It's counterfeit money, printed by leprechauns. You'd get arrested if you tried to spend it," Ron added.

"No, it's gold alright, but it's one big piece and can't be moved."

"If you touch it you turn to gold."

"You're all wrong; it's a trap to catch people. Leprechauns are cannibals."

"No, they aren't; they're friendly." We ranted on and on, debating rainbows, leprechauns and gold.

Once, just after a rainbow had diminished from the sky, Ron said, "Sometimes my dad calls my mom Rainbow. He says it as if it's her name."

"What's your mom's real name?" I asked.

"Her name's Iris," Ron responded, "but she doesn't like it. Nobody calls her that."

"Does she like to be called Rainbow?" I asked.

"I don't know. But she likes it when my dad says she brightens his day like a rainbow," he answered.

Thinking about the marvel and majesty of what we had observed, I said, "I think anyone would like being compared to a rainbow."

Rainbows appeared and thrilled us when we least expected

them: in the mist from a garden hose, in an oil bull's-eye spilled on the road, in soap bubbles, in a water droplet on the eye of a fly, and radiating from the feathers of starlings and pigeons.

WHAT ARE YOU WAITING FOR?

Some of my closest friends had BB guns. In order to be one of the gang, I had to accept and use one. Our parents would have been horrified about some of the things we did, but of course we had our allegiance of boyhood honor and never told an adult about our escapades.

Along a distant railroad siding, an abandoned factory loomed like a sleeping giant just begging to be explored. From the outside it appeared lifeless: rusty, dirty, paint chipping and falling away everywhere you looked. Weeds and trash covered the cracked concrete paving. Many of its 100s of windows were cracked or broken.

Inside, the building was exciting. There was row after row of motionless machines. Great storage tanks towered above everything like silent, vigilant guardians. The tanks were linked one to another with unending catwalks high above the floor. Initially we explored the new territory, racing on the catwalks, pushing buttons and pulling every lever we could find. We even swung from storage tank to storage tank using the many chains that hung from the girders of the roof.

This satisfied us for a while, but soon BB tag became our obsession. And, boy did it hurt! No one wanted to be tagged by a BB! There was always a yelp and a welt to prove that someone had been tagged. For us, the incentive of pain if you were tagged, only added to our enthusiasm for the game. Our only rules were that you couldn't leave the building and no shooting anyone above the waist.

Once I was hit in the ear, and it hurt for days. Fortunately, our parents never found out and nobody was ever seriously injured. BB gun tag gave us familiarity with the weapons that would later lead to a very uncomfortable situation for me.

As far back as I can remember wild creatures have been a part of my life, but the circumstances I often found myself in created great confusion. As with most young people, peer pressure dictated my life more than my own desires did. Inside, my heart was a marshmallow when it came to frogs, birds and furry animals. But on the outside I wanted to appear tough and uncaring just like the vast majority of my friends. Great emotional sacrifices were made to achieve this goal of appearing to be a tough guy. My success at being "one of the gang" surprised even me.

I grew to hate BB guns. Most often our targets wore feathers. Usually the birds we pursued would escape unharmed. Occasionally one was killed and I would yell and rejoice along with everyone else. Inside I was dying.

BB guns are grossly inaccurate. The BB curves and deviates sometimes as much as several feet from where it is aimed. One boy had a BB pistol that basically couldn't hit the broad side of a barn. But I remember one day that it did kill.

Standing in the woods with a group of my friends, I pointed the gun toward the treetops and fired. Birds flocking in the trees took to the wing in different directions—all except one. Horrified, I watched as one bird fluttered for a short distance and then fell. I ran to it and found it still very much alive. Shiny black with brilliant red and yellow bars on each wing, it was beautiful. Breathing very heavily, it was turning its head in all directions as we surrounded it. Its eyes were full of fear. I didn't want to hurt it anymore and I was relieved that it wasn't dead.

Then the inevitable happened. The taunts began, "Kill it. Hurry up, kill it. What are you waiting for? Cm'on, kill it."

My stomach sickened and my heart cried out, "Please, oh please, help me God. I don't want to kill it. Oh God, I'm sorry." My mind raced trying to find a way out of this awful dilemma. My heart or my friends? The bird or the group?

I pressed the barrel against the bird's body, closed my eyes and pulled the trigger. When I opened my eyes the bird was still alive, but it was bleeding.

"Shoot it again," someone yelled. I did and this time it stopped moving. It was dead.

From that day on, I always had an excuse when the BB guns were brought out: "No, I'm going to play some basketball," or "I have to be home soon." Never again did I join the BB gun games.

Thoughts of killing that bird have haunted me ever since; even today I can recall every detail of the awful event and my anguished feelings. It is a regret I will carry with me all the days of my life. It cost the life of one of God's creatures to teach me to think before I follow the dictates of the group and that the most important thing for me to go along with is my own set of values.

WOLF CREEK

The only outdoor interest my father actively pursued was fishing. Fortunately, he also insisted that I like fishing. And I did, sort-of. My father began taking me with him when I was six years old. What I actually liked most wasn't the fishing itself, but the being outside in wild places. Almost always we went to the same two fishing destinations very near Slippery Rock, Pennsylvania. Most often my Dad, uncles, childhood friends and I went to Wolf Creek, a medium sized, small-mouthed bass stream. Today a portion of the area is a Nature Conservancy Property known as the Wolf Creek Narrows and another part is owned by Slippery Rock University.

I knew few birds that early in my life, but I was very aware of them. My father and uncles were "sit-and-talk" fishermen, but I could only sit so long. From somewhere I had obtained the explorer gene. I had to move, find and see.

My father and I always went through a routine shortly after arriving at Wolf Creek. At first we would settle in and start fishing, but soon I would stand up and say, "I'm going to go and see what I can find downstream."

Right away my father would answer with, "Don't go too far. And I want you back here for lunch."

The unspoken agreement was, "You can go and fool around all you want before and after lunch, but I want you to be here for lunch." I believe it was my father's way of keeping an eye on me without really keeping an eye on me.

Wearing my fishing vest and carrying my rod, minnow seine and bucket, I was soon on my way downstream, fishing as I explored. Often I caught a movement from the corner of my eye and spun to see a giant, long-legged bird flying away from me. It was the biggest bird I had ever seen. What fascinated me most was that it seemed to fly in slow motion. The large wings would pull at the air as the bird gained height and moved forward.

The languid movements made time seem to slow down so that each moment seemed like a second and a few seconds seemed like a minute. It never landed where I could see it. Instead it followed the stream and disappeared around the next bend. And that is where I would almost always find it. At the next bend I only caught that movement in the corner of my eye again and then watched the bird in slow motion, as it slowly got airborne and escaped. Time and again, with each trip to Wolf Creek, year after year I witnessed this giant bird and its slow motion flights. It provided me with hours of fun and training.

There were times my explorations took me away from the creek, sometimes following a feeder stream to its source and then trail blazing through a woodland to where I thought I could find Wolf Creek again farther downstream. After one of these explorations I was resting on a high bank overlooking the creek when my giant bird landed in a shallow open inlet on the other side of the creek. I dared not move. It stood motionless for a long time before taking several long cautious steps into slightly deeper water.

Usually my patience was limited, but on this occasion I was immobile for a very long time. The bird seemed like a statue, not moving at all. The body looked fat and heavy, but everything else about the bird was streamlined. The bill was long and narrow and appeared to be very sharp. Thin, black feathers pointed out from the back of the head. It had a long S-shaped curved neck and long skinny legs.

The shape and behavior all seemed very odd to me. I wasn't used to seeing any kind of animal be still for such a long time. At one point I thought, "Maybe the bird fell asleep." In a startling almost instantaneous motion the bird thrust its long narrow bill, head, and neck into the water. It shook its head violently, and then stood upright again. Hanging from its mouth was a large frog, still very much alive and pushing against the bird's bill. For about a minute as the bird was still again, the only movements were from the frog struggling to get free.

As if things couldn't get any more bizarre, suddenly the bird flipped the frog in the air and caught it. It did this several times. After a final toss, it caught the frog headfirst with the head and body wholly in its bill and mouth, legs sticking out. Then with one jerking gulp the bird swallowed the frog. I was stunned, barely believing what I had seen.

Once after observing the huge bird on a mud flat I found myself fishing from the same area and noticed the large four-toed footprints the bird left behind. Many times later I would see these now-familiar footprints. When my Dad and I saw the bird, he would always call it, "some kind of crane." After I began birding I discovered it was a great blue heron I had been chasing and these memories flooded me all over again.

My father was afraid of snakes. I remember him removing

a snake from our yard on the end of a rake but not harming it. Still he couldn't tolerate being near them. Wolf Creek had lots of snakes and I loved it. My father wanted me to fish, but tolerated other activities since I was such an expert at catching lots of good bait for him. I was born to seine. With a seine in my hands I was in my element. Many times I disappeared with my seine and minnow bucket returning later with a bucket-load of large minnows, soft-shelled crayfish, and over-sized hellgrammites.

One time I caught a large water snake and wanted to keep it for a time. Into the minnow bucket it went. As I got nearer to where they were fishing I heard my dad say, "There's Bill. Now we will have some real bait!" As soon as the minnow bucket hit the ground and my dad lifted the lid, my snake leaped out, coiling and unwinding as it thrashed around on the ground, then slithered toward the creek trying to escape. My dad and uncles, who were between the snake and the water, danced around bumping and pushing into each other trying to avoid it.

Once the snake was swimming away in the water, my dad scowled at me and said, **"Don't you ever do that again!"** If I hadn't been supplying him with good bait, I think he might not have allowed me to take the seine and minnow bucket again.

All this took only a minute to happen, but to hear my dad tell it, "The snake was chasing us for a long time, trying to bite us."

I would rebut his story explaining, "The snake was only trying to escape and you all were in its way."

Most of the snakes I saw tried to escape so it was easy just to reach and grab them by the tail, but some of the larger water snakes I caught were very aggressive and tried to bite.

I developed my own way of dealing with the larger snakes. Grabbing the tail, I swung the snake between my legs, closed my legs holding the snake between my thighs, and slowly pulled the snake backward towards me. Once the head was touching the back of my thighs I could safely grab the neck behind the head.

From a distance my dad once saw me do this and later told me, "I don't know what you were doing with that snake you had, all that jumping and dancing around. Whatever it was, please do it when I'm not around."

I think my dad knew he couldn't keep me from catching snakes, but he could control where I did it to some extent.

Many years later I took my dad to Wolf Creek. Usually we walked along trails through the woods to our favorite fishing spots but this day we decided to walk the creek and catch some bait along the way. Right at the creek's edge I spotted a large northern water snake coiled against the base of a tree. I pointed it out to my dad.

"Let's get away from that thing," he said.

"No," I said, "I want to show you something." Approaching the snake from the stream so I was between it and the most obvious route of escape, I said, "I want to show you how I catch snakes."

"I don't think you should do this. Let's just go fishing," he said.

I answered, "It'll only take a minute."

"Are you sure it's not poisonous?" he asked.

"It's safe. This will be easy," I said.

Since the snake was coiled, I got as close as I could and waved my left hand off to the side to get it to raise its head. As the snake moved its head toward my hand I quickly snatched at the head with my right hand. I had successfully used this technique dozens of times. But this time I was a tiny bit too slow. Faster than the eye could follow, the snake turned toward my grabbing hand, sank its teeth into me directly between my thumb and pointer finger and held on. The look on my dad's face was one of horror. I remained calm as I pried the snake's mouth from my hand and then carefully released it toward the creek.

My dad needed reassurance. "This has never happened before," I said. "I would never try this with a poisonous snake. I must be getting slower."

He responded with, "Are you sure you are okay? I think we should find a doctor."

By his tone and his look, I was sure the kind of doctor he might have been referring to was a psychiatrist. My hand was dripping blood, alarming my dad. I tried explaining that the northern water snake's saliva contains a mild anticoagulant which can cause the bite to bleed more than other snake bites. Every time he looked at my hand he would say something pertaining to the bleeding, or that maybe the snake was poisonous, or why in the world would anyone do such a thing. I wrapped my hand in a paper towel. More than an hour later as we stood side-by-side fishing, he looked at the bloody paper towel and we had the same conversation all over again.

"Are you sure you are alright?"

"Yes, I'm fine."

"Maybe we should take you to a doctor. You're still bleeding."

"The bleeding will stop soon."

Earlier I had reassured him that the bleeding would stop shortly but it hadn't, so he was not inclined to trust what I was saying. Later the bleeding did stop and we had a wonderful rest of the day fishing together.

There were other birds I saw along Wolf Creek, but as a

youngster their identification was beyond me. As I fished, they flew above my head, caught insects and then landed on some nearby overhanging branch. From the highest branches came birds darting after insects way above my head and sometimes I saw hints of red and yellow. In later visits as an adult, I saw all these same birds, but now they had names and were more familiar: American redstart, flycatchers, and cedar waxwing.

After becoming a birder and returning to Wolf Creek, it seemed to me as though the bird fauna had changed: it was much more diverse than when I was a young. But it hadn't changed at all. I was the one who had changed. I was more diverse.

Fishing was fun but, unlike my dad, I had my limits. My dad didn't venture far downstream like I did. It was a long, slow, slippery, strenuous hike. At times I would hike the entire 2.5 miles to where Wolf Creek entered Slippery Rock Creek. So after catching a few fish with my dad I would say, "I think I am going to head out and fish farther downstream—see what's down there." And I would go off chasing more than just fish.

There were two other birds I remember from my childhood at Wolf Creek. One I used to watch for long periods of time. Not that I made any kind of effort to watch; it was just a coincidence. I would be fishing and a kingfisher would show up. Sometimes I saw it arrive, but most often it flew in without me noticing it. As quickly as it arrived it would be gone again, rattling as it flew farther away along the stream.

On rare occasions a kingfisher would stay and compete with me for the fish. The kingfisher wanted a fish small enough to swallow. My goal was to catch a fish much larger than the bird itself. I remember one who made many unsuccessful attempts to catch a fish. For every fish it caught, it missed nine others. There were others that were more successful. They would dive perhaps seven times to catch three fish. The kingfishers nested in the banks of the streams, high above the water level. I saw them enter their holes in the dirt many times, usually carrying fish to feed their babies. Although I was tempted to approach the holes and reach in, I never did.

Only once do I remember tampering with a nest and it was not a good experience. I was in a woodland near the projects where I grew up and I saw a bird's nest. I wanted to see what was in it. I climbed the tree and pulled the top of the tree toward me. Not being quite able to see inside, I tipped it even farther. An egg rolled out and broke on my chest. It smelled so bad I almost vomited. All the way home I was heaving. When I went into the house my mother couldn't be near me without gagging. She called my grandmother who lived nearby. My grandmother came right over, took me outside and hosed me off. The only other time I remember heaving like that was when I was sprayed by a skunk. I believe the rotten egg experience made me more careful—I learned by that mistake to be more wary of bird's nests.

Another nearby place we fished was Cooper's Lake. It was about 10 acres and most of the time we had it all to ourselves. The lake couldn't be seen from any road. A small stream that had been diverted to wash gravel fed into the lake through a large cattail swamp. We knew about the lake from talking to an older gentleman, Mr. Cooper, who owned the gravel company.

He invited us to fish there and said, "I stocked it years ago and there are some pretty big fish in there."

That's all my dad had to hear. My favorite area of Cooper's Lake was the cattail swamp, but my dad avoided the marshy area. It was muddy and difficult to traverse. My dad always wore waders that stuck in the mud making it challenging to walk as his foot almost pulled out of the boot. I wore GI boots and camo pants so when my foot went into the mud I could easily pull it out and continue.

For me the most difficult parts of the swamp were the large spider webs I had to walk through and the birds. At certain times of the year birds swooped so close to the top of my head that I would hold a hand in front of my face to protect my eyes. These birds were noticeable, not only because of their behavior, but because they were a beautiful rich black all over except for bright red wing patches bordered by a thin row of yellow.

By the time I arrived at the opening where the swamp met the lake I was a sight. I could feel sticky webs covering my face and there were spiders crawling all over me. The spiders never bothered me but trying to clear the tenacious invisible webs from my face was annoying. The oddest part of my appearance was the yellow powder all over my head, face and upper body. At a later time I would discover that the powder was pollen from the flowering cattail heads and the birds were red-wing blackbirds. Even now I can visualize those days in the cattail swamp and hearing the male red-wings scolding me as they clung to the tops of the cattails blowing in the wind.

On those childhood fishing trips, I always loved to seine for bait and other creatures and was most excited when I caught something unusual: a frog, giant tadpole, perhaps a turtle or snake and, once, even a young muskrat. And the birds always caught my attention although they were always out of reach. What I didn't realize at the time, but know now, was that I was growing into birds.

"SPECIAL PROBLEMS"

My last semester of college was in the spring of 1972. One course required for my biology major was titled "Special Problems". The faculty suggested I do a winter bird survey of the college arboretum. No one had ever done a bird study of the area and the fact that I didn't know anything about birds didn't seem to matter.

The term "spring" semester is a misnomer, since the semester actually began in the dead of winter. Other biology majors started their research when the warmer temperatures began to return sometime in March. Afterwards they would scramble to interpret their data and would work feverishly to write their papers so they could turn everything in before the semester ended in May. Having observed that, I wanted to begin my research right away.

The one drawback I had to doing any kind of activity akin to "bird watching" was my ego. Attitudes formed as I was growing up in a housing project presented me occasional problems in my college years and beyond. Chasing birds was not the "manly/tough guy" image to which I had become accustomed. Thinking about it logically I knew there was nothing wrong with me chasing after birds, but somehow it just didn't feel right.

Still harboring this ambivalent attitude, I gathered my supplies and began the bird survey. While I did have a pair of binoculars hiding in my closet, they had never been used to look at birds. The *Birds of North America* guide I used was borrowed from the campus library.

On my first day of the survey I hiked to an open field. At the far end of the field I could see movement in a line of short staghorn sumac trees. Through binoculars I saw bright scarlet berry clusters on the ends of most branches and on several berry clusters were vivid blue birds with orange breasts. At that moment, to my surprise, I didn't care what kind of birds they were. What did matter was that I had never seen anything so amazingly beautiful before. As I had hiked to the field earlier, everything had been a mix of wintry grays, browns, and blacks against a white snowy background. All of a sudden here were bright scarlet, blue, and orange. I was hooked. Although the biology faculty's requirement was to do just nine surveys of three different habitats, I did a total of 24.

Each survey took about three hours to complete. The three habitats surveyed were a meadow, wild black cherry/ American elm woodland and mature beech woods.

After three days of surveys I thought, "I hope I am doing this right."

My advisor was on the Special Problems committee so I went to his office for some advice. After a half hour of discussion he said, "I don't think there is anyone in the Biology Dept. who knows anything about identifying and surveying birds, but Dr. Eddy in the Geology Department is a bird watcher. Maybe he can help."

Dr. Eddy had been my instructor in both Physical and Historical Geology. He had introduced me to spelunking, fossil hunting and rock formations on geology field trips.

And I remembered him wandering off on those trips with binoculars in hand as we students broke rocks and looked for fossils along road cuts.

The day finally arrived when Dr. Eddy was to go with me. I was nervous. Suddenly I remembered an event that had happened a few months earlier. Several of his former students were at a table in the Student Union talking one evening when Dr. Eddy had come over and sat down. He and his wife had just had their first child, a boy who they named Graham. I had asked what the middle name was.

"I don't like middle names. He won't have one," he had said.

Someone suggested "Cracker" and we had all laughed. Dr. Eddy didn't seem to find it as amusing and had gotten up and left. I knew that Dr. Eddy was a matter of fact kind of person but with a sense of humor. Would he hold a grudge?

When we met, he looked at me head-to-toe, as if sizing me up...for something. At least, that is how it seemed to me, possibly because I was so anxious. Off we went. Getting to my first survey area, a meadow, required descending a long hill, crossing a stream and making a steep climb to a plateau overlooking the campus.

When we arrived at the meadow I said, "What I do is see all the birds I can and list them for this habitat."

Dr. Eddy said nothing. After about 45 minutes at the meadow, we headed toward the wild black cherry/American elm woodland. I led and Dr. Eddy followed. I repeated what I had done at the meadow: looked around carefully, and then listed all the birds I saw.

Finally, I got up the nerve to ask him, "Well, what do you think about what I am doing?"

He answered, "I think you're nuts!"

I was shocked and confused. I didn't know what to think or say.

He noticed my bewilderment and asked, "Aren't you cold?"

"What do you mean?" I asked.

He answered, "In case you haven't noticed, there is a foot of snow on the ground, it's 20 degrees and it's windy…and your shoes are low-cut, soaking wet, and you have meager clothing on for a day like today, especially to be out for hours."

"Well, yes, thinking about it, I am cold, but these are the warmest clothes I have, and this is something I have to do." Then I asked, again, "What do you think about what I am doing," and added…"with my bird survey?"

He asked, "What about the songs?"

"What songs?" I asked.

He answered, "Don't you hear some birds singing and making noises while you are out doing these surveys?"

"Yes, sometimes I hear that," I said.

"Unless you report, not only the birds you see, but also those you hear, your surveys are not valid," he said.

I laughed, thinking this was his attempt at joking around, making me feel at ease after his, "I think you're nuts," comment. But it wasn't; he was serious, and I again was confused and a bit panicky.

"How can anybody know that?" I asked.

"It takes a long time and a lot of work," he answered. He suggested I go to the library and borrow records of bird songs. He also invited me to a winter bird count at Oglebay Park not far from the college. I spent a lot of time in the next few weeks listening to bird songs and studying that bird book.

My bird surveys were laborious because I didn't know the identification of many birds. Cardinals I knew, although they had always been referred to as "red birds." A bird landing on the side of a tree made me immediately think "woodpecker." I was right; it was a downy woodpecker. With each "new" bird I encountered, I would leaf through the pages of the field guide looking at drawings. Song sparrows, tufted titmice and chickadees were all new to me.

In the mature beech woods on a cold day with the temperature around 10 degrees, I saw a tiny bird flitting about in some gnarled roots and thick shrubbery. As I watched the bird I thought, "How can anything so tiny and so active survive on this cold wintry day?" I had just seen my first winter wren.

Minutes later my attention was drawn to some high-pitched sounds far above the ground in the dry leafy branches of an old beech tree. I spotted another tiny bird, a golden-crowned kinglet. The excitement I had doing these surveys didn't allow me time to think about my meager clothing. I was cold, but I was having too much fun to care.

My first pileated woodpecker reminded me of the sounds from the Tarzan movies I watched as a young boy. What a spectacular bird and song! The ruffed grouse exploded from a nearby location in a burst of furiously flapping wings that made my heart feel as if it were lodged in my throat, beating uncontrollably. As a youngster I had heard the grouse drumming far off and thought some poor guy was trying to start his mower, but instead of running smoothly, it would run for a short time and sputter to a stop. Red-bellied woodpeckers were a quandary since I could never find red on their bellies. Sometime later when I held one in my hand I finally understood. The white-breasted nuthatch appeared streamlined as it slowly and deliberately circled down the tree in an upside-down spiral, its long slender beak probing the tree's bark for hidden insects and spiders.

One day I noticed in the college's weekly newspaper that Dr. Eddy would be leading early morning bird walks every Tuesday until the end of the semester. The walks began at 7:00, lasted an hour, and everyone was welcome. That first walk, all the birds we heard and saw were familiar to me, with the exception of one.

We were below a large stand of mixed white pine and Norway spruce bordering the college reservoir when Dr. Eddy said, "I hear grosbeaks and there are a lot of them."

No sooner had he gotten the words from his mouth when a large flock of robin-sized yellow, black and white birds descended on and into the evergreens. They were beautiful. Most birds on my survey routes were the same muted colors of the wintry landscape but these were bright yellow in places, a brilliant contrast to the green spruce and pine needles in which they moved.

Dr. Eddy asked me, "Do you know what kind of birds these are?"

"You said they were grosbeaks," I answered.

"Yes, but what kind of grosbeak?"

Checking my field guide, I answered that they were evening grosbeaks.

"Boy do they hurt when they bite," Dr. Eddy said.

"They bite people?" I asked a bit confused.

"Only when you have one in your hand," he answered.

"How in the world does a bird like that end up in someone's hand," I wondered.

"Do you know what bird banding is?" he asked.

I didn't know.

"Maybe I can show you sometime," he said.

One of Dr. Eddy's bird walks yielded a bird called a yellowlegs and I discovered how difficult it can be to identify certain birds. It turned out there are two different kinds of yellow legs: a greater and a lesser. After some discussion and rechecking the bird several times with binoculars Dr. Eddy asked, "Bill, what do you think?"

If I had answered honestly I might have replied, "You must be crazy for asking me. I have no idea." Instead I responded, "I can see it's a yellowlegs. Which one, I don't know." It did feel good that I was asked. With every bird walk I felt more and more comfortable and was learning a lot about birds.

All of Dr. Eddy's early morning bird walks were attended by only three people, him, his wife Anne, and me...except for one walk. One morning only Anne and I were there: Dr. Eddy forgot to come.

BROOKS BIRD CLUB COUNT

The Oglebay Park bird walk that Dr. Eddy had invited me
to was sponsored by the Brooks Bird Club. People met at the
Brooks Nature Center at 8:00 and everyone was to meet back
at noon to report their results. I was surprised that there were
over 20 people there. Everyone was milling around talking
about birds but soon they began to break into smaller groups,
deciding where in the park they would go. The goal was to
cover as much of the 1,700 acres as possible.

Dr. Eddy took me by the arm and said, "There is someone
I would like you to meet. You can go with him on today's
count." The man's name was Glen Phillips and he was a very
serious birder. It was all business with him. He worked as
a lineman for a local utility company and according to him,
"birds are my life...I love birds." The other person in our
group was Dorothy Broemsen, who everybody referred to as
"Dot". Little did I know at the time that both of these people
would become great friends of mine as well as important
influences in my life.

Like most winter days in the 1970s, it was cold and
snowy—lots of snow on the ground with more falling. Glen
and Dot had decided to survey an area below the Nature

Center. Most of the time we walked quietly and stopped occasionally, especially when a bird was calling. Glen would identify the bird, Dot would confirm it and record it on a checklist and I would observe. I didn't say much but I sure paid attention. What surprised me most were how many birds we encountered that were the same as those from my surveys at the college: cardinals, Carolina chickadees, tufted titmice, song sparrows, red-bellied woodpeckers and others. But on this walk most were identified by the sounds they made.

Sometimes all that was heard was one note and that note translated into a downy woodpecker or perhaps a white-breasted nuthatch.

At one point Glen said, "Now that chickadee is a black-capped. Its "chick-a-dee-dee-dee" song is noticeably slower than that of the Carolina."

In between stops we were noisy, but we couldn't help it: the combination of single digit temperatures and "frozen" snow made each step scream a crunching sound, as if to say, "Here we are! Over here!"

When we stopped it was peacefully quiet and beautifully snowy with no sounds except an intermittent birdcall or slight gust of wind. The Caddy Camp bordered a golf course and between the openings of the fairways and greens were stands of pines trees. There was a repetitive tapping sound coming from one of the pine stands. It reminded me of two small rocks hitting together. At times the sound was erratic and at other times, patterned.

"It's a woodpecker," Glen said.

I thought, "Doesn't sound quite like a woodpecker to me, unless, of course, it's banging two rocks together."

As we edged closer I saw movement and there it was, a woodpecker, tapping on one of the pines. We all watched until it flew away, and then we walked over to the tree. Glen pointed out the straight horizontal line of small holes that were indicative of a yellow-bellied sapsucker.

"I thought you said it was a woodpecker," I blurted out.

"Sapsuckers are woodpeckers," Glen answered. "They are a kind of woodpecker that sometimes catches an insect and dips it in tree sap before eating it—kind of like you having syrup on your pancakes."

When Dot saw the bird she had known it was a sapsucker; she had even known it was a male by the red throat, but she hadn't been sure about the tapping sound. I, on the other hand, hadn't even known that sapsuckers were real birds, honest-to-goodness woodpeckers, which inhabit the forests, and not just a silly cartoon bird.

As we continued, Glen stopped and said, "Listen!"

There were birds high in the tall Norway spruce trees above us. The trees on the edge of the woods had snow laden limbs with patches of green needles poking through, but our trail had taken us through the center of the stand where the ground had little snow and the branches were mostly snowless. Standing in the spruce shelter, I knew the calls sounded familiar, but I couldn't place them. Most of the time when a bird made a sound I had no idea what it was, but this sound I knew I had heard before.

We listened for a while and then Glen announced, "We can add golden-crowned kinglet to the list.

Looking up through the needle-covered branches I could see tiny birds flitting in and out but wasn't able to see any markings. I understood even more how important it was to learn the songs.

Then he asked, "How many do you think there are?"

Glen and Dot talked about the kinglets…how they

always seemed to be in that stand of spruces…how they had expected to hear them there…if we hadn't heard them there, it would have been unusual. They talked a lot which was a bit surprising since we had all been so quiet early in the survey. One of the subjects they mentioned became important to me later in my surveys at the college: how significant habitat is in determining what birds might be encountered in a given area. I found that insightful and I have carried that idea with me throughout my life.

We had been out for almost four hours and weren't far from the Nature Center, so we started the last part of the circuit.

Our last bird for the morning turned out to be special since we were the only group to find one. Within sight of the Nature Center and several other people returning from their surveys, we heard what might be described as a soft short trill.

Glen said, "This bird has a very beautiful song which I doubted we would hear this time of year, but the call note is distinctive."

We easily found the bird. Its movements were reminiscent of a woodpecker or perhaps a right-side-up nuthatch. It "crept" up the tree sometimes moving in a spiral pattern, often with a jerking motion, searching for tiny invertebrates with its long, curved bill. When it arrived near the top, it flew to the bottom of a nearby tree and began the process all over again. The brown creeper's breast was bright white but still it was almost perfectly camouflaged. Holding its belly close to the tree most of the time, the creeper showed only its lightly streaked brown back.

We finally returned to the nature center and shook off the snow. Everyone sat around talking about the morning's birds, except me—I listened. Chuck Conrad, one of the original

founders of the Brooks Bird Club, got up and said, "It's time
to begin with our survey reports. First, I would like Greg to
introduce someone."

Dr. Eddy had me stand and introduced me as, "a student
from West Liberty who was doing a bird survey as part of his
graduation requirements."

Then the oddest thing happened. Everyone reached high
over their heads and began to wiggle their hands and arms
in a twisting kind of motion. Before I had started my college
bird survey a few weeks earlier, I had thought that chasing
birds was an activity for the unusual among us. Just when I
thought I had overcome that image, here were birders doing
something weirdly unusual again. After I sat down Dr. Eddy
leaned over toward me and whispered, "We do the waving of
the hands instead of clapping so we protect our hearing."

Well, there was the explanation, even though I didn't really
understand it.

People began reporting about the birds they had
encountered and the numbers of each.

One man stood up and said, "We saw four eastern
bluebirds feeding on poison ivy berries near the old Girl Scout
Cabin."

As people reported their results, others had comments or
questions.

"Kinglets were so close we didn't need binoculars to see
their golden and red crowns."

"The numbers of resident birds like chickadees, titmice,
white-breasted nuthatches, and downy woodpeckers are
down, but the migratory bird numbers are up."

I wasn't sure what all that meant but still found it
interesting. Everyone in the room was dedicated and really
liked birds.

One person mentioned, "The rough winter weather has kept some bird club members at home, otherwise we would have had a lot more people to cover the entire park and the reported numbers of birds would have been higher."

Until then I had thought that all of the people in the Wheeling, West Virginia area that liked birds was there. Now I learned that there were more. I had no idea there were this many people excited about birds!

Our brown creeper report brought some oohs and aahs.

After the reports, I sat down at the large picture window and watched the birds at the feeders. All the reported feeder birds which I had never seen before were, one by one, added to my list of new birds for the day.

I went home feeling accomplished, knowing a lot more about birds than I had when I woke up that morning.

AVALANCHE OF BIRDS

Everything, at least everything relating to birds, seemed to be proceeding like an avalanche in my life.

At first it was a gentle snow consisting of a series of thoughts about the bird surveys I had to do to graduate. Then I saw the eastern bluebirds on the red sumac and the blizzard began. That moment changed my life forever.

The survey walk with Dr. Eddy was the event which caused the mountain top of snow to break and begin its far away, rapid descent.

By the time of the first winter bird walk with Glen and Dot, I was hopelessly buried......in chasing birds.

Most avalanches are not a welcome fun experience but mine was enjoyably difficult and rewarding. My normal routines of life, family, times out with friends and even meals were being regularly interrupted by my new interest in birds. I found myself studying the *Birds of North America* because I wanted to and eagerly going out on some of the coldest days to chase birds in my Special Problems study plots. I went to bird-related events scheduled by the Brooks Bird Club, too.

Winter began changing to spring. The deep snow was slowly melting and my trips to the woods were significantly easier. It wasn't as cold and climbing some of the hills even had me breaking a sweat. Tree branches were devoid of snow. But new challenges presented themselves.

None was more perplexing than one that began to happen on a regular basis in the wild black cherry/American elm woodland. One day while surveying, I heard a faint sound that caused me to stop and quickly look behind me. A huge bird was flying rapidly away from me through the trees. No color or markings seemed noticeable to help me identify it. Two days later when I was in the same woodland it happened again. Next trip...same woodland, same bird, same happening. However, this time I decided to back-track to where I suspected the bird had begun its flight. There I found a dead squirrel, pretty much intact, but without a head. This mystery was on my mind to the point that I decided to present it to some of the Brooks Bird Club members at an upcoming walk.

The general consensus was that it must be a great horned owl. Everyone agreed I was very fortunate to see one, even though I hadn't seen it well enough to identify. At the college library I found some articles and books about great horned owls. Before long I was familiar with the habits and identification of all the owls that might be found in West Virginia.

The next time I surveyed the woodland I changed my routine. Approaching the grove, I stopped and carefully checked each and every tree through binoculars looking for the owl. Not finding it, I walked on to the very edge of the woods and again checked the trees. Nothing. I went into the woods cautiously checking from the very tops to the lowest branches. My binoculars scanned every tree in sight. Slowly and silently I moved deeper and deeper into the woods.

Then, "OH CRAP!" I thought as I turned around only to see the owl flying away behind me. I had checked every tree and branch many times and had seen NOTHING! I stood there troubled and perplexed, thinking, "How in the world did this owl escape my careful search?"

Days later I thought I had the owl dilemma all figured out. The only logical explanation for not finding the owl on the previous survey was that it must have been perched on the opposite side of one of the trees I had checked. This time I would also move around to different vantage points so I could see all sides of all the trees and could check every tree even more carefully.

My mind was working overtime trying to win this competition. Lying in bed the night before the survey I had gone over every detail and had tried to think of anything different I could do to find my nemesis before it found me. Finally I again approached the woodland for my fifth attempt to find the owl before it flew. One thing I noticed was the dead silence of the woods interrupted only by infrequent bird calls or songs. My footsteps seemed to be like thumps amplified through loud speakers when compared to the stillness of the woodland.

"Surely the owl hears me," I thought, "but why does it wait until I walk under or past before it flies? Why doesn't it fly now?"

When I was almost through the woodland, near the side where I had always begun my previous surveys, I began to breathe more slowly and thought, "The owl's not here today."

Then, "HOLY CRAP!" I heard it again!

As I turned, there it was flying away from me.

"Oh, well," I thought, "life goes on," and I continued my survey.

But I realized that life wouldn't go on, at least not the way I wanted it to go, unless I could see the great horned owl before it flew.

The next day I had classes all day after 10:00. There wasn't enough time to do a survey, but there was enough time to look for the owl. When I arrived at the woodland there were more bird sounds than usual and they all seemed to be coming from the same area. There were more birds in just this small area than I had thought there were in the entire woodland.

As I watched through my binoculars, I wondered why they seemed to be upset with each other. Walking a few feet closer I noticed the birds seemed to be flocking around one particular tree. As I looked closely…THE TREE MOVED…or so I thought. There was movement all right, but it wasn't the tree. There was a large curved feathered bump right up against the tree. I had found my owl! It was leaning against the trunk, wings loosely hugging the tree, eyes closed or perhaps peeking through thin slits and calmly resting or sleeping as the smaller songbirds harassed it.

As I watched it I thought, "I probably looked right at it before and never thought it was anything more than a bump on the tree."

I watched the owl for a short time and then walked towards it as if I were doing my survey. As I walked under the owl, I turned and began walking backwards, watching it as I slowly moved away. The owl stood up, glanced around and left its lofty perch. At the moment it flew from the branch I heard a familiar faint scraping noise. It was the sound of its talons scratching the bark as the owl left the branch. That sound must have been what had alerted me before when I had turned around, only to see the owl as it flew out of sight.

Standing in the snow, grinning, I looked around and thought, "There's a new sheriff in town!"

My bravado didn't last long. I glanced at my watch and realized there were only 10 minutes until class started. Off I went sprinting through the snow, across the meadow, down the hill, over the stream, up a hill, across the hockey field, through the woodland behind Boyd Hall and finally into Main Hall. I was late for Physical Chemistry but not by much. Huffing and puffing I darted into the classroom and sat down. Dr. "Cip" gave me a stern look and immediately began teaching.

Spring brought the early wildflowers, most of which I was already familiar with thanks to Mr. Berry's plant taxonomy class. And spring also brought new birds into my survey areas. The surveys for "Special Problems" officially ended on the last day of winter, March 20, but my trips to search out new birds did not.

Early April brought the first warbler to one of the survey areas: a Louisiana waterthrush. I couldn't help but notice the bird as its song was loud and frequent. The small bird appeared nervous as it bobbed from rock to rock along the stream.

One place I hadn't looked for birds was the college reservoir. It was formed by a broad concrete dam with a wide spillway holding back the water from a small stream. The route to my meadow survey went by the bottom of the spillway with the breast of the dam high above me, so I could not see the water. The first time I returned to the area after finishing the "Special Problems" surveys, I thought, "Now I can go anywhere I want to search for birds."

Climbing the hill and reaching the breast of the dam, I was surprised to see three birds in the water right in front of me. I quickly lowered myself to the ground and slid back down the hill a short distance. To the left of the birds I noticed a leafless honeysuckle shrub. After crawling back up the hill and hiding behind the honeysuckle, I could see the birds right through the bush. They were spectacular: some kind of tiny duck, unlike anything I had ever seen before. They had iridescent dark green heads that sometimes looked black, with a white hood covering the back half. Their bodies were mostly white… bright white, like shirts in a TV laundry detergent commercial. I could barely get my field guide out fast enough as I slid back down the hill.

Carefully I examined each page of ducks. My ducks were buffleheads. Again I scooted up to the bush and watched the buffleheads—two males and one female. They swam slowly along the shoreline, into a small inlet and out of sight.

I continued to think, "Bufflehead…bufflehead. What a neat name! What a beautiful bird!"

Most of my early birding was done in the West Liberty State College (now University) Arboretum, where my surveys had been done. Arboretum was perhaps a misnomer since none of the trees were labeled and there were no paths or easy access to the area. Still, these 154 acres provided a variety of habitats that many different kinds of birds visited and nested in.

Because of its lack of easy accessibility, it was rare to see another person in the Arboretum. Being alone in natural quiet places has always called to me, as if saying, "Come to me and I will give you peace; the troubles of the day do not exist here."

In those early birding adventures, my mind and thoughts were absorbed with the glories of wild creatures. I was often reluctant to face my worldly concerns. And right then my biggest and most pressing concern was that I was graduating in a month and I needed a job.

WILD BIRDS — WILDFLOWERS

When I wasn't chasing after birds or wildflowers, I thought about looking for them and where I might find ones I hadn't seen before.

In the spring semester before my Special Problems course I had taken Systematic Botany, today commonly referred to as Plant Taxonomy. The textbook was *The Flora of West Virginia*. I would come to know its 1,000+ pages very well. Mr. Berry, nicknamed "Thunder Frog" for his deep booming voice, was the instructor. I grew to have a great appreciation of him.

Taxonomy and I fit together well. Mr. Berry recognized my eagerness to search out and identify every wildflower in West Liberty. Beginning in March there was a lab once a week with about a dozen different wildflowers for each student to identify using the keys in the *Flora*. Some students would struggle for the whole two hours with several of the more difficult ones. I was usually finished in about 5 minutes—10 if there was one I hadn't seen before. And that was what made the difference for me: having seen the wildflower before. I was in the woods, along streams, and exploring meadows all the time. Once Mr. Berry introduced me to plant keys, wild horses couldn't have kept me out of the woods.

Right away, Mr. Berry recognized my value. The day of the second lab test, I took my usual five minutes (writing the correctly spelled common as well as scientific names took me a while) and went forward to hand in my answers.

Mr. Berry said, "Here, take this. Read it and watch over the other students. Answer any questions they may have and make sure they do not cheat. I will be in my office if you need me."

He gave me a book on poisonous plants and I did as requested. By the end of the semester I had been given a mini botanical library.

After retirement he went to the southwest to photograph cacti and, unfortunately, soon died. I was sad to hear of his passing. Later that year I received a call from his wife.

"Of all of Malvern's taxonomy students, you were his favorite," she said. "He once told me that upon his death, I was to contact you and ask if you would like to have his library."

I was stunned and honored. I accepted gratefully.

Mr. Berry had been the one who had introduced me to keys. Once I had the means to attach a name to the things I was seeing, I was able to go to other sources to learn more about the birds and wildflowers and other things I found. After that there was no putting the genie back in the bottle. I have always felt greatly indebted to Mr. Berry.

Every week during my last spring at college, I saw Dr. Eddy on his Tuesday morning bird walks. After one of the walks he said, "Do you remember me asking you about bird banding a while back? Well, this Saturday I will be banding birds at Oglebay Park. I thought you might like to stop by and see what it's all about. Bring your *Flora of West Virginia.*

You can teach me how to key plants and I will show you bird banding."

Arriving at the park I followed a trail through a large stand of red pine trees. At the bottom of the trail was Dr. Eddy, sitting in a lawn chair, reading. Another lawn chair sat there for me.

A short distance away a fine net was strung between two poles. Although the net was 40 feet long and 10 feet high, it was almost invisible. We could have sat there all day and I never would have noticed it.

"There is another one over there," he pointed out.

"This is how we catch birds and then we band them."

"Do we chase them in?" I asked.

"No, we just sit and wait…and hope we catch something," he answered. "In the meantime, let's find some wildflowers and you can teach me some things," he added.

All of a sudden a bird hit the net closest to us. We hurried over and there, in a loose pocket that ran the length of the net, was a downy woodpecker. Having no idea what to expect I remained quiet and watched. Dr. Eddy reached toward the woodpecker. The bird jumped around a bit and then hopped right out of the net and tried to fly away. I was horrified by what I saw next. The bird was flying but going nowhere. Its tongue was still attached to the net. And the tongue was pulled out about four inches!

Dr. Eddy quickly grabbed the woodpecker and said, "That wasn't good." He reassured me that things like that were rare.

In time, I would eventually remove tens of thousands of birds from mist nets, but I would never again witness what I had seen that first day with the downy woodpecker. Slowly and gently Dr. Eddy pulled the net from the bird; first the feet, difficult because of the way woodpeckers hold their legs against their bodies, followed by the wings and tail. The entire time the uncooperative bird tried to peck and bite Dr. Eddy's hand. The tongue looked impossible to remove, especially with the woodpecker constantly trying to bite, but it was soon untangled.

"Do you want to hold it? Put out your pointer finger and your middle finger forming a V. The neck goes between those fingers and the rest of the bird will be in your hand with your thumb and other two fingers around its body," he told me.

It was amazing. The bird was soft and warm and I could feel it vibrating…partly its breathing, but mostly its heartbeat. Dr. Eddy showed me the tiny band the bird would wear for the rest of its life. With special pliers Dr. Eddy opened and then secured the band onto the woodpecker's leg. Made of aluminum, the band was lightweight and wouldn't interfere with the bird's ability to fly or find food. As I held the bird, Dr. Eddy recorded the species, AOU #, age, sex, status, region, latitude and longitude codes and date on a line adjacent to the unique nine digit band number.

"Release the bird when you want to," he told me. "You don't have to toss it…just open your hand."

After a short time of examining it more closely, I opened my hand. I was sure the bird would drop to the ground, but in an instant it was 10 feet away and soon out of sight.

As Dr. Eddy and I sat talking about wildflowers and birds, we could hear someone walking down the trail toward us.

Dr. Eddy got up, walked toward the man, and said, "Hi John. I thought I might see you today."

Then Dr. Eddy introduced me. John Christie was the Director of Nature Education for Oglebay Institute at the Brooks Nature Center there in Oglebay Park. I was surprised to discover that Dr. Eddy was the head of the Nature

Committee at the Brooks Nature Center. The two began discussing a dilemma they were facing. The Naturalist at the Nature Center was leaving in two months and they needed to find a replacement.

John said, "I dread the thought of going through dozens of applications and then the subsequent interviews to find a new naturalist." They discussed ways to avoid that problem.

After they had talked for a while Dr. Eddy turned toward me and said, "What about Bill here? Would you like to be a naturalist?"

Right away I found myself answering, "Sure!"

John said, "Why don't you come by the Nature Center before ten on Monday morning and you can see if it's something you might like."

"I'll be there," I answered.

When John left and was out of sight, I turned to Dr. Eddy and, with great concern, asked, "What's a naturalist?"

"Don't worry," he answered, "you can do it."

Up to that day I had had only one other promising job opportunity: a wood preserving company in New York was looking for line foremen who would inspect newly set telephone poles. The pay was good, I would have had a company car and I would have been the leader of a crew of four. The day ended with lots of new things for me to consider.

JOB

I awoke early on Monday. Everything seemed fine until I began over-thinking my options.

Growing up near Pittsburgh, I had always thought I would stay there with my high school friends and never go to college. Now, here I was in West Virginia, finishing college and needing to find a job.

West Virginia was, in many ways, the opposite of what I had thought I wanted. The biggest difference, and the thing I liked most, was that in West Virginia it was a lot easier to walk into a quiet place and be alone.

I arrived at the Brooks Nature Center and was greeted by Dot, who I had met on my first Brooks Bird Club walk. She was the secretary there. John Christie wasn't there yet but the naturalist, George Lippert, was. George began explaining to me what I would observe when the high school students arrived and how the morning would progress. While he was describing my role as an observer learning about being a naturalist, the school bus arrived and the phone rang at the same time. Dot answered the phone. The conversation was short.

She yelled, "George, Louise isn't here because her car

won't start." George looked at me and said, "Bill, you are going to have to take a group. One of my volunteers can't make it."

Before long, I was on a trail with a group of high school students and their teacher. Besides feeling very inadequate, I had no idea where the trail went. There were birds singing, but I didn't recognize the songs, so I couldn't talk much about them. So what I talked to them about were concepts: how important plants are because of essential things they provide, that water is the life blood of the earth, that birds provide beauty and music and that there is a balance in nature. Those two hours seemed like the longest hours in my life.

One day John Christie said, "Bill, we need to talk."

"Why don't you work for us through the summer," he said. "If we don't like the job you do for us or you don't like the job, then we'll part company."

I agreed. Almost all of my time for the next three weeks was spent with George. About the only time I was away from him was when I was leading school field trips and public nature walks. Even then he would accompany me on some of those and afterwards we would talk about how I might have done something differently or better.

George was a good birder and taught me a lot. Birds were becoming something I was able to talk about more readily.

Seemingly insignificant things can change one's life. My plant taxonomy class had propelled me outside into natural areas, the Special Problems course had immersed me in birds and now I had a job that would allow me to stay in West Virginia.

My job as a naturalist kept me very busy. In the morning before work I would be in the field chasing bird songs I didn't know. After work most days I did the same. Saturdays and

Sundays I spent birding, mostly by myself. I was finding new birds and learning more each time I went out.

I frequently thought, "I wish I knew it all RIGHT NOW!" Nowadays I know that just doesn't happen—it's a lifelong pursuit. One never learns or knows it all. The joy is in the chase.

For me, one of the most shocking things about birds was my first spring migration. I overheard two Brooks Bird Club members talking one day in April.

"Phoebes are back and I heard my first Louisiana waterthrush, chipping sparrow and field sparrow the other day," one person said.

The other person replied, "I haven't heard the waterthrush yet, but we had a Baltimore oriole yesterday. All hell's about to break loose! Don't you love it?"

At that time I had no real idea of what they were talking about. Like most people I thought, "Birds migrate north in the spring and go south in the winter. Big deal." Boy was I in for a surprise.

Keeping a "life list" is something most birders do and I followed suit. Every new bird was added to my list. Early April birds that were new to me included the eastern phoebe, yellow-shafted flicker, eastern meadowlark and Cape May warbler.

There was one early April bird that I often heard, but didn't see for a long time. In the college arboretum during my early morning and weekend birding I often encountered one particularly unbirdlike sound. I thought it might be a bird but I wasn't sure. The sound always came from a distant ridge. Walking along very quietly I would hear, "**caw-KUCK**." The sound wasn't loud from where I stood, but since it came from such a distance, I knew it was forceful. I heard it several times on each visit to the arboretum but always from a great distance.

On one beautiful chilly spring morning I decided to hike to that far ridge. Once on top I was surprised to see large open fields where last year's corn had grown. Not wanting to walk through the fields because I assumed nothing would be there, I skirted the area sticking to the edges where woodlands and natural meadows arose.

"**Caw-KUCK!**" I heard it. The sound came from the stubbled cornfield. I saw nothing. I decided to crisscross the field . A flock of horned larks flew up and away. I followed, keeping a close eye on them through my binoculars.

I was pretty sure my mystery sound could not have come from such tiny birds. But I had already learned a lesson: don't take anything for granted. There are a lot of amazing and unusual things that happen in nature.

Getting closer and closer to the horned larks I was able to see the long black sideburns on their heads. They reminded me of Elvis Presley. The larks also had tiny horns barely visible on the tops of their heads. I am not sure why but I breathed a sigh of relief when I heard their sounds: light and airy high pitched musical notes. It had seemed unsettling that the loud, harsh, "**caw-KUCK**" sound might come from these small birds.

"**Caw-KUCK!**" There it was again! I began walking toward the sound. A wild flurry of wing beats took me totally by surprise. Flying away from me was a large full-bodied bird with a very long tail. I had found the "**caw-KUCK**" bird: a ring-necked pheasant. It wouldn't be until many years later, while photographing close-ups of bird feathers for *National Wildlife Magazine* that I would discover how remarkably colorful this bird really is.

Working at the Nature Center afforded me inside information about birding events. My secretary, Dot always knew what was happening.

One activity was an annual event called Century Day. The objective was for the total of everyone's bird sightings for the day to be at least 100 species. Members went out in the morning as early as they wanted and then met in Oglebay Park at noon for lunch and to report their results. After lunch they went out again to look for more birds. Century Day was always the first or second Saturday in May.

May 6, 1972 was my first Century Day. My plan of attack was to search for birds in the college arboretum before I went to the park. This day I got up early enough to begin just as the sun was coming up.

Have you ever been awestruck? There were so many birds singing. It was as if all the birds in the county had gathered in this one spot and were loudly trying to decide who would go where to feed, collect nesting material, and fuss at the crows or great horned owls.

As the sun rose over the horizon I ventured into the woodlands. A mist rose from the ground and up through the new leafy tree canopy. The sun's rays, caught in the tiny water droplets, comforted every part of me as if saying, "Here I am. Come to me. I am the peace you seek." At times like that I always did find peace.

Now the birds were singing less frequently. Carolina chickadee, tufted titmouse, mourning dove and white-breasted nuthatch were birds I identified that morning by the song or a call note they made.

As the morning progressed the earlier jumble of songs had subsided a bit and I was beginning to feel more comfortable and competent with my meager birding skills. On top of the

first hill was a ridge lined with old tall black willows. High in
the willows was a song I didn't know. Raising my binoculars
for a closer look I saw a small bird that was mostly yellow
with a black circular cap on its head. Right away I thought
"warbler." Leafing through the warbler pages of my field
guide I quickly found it: Wilson's warbler, a new life bird.

Suddenly a song arose that would make anyone, birder
or not, stop in their tracks. It was the most beautiful musical
sound I had ever heard. The song was light, airy and hypnotic.
I imagined an accomplished flutist, hiding a short distance
away, expertly playing in a most enthralling manner.
Scanning the woodland I soon saw the bird: a wood thrush,
another new bird for my life list.

As the light struck the tops of the trees I occasionally saw
a bird sitting still in full sun. It appeared to be afire with color.
While following one bird in my binoculars, another would fly
across my field of view in the opposite direction and I would
follow that one, only to have another come whizzing by and
grab my attention. These were mostly warblers.

In future years I anxiously awaited spring migration,
hoping each time I entered the woodlands I could again ride
the recurring waves of warblers as they stopped to feed on
their long journey northward to distant breeding grounds.
That morning I added the American redstart, the black-
throated green, hooded, chestnut-sided and black-and-white
warblers to my life list. I saw other birds I had never seen
before but I wasn't sure about their identification.

I had begun the morning at 5:30 waiting to enter the
woods. Five and half hours later I hurried back to my car
and drove to Oglebay. Since this was my first Century Day
I wasn't sure what to expect. All the excellent birders I had
met and others I had only heard about would be there. Surely

there would be something exciting I could report from my "new" birds and I hoped others would be as excited as I was. I envisioned myself standing proudly and announcing "chestnut-sided warbler" or perhaps "wood thrush" and everyone would "oow" and "aaw" about my finds. I would humbly sit down and accept my accolades with unassuming modesty.

When I arrived at the picnic site I found Dr. Eddy and Glen who had saved a seat for me. Dot was there, too. Some of us had bag lunches, but to my surprise, many had coolers or picnic baskets and there was a lot of sharing.

Finally Chuck Conrad stood up and announced, "We had better go over the bird list so we can get to our afternoon destinations."

Earlier I had wondered how many birds we would have from the morning's surveys? Having no idea what to expect, I thought 75 would be a respectable number.

Chuck started through the checklist. "Did anybody see any loons?" No loons. "How about grebes?" Someone had seen a pied-billed grebe. "Did anyone see any herons?" Three different kinds had been seen. "Now the ducks…let me go through the list rather than everyone yelling at me."

I was shocked at how many different kinds of ducks people saw. There were some questions about where the ducks were seen. Some people planned to check those same places later. The number of birds was quickly adding up. People had seen hawks of all kinds, gulls, terns, sandpipers and so much more.

"Where in the world did they see all these water birds?" I thought. Then, I remembered that the Ohio River was not far away.

We went through the entire list. My head was spinning.

The scanty list of birds I had identified from the college arboretum didn't even warrant mentioning. Everyone there had seen all that were on my list and more.

"So much for my moment in the spotlight," I thought.

Chuck asked several people to count the birds he had marked on the checklist. The final tally was 105. Surely there were no more kinds of birds to be found this afternoon or any afternoon. Minutes later I would be proven wrong.

As we left for our afternoon trips, several people were looking at birds in a nearby stand of Scotch pines. An elderly man, Judge Worley, had found a bird that he and others were having trouble identifying. It flitted and darted in and out of the pine needles only sitting still in places where we could see just small parts of it.

The general consensus was that it was a warbler, but which one?

Finally, it came out into full view.

I thought, "If it is a warbler, it has no *jump-out-at-you* colors or markings like the warblers I saw earlier this morning."

The mystery bird sang a weak chippy-like trill several times and then some people pieced the puzzle together—an orange-crowned warbler. After looking in my field guide I, too, could see it—and a new life bird for me. Everyone who saw it was very excited and all thanked Judge Worly for finding it. I later realized that this was one of the rarest birds ever reported on a Century Day count. I have never seen one again in Ohio County.

Also in those same pines we found a red-breasted nuthatch. Glen explained that they had been common during winter, but this was very late in the season to see one. Those two birds brought the Century Day total to 107 almost before we had started back out.

Dr. Eddy and Glen decided we would survey areas around West Liberty. We three went birding in Dr. Eddy's car. Three pairs of eyes scanned the horizon as we drove by. On one back road along a grassy field we stopped to look at a bird perched on a strand of barbed wire.

Looking through his binoculars Glen said, "It's a thrush!"

Dr. Eddy remarked, "The back is gray-brown with no noticeable reddish-brown colors."

"Check the cheeks," Glen said.

"No gray," Dr. Eddy answered.

It was a Swainson's thrush, another life bird for me. Dr. Eddy and Glen bantered back and forth about how strange it was to see the thrush "out of habitat."

Glen laughed and said, "Well, it IS migration," and that settled it.

As we drove I thought about how much fun I was having seeing so many different kinds of birds, when we abruptly came to a stop.

Dr. Eddy exclaimed, "On the wire. New bird!" We watched a sparrow hawk (now American kestrel) scanning the meadow and road edges for food. It was another life bird for me.

I always consider this one of the most fun days I ever had while chasing birds. What made it so special was how excited Glen and Dr. Eddy were each time I saw a new life bird.

For years to come, in front of other BBC members and friends, Glen would ask, "Bill, on that first Century Day, how many life birds did you get?"

And I would answer, "Forty-six!"

BROOKS NATURE CENTER — JOHN

Dot, my secretary, was a very good birder and I admired her for it. She always encouraged me. Our friendship has lasted for decades. When I had questions concerning a bird I had heard or seen, Dot was the person I asked and she often had the answer I was looking for. Nowadays she often says to others, "There was a period when I knew a whole lot more about birds than he did," and that was so true.

My tenure as naturalist at the Brooks Nature Center lasted 18 years. The first Director of Nature Education I worked under was John Christie. He had once worked for the Peace Corps in Africa and had acquired a passion for wild creatures and places.

John was, to say the least, an idealist. Besides my regular duties of teaching school programs, adult workshops, leading public nature walks, building exhibits, fielding calls from the public pertaining to every kind of wildlife topic or problem imaginable, John informed me early on that for me to continue as a naturalist for him there were two things he required: 1) for me to read all of the publications we subscribed to, and 2) for me to get a Bird Banding License. He explained to me that the Brooks Nature Center and those associated with it had a long tradition of bird banding and bird research.

There are 5 requirements for a Master Federal Bird Banding Permit. 1) The applicant must be fully trained prior to applying for a bird banding permit. Fully trained means knowing how to identify, age, and sex each species of bird one might capture and also knowing how to use and safely extract birds from mist nets if such nets are to be used. 2) The applicant needs to submit a detailed research proposal documenting the goals, purpose and procedures of a bird-related project they will do. 3) The applicant must submit a resume of their banding experience including numbers of hours worked, level of supervision, species diversity and numbers of birds handled. 4) Three references from other bird banders or professional ornithologists are required. 5) The applicant must be 21 years or older.

The good news was I already met one of the requirements—I was 23 years old. One advantage I had was the fact that there were several Master Bird Banders in the local BBC who were more than willing to help me, including George Lippert who I had replaced as naturalist at the Nature Center. Although George had left the Nature Center, he still worked locally. But my greatest advantage was that Dr. Eddy wanted to teach me banding.

As the seasons changed my focus at work also changed: in spring I was busy with school groups visiting for nature programs and walks; in summer I offered a variety of programs for park guests; in fall I worked with school groups again; and in winter I was to do bird banding on days when I didn't have other obligations.

One day during my first spring, John came to my office and said, "So you don't have any programs today? You don't know the birds well enough. I want you out in the park chasing and studying birds. Take your lunch...I don't want to see you back until quitting time."

John didn't know that when I arrived at work each morning at 8:30, on most days I had already been out chasing birds for two hours. And now, I was in the position of being paid for what I already had been doing on my own time.

My first scarlet tanager was mesmerizing. I had seen the drawings in the field guide and wanted to spot one in the wild. One day in the park I heard the characteristic "chip-churr" or "chip-burr" call note associated with the scarlet tanager. At the time I didn't know the call so I chased the sound. Soon through my binoculars I was looking at one of the most beautiful birds in North America. I watched and followed its every move until my arms got tired from holding the binoculars.

During my years at the Brooks Nature Center I occasionally received phone calls from people who had seen their first scarlet tanager. The conversation usually went something like this:

"I saw this incredibly beautiful bird. I think it's a jungle bird—maybe someone's pet."

As the caller's description went on and on I would relive the thrill of catching sight of my first scarlet tanager. Eventually I would explain, "The bird you are describing is a scarlet tanager and they are quite common. We don't see them often because they remain hidden in the leafy tree canopy. If you knew their song, you would realize how abundant they really are. I hear them every day."

Glen Phillips had told me early on, "Learn the robin's song. It's a key to several other common species." "Cherry-up, cherry-o…cherry-up, cherry-o," over and over again is the robin's repeated song. It was one of the first songs I learned. Glen was right—field guides often describe the scarlet tanager's song as sounding like, "a robin with a sore throat,"…the rose-breasted grosbeak's song like, "a robin with rocks in its mouth,"…the summer tanager's song as, "a cross between a robin and scarlet tanager." Already knowing the robin's song definitely helped me to recognize those other similar songs more easily.

The cares of the world keep us unaware of the miracles of life, or so it seemed to me at the time. For most of my life, I hadn't been aware of bird songs. I hadn't been listening. Other cares had garnered my attention and had kept me oblivious to what I now couldn't and didn't want to keep out of my mind. I was having the time of my life.

During my first spring as a birder I slept with the bedroom window open. Beyond my back yard were 14 acres of woodland with a ravine and a stream running through. Past the woodland was a meadow plateau. During early spring it was mostly quiet but as the season progressed there came to be a myriad of sounds. Nearby night sounds of grasshoppers, katydids and crickets were accompanied by a distant, bizarre, greatly varied sound from what I thought might be a bird. I mentioned this to other BBC birders and they were sure it must be a yellow-breasted chat, North America's largest warbler.

When I checked my *Birds of North America* field guide I read, "Song is an amazing alteration of caws, whistles, grunts and rattles, frequently given in flight and even at night."

That had to be my bird and it would be new to my life list. Early the next morning I was on my way to the meadow. It had been a clear night and the dew was heavy. When I got to the meadow my socks and shoes were soaking and I was cold.

A short way into the meadow I was soaked to my knees.

Getting soaking wet was common for me. On this day, sunlight was filtering through openings in the tree line and striking the droplets of dew. The meadow was sparkling with tiny jewels of water...some brilliant white and others of green, blue, red, yellow, and purple. When viewed individually each water drop was a world of color all its own. As a whole, the meadow reminded me of a rainbow where the individual bits of color hadn't yet come together. It was spellbinding.

After a short time of standing and listening, I heard the chat. Soon the chat was vocalizing from the highest point of a large multiflora rose bush. Its bright yellow breast glistened in the new sunlight. I don't believe I have ever seen a brighter yellow...as if it were on fire with a yellow-hot undulating flame. Dazzled, I was sure this was the ultimate birding experience...until...until the bird lifted from its perch and became airborne. With its breast blazing in the sun, the chat flew in a high arc. At the top of the curve, it hovered with long, slow, deep wingbeats. Its legs hung loosely as the chat pumped its tail against the air. It seems like a small brilliant sun floating forever in the sky. The entire time it was in the air the chat caroled its varied repertoire of sounds. I was in awe.

The fall season at the Brooks Nature Center brought a change of exhibits and many requests for programs. Another duty I had was to maintain a bird feeding station and keep track of the kinds of birds that were visiting. We had a variety of feeders and offered several kinds of food.

Most of what we provided was striped sunflower. There was also a large feeder with mixed seed: white and red millet, cracked corn, milo and sunflower. For woodpeckers and other primary insect eaters, we also provided suet that a local supermarket saved for us. From the reading John had me do, I learned about studies concerning the kinds of seeds birds preferred, might tolerate or didn't eat at all. Eventually I made my own wild bird mix using equal parts of black oil sunflower seed and white millet.

Since Oglebay Institute is a non-profit organization we held three bird seed sales each fall/winter as fund raisers. A tractor trailer loaded with seed was dropped off in our parking lot. Much of the seed had been pre-ordered by people from Wheeling and surrounding areas. We sold over 80,000 pounds of bird seed each year. During the sales people also bought feeders, field guides and bird books.

Birding in the fall wasn't the same as chasing birds during the springtime migration to their breeding grounds. During fall migration the birds are more furtive and quiet with a few exceptions. The most notable exception is the chimney swift.

Swifts have a remarkable flight. They are masters of the air. Thinking back to the projects where I grew up, I wondered why I didn't remember seeing their dazzling flights around any of the 500 homes. After a little reflection I realized that these birds nest in chimneys and none of the homes in the projects had chimneys. Before Europeans began to populate North America, swifts nested in big old hollow trees and occasionally cave entrances. Now our older buildings provide a wonderful substitute for their original homes. Chimney swifts are not colorful birds, but, boy, can they fly! They are fast accurate fliers, rapidly gliding and zooming above the houses and tree lines in search of insects. It almost seems like one second they are going too fast to be seen and then the next second they stop on a dime. Chimney swifts appear to have alternate wing beats but that illusion is caused by their quick dynamic flight.

One evening on campus I was walking home from the woods. I heard a loud chattering mass of chimney swifts flying in a wide circle. As I stood watching, a student walked by, looked up, and said, "Bats! Yuck."

I felt like grabbing the guy, shaking him and telling him how misinformed he was. But I knew better so I just continued to savor the event. I glanced at my watch—it was 7:20. More and more swifts showed up and joined the circle. There were 100s of them.

As the darkness came, the circle got smaller and smaller. An occasional bird would flutter into the building's huge chimney. Soon there were dozens dropping, one after another. The circle continued to tighten. More and more dropped into the chimney, now several at a time. All of a sudden there were none left—they were all in the chimney. By 7:50 the spectacle was over.

The next night and for several nights afterward I returned to watch the swifts. Then one night there were no swifts. Something had told them it was time to go. Chimney swifts migrate at night using the stars as navigational beacons. They had begun their long trip to the upper reaches of the Amazon River in Peru where they winter.

Recently I have been able to watch the agile acrobatics of these amazing birds each evening at my home. Just before sunset, they spend almost half an hour doing what appears to be practice for entering their home—the chimney of the house next door. As the swifts approach the top of the chimney, they seem to slow a bit but somehow overfly and miss the optimum opportunity. Then speed up as they swoop and fly by the opening. Eventually, as the evening gets darker, each bird swoops down toward the chimney, abruptly stops its forward motion and, with a gentle flutter, drops into the chimney.

BIRD BANDING

In the fall schools that wanted to visit the Nature Center would try to schedule dates before temperatures got cold. From mid-September through October I had schools visiting every weekday. Beginning in November the visits dropped off dramatically. That was when bird banding began.

The banding of birds with uniquely numbered aluminum bands allows for the approximation of populations of individual species. When a banded bird is afterwards encountered through observation, trapping, or recovery of the band when the bird is dead we can discover such information as dispersal, life-spans and population growth. Of great importance is the study of migration. Not all birds that nest near our homes stay there all year long. Many migrate to warmer climates (sometimes thousands of miles away). We know the where, why and how of migration from recovered bird bands. All the data gathered from bird banding also aids in the protection of certain species in danger of possible extinction.

Dr. Eddy came early and set up mist nets outside near the bird feeders. Inside I had a fire blazing so we could sit and watch the nets and feeders through the large picture windows.

On each banding day there would be an initial rush of birds. As the morning progressed we caught fewer birds.

After years of banding I recognized the ideal conditions for netting birds during fall and winter months: 1) overcast sky, 2) snow cover on the ground, 3) temperature 15 to 30 degrees and 4) little or no wind. Another good time to net birds was during a snowfall or just before a winter storm.

I remember January 25, 1978 vividly. There was a winter storm warning and a storm was to hit around mid-day. In the middle of the morning we received a phone call from Oglebay Institute's main office telling us we could close up and go home. Everyone rushed out the door—I stayed.

I thought, "I wouldn't miss this for anything." Besides I had a Volkswagen Beetle that was terrific in the snow.

What I wanted to observe was how the birds reacted to this drastic change in air pressure and if their feeder activity would increase. As the storm got closer I could actually see the barometer needle of our weather station creeping lower. In the 18 years I worked at the Nature Center, there had never been, nor ever would be, as many birds clamoring to get food at the feeders as there were that day.

One of the ways I used to determine feeder use, although not 100% accurate, was to count the number of cardinals since we usually had lots of them. (One winter I banded 129 cardinals at the Nature Center.) My method was to count the males and then double that number. Since cardinals are large and the brightest feeder bird, they are easy to see. There were many days I counted more than 30 cardinals but on this day I counted 48. They looked like Christmas ornaments adorning the wintry snowscape.

And it wasn't just cardinals I saw. Chickadees were everywhere as were tufted titmice, white-breasted nuthatches, downy woodpeckers, song sparrows, white-throated sparrows and slate-colored juncos. Large flocks of evening grosbeaks, purple finches, American goldfinches and pine siskins were also there. Blue jays, red-bellied woodpeckers, hairy woodpeckers and others frequently flew in for seeds, too. I had never seen so many birds at a feeder.

Since I was no longer a poor college student, I now had adequate clothing for days like this. Out I went into the Blizzard of 1978. It was extreme. The wind was fierce and the gusts were incredible; some places in the Ohio Valley had gusts of nearly 90 mph. The tops of the trees, barely visible through the snow, were groaning as they whipped around in every direction. At one point the trail just disappeared—a whiteout. Trees only two feet in front of me were faint shadows and anything farther was gone altogether. I kicked around a bit, found a log and sat down and kept my head facing down.

As I sat there I was sure I saw a bird alight on my knee. I thought it was a Carolina wren but even at that close distance it was a blur. My incredible whiteout only lasted minutes, but it is the only one I have ever experienced.

As I returned to the Nature Center the winds subsided, but the snow continued to fall. Driving home it was beautiful— snow clung to every branch and the roadway was covered. No other cars were on the road helping to make my drive safe and uneventful.

On days when Dr. Eddy came to band I was often already working on a project but would stop and help him set two nets. It wasn't unusual to catch 15 to 20 birds or more in the first 10 minutes. Then we would go out, untangle birds and band them. After a while I would go back to my project and Dr. Eddy would read or perhaps grade papers.

Net tending in the winter is far more difficult than in warmer weather. Some of the birds we regularly caught in cold weather got far more tangled than the kinds we caught in the summer months. Chickadees are the most difficult to take from nets. Since they are small, parts of them easily fit through the one-quarter inch mesh squares. And chickadees are fighters; constantly biting and kicking. The best way to avoid them being badly tangled is to extract them right away.

Several other birds also present difficulties. Woodpeckers' tongues are barbed and sometimes become entangled in the mesh. Their legs, held tightly against their bodies, seem to indicate, "It was your net but it's mine now. I'm not letting go."

Blue jays also have a strong foot grip and are also reluctant to let go of the net. Cardinals, purple finches and evening grosbeaks bite hard enough to cause significant pain, especially if they catch the cuticle.

My favorite birds to band were the tufted titmice. Although they were not the biggest bird, they were always, by far, the most aggressive and least fearful. Like the chickadees, they would bite and kick, but they would also scream. They have a great repertoire of screams but I never thought any of the sounds indicated they were at all afraid. More the opposite, as if screaming, "How dare you! Unhand me! Just wait until I get lose, you will regret this!" Their "attitude," for such a small bird, gained my appreciation. I always view the titmouse as a small bird who thinks of itself as the biggest bird in the woodland.

By the following March I was ready to apply for my own Master Federal Bird Banding permit. All the banders I had net tended for thought I was ready. I was 24 years old and, according to the banders who wrote my three letters of recommendation, fully trained. The only hurdle I faced was the research project proposal.

There was one group of birds whose biology interested me more than any other: the owls. One owl species in particular interested me, partly because it was so secretive and partly because not a lot of research had been done on the bird. So I decided: the eastern screech-owl, *Otus asio* (now *Megascops asio*), was the bird I wanted to study.

Master Personal Bird Banding permits are not easy to acquire due to the stringent requirements. However, I had gone from the most novice of bird watchers to being a licensed bird bander in fifteen months. I had worked very hard to achieve my permit.

Besides banding birds at the Nature Center, I also began to trap and band birds at my home. My children were often involved. I wanted them to have a similar appreciation for birds as I had. Usually they loved the intimate contact with birds. However one day my oldest daughter said, "Mom told me it was okay to have some friends stay over this weekend but I don't want you banding birds. They might think it's weird." What actually happened was that somehow her friends already knew about the banding and they wanted to "trap some birds." So we did and they loved it.

On average, I banded approximately 1,000 birds per winter while I was at the Nature Center, but from 1972 to 1979 the average was much higher. The reason was the weather. The average winter temperature during that time was much colder than it is nowadays. For example in many parts of the Ohio Valley during January of 1977 we spent the entire month at or below freezing. Low temperatures force the metabolism of a bird to work harder and this requires the bird to find more food. If the ground is bare, that is not too much of a problem.

But during those years, snowfall was higher too. Our first significant snowfall of at least six inches usually occurred by mid-January. A week later another five to ten inches would fall. Within a week or two there was usually a major storm dropping 12 inches. And, because of the low temperatures, this snow didn't melt—it kept accumulating. We didn't see bare ground again until the spring thaw in late March or early April. For these reasons our bird feeders were crowded.

When I was introduced to bird feeding there were significant winter flocks of evening grosbeaks, purple finches and pine siskins at most feeders in the upper Ohio Valley. I expected that winter bird feeding would be like this for my entire life. But it didn't continue. For the most part, "real" winter weather ended by 1980. Now, although we may see some of these birds during certain winters, the large flocks we had in the '70s haven't happened again. When compared with the decade of the '70s, the winters we have today are hardly noticeable. At least that's how it seems to me.

When I netted a lot of birds, I put them into holding cages until I could band them. A cage has 12 individual compartments, each with its own swinging door. One side of the whole set-up is covered with window screening. A hand holding a bird pushes into a compartment by tipping up the swinging door, the hand is opened, the bird immediately goes toward the open-looking screen side and the bander pulls the hand back out letting the door swing closed. When it is time to band a bird from the cage, all I have to do is reach into a compartment: the bird inside, facing the screen looking out, is in just the right position for my hand to fit around it and take it out.

That's how easily the holding cage worked with almost all birds...except the Carolina wren. When I reached in for a Carolina wren, the bird was, more often than not, facing the door, watching and waiting. Many times a Carolina wren flew right up my coat sleeve. Chasing the tiny bird out of my clothes and then out of the building made for some interesting experiences.

Early on I had difficulty separating their loud "teakettle-teakettle-teakettle" (or sometimes "kettletea-kettletea-kettletea,") song from the wide variety of cardinal songs I heard during the warm weather months. Then in winter, instead of the song, I had to learn their more common long, "churrrrrrrrr" sound. At the feeders, when they were not eating peanut butter or a suet/peanut butter mix, it was not unusual for the Carolina wrens to squeeze between the glass and roof of a hopper feeder and eat the sunflowers seeds "indoors." When I saw seed being launched off the feeder from just under the roof, I always knew who was doing it.

I have always thought of Carolina wrens as a bit more intelligent and maybe more curious than other birds. They certainly were opportunistic eaters. As part of maintaining the snake exhibits at the Nature Center, I would feed the snakes live mice that I trapped nearby. I would put a smear of peanut butter on the pressure sensitive plate inside a small aluminum trap. Once the mouse went inside and touched the plate, the door would close behind it. Besides mice and shrews, Carolina wrens were also caught regularly. It is impossible to see inside the trap when it's closed, but the sound of the Carolina wren's wings brushing the sides would give it away.

One of the most frequent questions I answered during the winter months pertained to the welfare of the birds. People would call, especially when below freezing temperatures were forecast, and ask, "What can I do to help the birds? How can I help keep them warmer?"

I answered, "All you have to do is to keep your feeders filled. Their feathers keep them warm enough on the coldest nights."

Sometimes I explain that birds are warm-blooded like we are: they maintain a constant body temperature. Food is their fuel and like us they burn the calories to maintain body temperature. So keeping seed in the feeders is what they need because that's their fuel.

Unfortunately, something tragic happened in the early morning hours of January 18, 1977 that showed that food is not always enough. The forecast was for minus 18 degrees for Wheeling. Before going to bed that evening I ventured outside wearing my warmest clothes. As I walked through the 14-acre woods behind the house it was quieter than I had ever experienced. When I stopped walking there were no sounds anywhere.

Minutes later the trees were creaking in the gusty wind and I thought, "How in the world can these plants and animals survive? THIS IS COLD! It's time for me to go back inside!"

That night the temperature dropped to minus 22 degrees: 54 degrees below freezing. Also that night, throughout the middle and upper Ohio Valley and northward, most of the Carolina wrens died...their stomachs emptied of food while trying to maintain their body temperature against such deep cold and they froze to death. It was five years before I heard or saw another Carolina wren.

BANDING WOES

Ninety-nine percent of the time, my bird banding operations ran as smooth as silk. However if I made a mistake when submitting my banding data, I received a letter requesting clarification. Mistakes such as a wrong AOU (American Ornithologists' Union) number or reporting the same bird twice with two different banding dates had to be explained and corrected.

Most people who chase birds learn to identify them by sight and then spend many more years learning the songs and calls. Banders, due to the nature of their activity, are able to learn certain nuances about each species which other birders cannot. I would guess that 99 % of birders have not actually seen a bird's ear. They are probably not familiar with eye colors of most species and how the eye colors can change over time. They don't know which birds are feisty and which are docile when in hand and they are not familiar with the proper handling techniques for holding a bird.

Early in my banding experience I was fascinated by how different the demeanor of each bird species was when they were caught. Chickadees and titmice were scrappers, while juncos and goldfinches were so still in the net one would hardly know they were alive. As I removed a junco, sometimes the bird would remain so still that the only indication of life was the eyes following my every movement.

Even among similar kinds of birds, personalities varied greatly between species. This was very obvious with the woodpeckers. Downys, red-bellied, northern flickers, and pileateds were aggressive and animated, while hairys and yellow-bellied sapsuckers were quite passive. The bites from woodpeckers were relatively painless; however pecks from a closed beak could hurt.

When removing a hairy woodpecker from a net I sometimes thought, "This bird is so much larger than a downy and its beak is far more impressive, but it hardly moves at all. Downys are like tiny feathered tigers, but this bird is like someone's pet pussycat."

Knowing how to hold a potentially pain-causing bird safely was an asset. Still, there were times I wasn't as cautious as I should have been. One particular instance involved my first yellow-bellied sapsucker. In the net the sapsucker was just like the hairy—showing no resistance at all. While I was removing it, I noticed a family watching me from inside through a large picture window.

I decided to bring the bird in to show the family. Experienced banders can hold most birds by the legs allowing onlookers the best view of the bird. Some birds when held this way bite at the bander's hand and others do not. Some birds, like cardinals and other heavily-beaked finches, are never held this way by banders because of the damage they can cause to a finger or thumb.

The sapsucker had remained calm the entire time of his lengthy captivity, so I decided to do something I will never attempt to do with any woodpecker again…EVER!

I decided to hold it by its legs. My intentions were good: I wanted this family to experience the full amazing beauty of the woodpecker. But when I grabbed the legs with one hand, held it up and let go with the other hand, the sapsucker immediately drilled my thumb with its bill. Blood spurted everywhere.

My happy visitors were now horrified by what they saw. The mother summed it all up in one phrase, **"OH MY GOD!"**

After changing my hold on the bird and wrapping my thumb, I put on my best happy face to try and defuse the horrifying picture burnt into these people's minds. I asked, as I always did, "Would anyone like to release this bird?"

They were still shocked by what they had witnessed so no one wanted to be anywhere near the sapsucker. Even today, I can imagine this family talking about their trip to Oglebay Park and the monster sapsucker, which instead of sucking sap that day, went after that poor man's blood.

Aging and sexing techniques for birds vary greatly among the species. Some birds, like chickadees, are so alike it is usually impossible to tell their gender. However, according to my banding manual, I can call a chickadee a male if it is showing a cloacal protuberance (I have never seen one on any bird), and call a chickadee a female if it has a large incubation patch. An incubation patch is a defeathered area on the lower abdomen where the skin has thickened and become rich with blood vessels to aid in warming the eggs. The key word here is "large" since, in some instances, the male will also incubate the eggs to a lesser extent and will actually have a small incubation patch.

So the problem with aging and/or sexing birds has to do with something I refer to as "frame-of-reference". Unless one has something to compare to on a regular basis, words like "large" and "small", "thick" and "thin", "long" and "short" are ambiguous terms giving no actual standard for judging or deciding.

Since I generally band birds during times of the year when they are not incubating eggs, I never see the patch. However, if I would catch a chickadee during nesting time and it did have in incubation patch, I would still have no idea if it was "large" or "small" since I have nothing to compare it to. The Bird Banding Manuals attempt to solve these problems by giving detailed information about characteristics to look for at certain times of the year.

According to me, I didn't have a problem determining the age or gender of American goldfinches. Sometimes when I caught a goldfinch during the cold weather months, I would mark the sex as U (unknown). From mid-October through December I would mark the age as U and from January through mid-April the age was listed as AHY (after the hatching year). I was comfortable with the way I interpreted the guidelines but, according to the BBL, I had a problem aging and sexing American goldfinches. One day I received the following letter from them:

> *Dear Mr. Beatty,*
>
> *I am writing in reference to the schedules which you recently submitted to the Bird Banding Laboratory with age and/or sex problems regarding the American Goldfinch. It seems that there is some confusion regarding the ageing and/or sexing of this species.*
>
> *American Goldfinches can be sexed by the color of*

their wings. Birds with black wings are safely sexed male; those with brown wings are safely sexed female. Occasionally you will encounter a bird with very dull black wings or very rich brown wings which may appear black. It is best to sex these birds unknown unless there are some black feathers in the crown. If there are black feathers in the crown, then it is safe to sex them male.

There is no accurate way to age the female goldfinches by plumage coloration. However, the males can be relatively easily aged by plumage. Birds with rich, black flight feathers <u>and</u> yellow shoulder patches <u>and</u> extensive white tippings to the secondaries and several of the primaries may safely be sexed AHY in the fall and ASY from January through the breeding season. Birds with dull black wings <u>and</u> brown to olive shoulders and little white edging on the secondaries and primaries may be safely aged HY in the fall and SY from January through the breeding season.

I hope these comments have helped to clarify the ageing and sexing techniques for the American Goldfinch. If I can be of any further assistance, please do not hesitate to contact me. Thank you for your continued cooperation in the North American Bird Banding Program.

Sincerely yours,

This letter didn't help me any more than the identical instructions in my Bird Banding Manuals. My confusion lay

in the fact that, when I had a goldfinch in hand, I wasn't sure
what the difference was between "black", "dull black" and
"rich brown that may appear black and brown". The letter
from the BBL did nothing to help my frame of reference.

For years, with each goldfinch I caught I thought, "This
one looks black, but is it 'rich' or 'dull' black, and if it's 'dull'
black, then maybe it's really just 'rich brown' that appears to
be black." Even the year I banded 14 goldfinches they were
caught one or two at a time so I still couldn't really compare
colors to build the frame-of-reference I needed to age and sex
them.

However, there came a day when my American goldfinch
problem was solved. In 1976 something happened that
changed everything: thistle/niger seed became available
for the first time. It made a huge difference to the number
of goldfinches visiting feeders. I caught 29 goldfinches that
winter, followed by 122 goldfinches during 1977-78, and then
229 in 1978-79. Now I can look out at the feeders in winter and
easily tell the males from the females and know which males
were born this year and which ones were born in a previous
year. Starting in 1977-78 the goldfinch became the most
common species of bird I banded.

Bird banding proved to be a very popular attraction for
the Nature Center's visitors. When I had birds in the holding
cages visitors would watch me band them. The children
especially loved it when I let them release the birds.

When birders stopped by I had new information to add to
their knowledge. I would explain the intricate details of aging
juncos and woodpeckers by eye color or mention that black-
capped chickadee wings and tails were just a few millimeters
longer than those of the Carolina chickadees or perhaps

explain an aging technique called skulling which is used to determine if the bird was born that year or some previous year.

Since people were so interested by the banding, we decided to publicize some dates when I would be live trapping and banding birds. We set aside one day each week for two months when the general public could stop by, observe and possibly release banded birds.

Right away we ran into problems. On the best banding days, when the weather was overcast, with snow on the ground, cold temperatures and no wind, few people came. We caught many birds on those days and everyone there was able to hold and release one or more. Those who did come out in that "bad" weather had a wonderful time. On the other hand, on the worst banding days with sunny skies, no snow and warm temperatures, we were overwhelmed with visitors but had very few birds to show. In future years we didn't advertise our banding.

RED-TAILED HAWKS AND GREAT HORNED OWLS

When I began working at the Brooks Nature Center we regularly received calls from individuals who found baby or injured animals. Most of the time I would explain that we did not take animals, but I could tell them how to take care of it. Some callers would continue to admonish me and almost beg me to take the baby or babies.

What I said concerning adult injured animals, was almost an order: "Leave it alone! Warm blooded animals can carry dangerous, sometimes fatal, diseases that humans can contract." Depending on the mammal, I sometimes referred them to the local conservation officer and provided the necessary contact information.

Sometimes the person at the other end would sternly say, "Well, if it dies, it will be your fault!" and then hang up. On rare mornings I found a box or some container at the front entry to the Nature Center containing one or several baby animals. A few years later when the Good Zoo opened in Oglebay Park I was able to refer all baby animal and injured animal phone calls to the Zoo. It was such a relief.

There was one group of animals the Nature Center did take, however—raptors. When someone called with an injured hawk, owl or sparrow hawk I would tell them that we did have a raptor rehabilitation program, but because the caller had possession of a bird and because the Nature Center was located in West Virginia's northern panhandle, with Ohio and Pennsylvania both close by, there was some additional information I had to relate.

According to federal law it was actually illegal for them to possess the bird and crossing state lines with the bird complicated matters even more. After explaining that to them, I would say, "I cannot give you permission or tell you to bring the bird here; that is entirely up to you."

At the time, my Master Bird Banding Permit was also considered a salvage permit, allowing me to possess feathers, birds, etc., but a Federal Rehabilitation Permit was also required for keeping young and injured birds for future release back into the wild.

The first raptor I received was a red-tailed hawk. On the phone the caller had said, "We have a hawk here. There's something wrong with it. When I came to work this morning I found it cowering in a corner of the gravel bay. I threw a blanket over it and have it here wrapped up in the blanket."

I explained the laws to him and before long a truck pulled into the parking lot. A man got out, opened the tailgate, picked up an armful of blanket and walked toward the building. Waiting at the doorway I welcomed him and invited him downstairs. In the classroom we unwrapped the hawk. It immediately flew into one of the large picture windows. I managed to gather the bird and, after putting it into a cage, the man went back to work.

Right away, I started examining the hawk. I couldn't

find anything wrong with it—the legs and talons were fine, both wings flapped strongly and evenly, and both were held squarely while the bird stood upright. To me the bird was obviously healthy and uninjured, so I decided to band and release it. Upon release the bird flew away, showing no signs of any problem.

Another red-tailed hawk caused difficulties of a serious nature. One morning a man showed up with one he had encountered while out deer hunting. The bird had been shot through the foot but the wings were apparently fine. I decided to keep the bird until the foot healed. For the few weeks I kept this hawk, the only contact I had with the bird was when I fed it and cleaned the cage. When I cleaned the cage, first I would pull the curtains on the windows so the bird wouldn't try to fly at the glass to what appeared to be the "outside." Then as I cleaned, I watched the bird hobble about the floor of the classroom. The foot was making evident progress in healing.

The day finally came when I decided it was probably ready to be banded and released, but two things still bothered me. When the foot had healed a large callous had formed near where the foot attached to the leg and the normal power in that foot was diminished. I could feel the difference in strength as it sat squeezing my gloved hand. A comment on my rehabilitation permit warned to be careful about banding *apparently* rehabilitated birds. It stated, "Release the bird unbanded if unsure about complete rehabilitation."

I decided to band the bird, which turned out to be a big mistake. A few weeks later I received phone call from the BBL about the #608-...-.. size 8 lock-on band issued to me. A woman had found the hawk, dead, near her pond. On the band she had found the BBL phone number and had called. She was irate! She had described to them how the hawk had been chasing her ducks and had killed two of them. The follow-up call I received from the BBL was a reprimand for banding a bird that was not fully rehabilitated and they requested that I call the woman to explain what had happened. The next morning I called. The woman was calmer by then, but was still somewhat upset about what had happened to her ducks.

She asked, "Why would this hawk kill my ducks? Nothing like this had ever happened before."

I explained the plight of the hawk—how it had been shot, the rehabilitation I had done and its release. I told her that the hawk had probably tried to hunt for its normal prey of small mammals like rabbits and squirrels, but wasn't successful. The ducks were easier prey and it managed to catch a couple, but even that was not enough to keep it from getting weak from hunger and eventually freezing to death.

My explanation helped her see things from a different point of view and she immediately became sympathetic toward the hawk.

She said, "I have the bird here in my freezer. Would you like to have it?"

When I arrived she was very gracious, welcomed me and asked if I would like a cup of tea. When I got up to leave she took the hawk from the freezer, handed it to me and then asked, "Can I keep this?"

In her other hand was the bird band.

I answered, "Yes."

She said, "I am sorry about your hawk."

And I said, "I am sorry about your ducks."

The first owl I received was a great horned owl, found along a roadway, probably hit by a car. I held the bird up and saw that the left wing hung noticeably lower than the right wing. I called a nearby veterinarian for advice.

Before long I was at the animal hospital with the caged great horned owl. Inside the waiting room were several people with dogs and a cat.

The doctor came out immediately, announced to the people there, "We have an emergency, but it shouldn't take long," and he rushed me into an examination room in the back part of the hospital.

"The first thing we need to do is to determine the bird's weight so I can put it to sleep for a short while," he said. He added, "Bird weights are deceiving. Even though it looks heavier, let's give it a shot for a seven pound bird."

After the injection, the bird went to sleep and we weighed it…four pounds. The doctor assured me by saying, "The anesthetic I used has great latitude and hopefully the owl will be okay."

The doctor positioned the injured wing and wrapped it with tape that went under the other wing and tightly around the body. The next thing he did was quite surprising to me: the entire bird was rolled up in what looked like butcher paper that was fastened with tape. Through one end of the tube I could see the top of the owl's head. The tail and feet showed at the other end.

The doctor explained, "Rolling the bird up like this gives it time to get used to the tape around its body. Once it regains consciousness, leave it rolled up for an hour before taking the paper off. Without the paper, when the owl woke up it would immediately try to remove the tape."

Finally the doctor said, "If it had needed a surgical procedure, that is something you wouldn't be able to do. But taping a broken wing is something you could do at the Nature Center. Leave the tape on for three and a half weeks. Good luck!"

Driving back to the Nature Center I heard the owl start fussing as he awoke. There was an occasional clacking of the beak and some rustling of the butcher paper. Inside the Nature Center I just put the rolled up owl on the floor. Most of the time the owl was quiet, but at times the tube of paper with owl inside rolled partly across the floor.

After about an hour I removed the paper. The owl totally ignored the tape on its wing and around the body. Three and a half weeks later I removed the tape. Putting the owl on my gloved hand, everything appeared to line up perfectly. After another week of fattening the bird up and letting it get accustomed to the use of both wings, I banded it and released it near where it had been found.

As a young boy I always liked having some extra money for bean shooters, comic books, or baseball cards. I remember one older neighborhood boy who sometimes made money by killing great horned owls. He would find a nest, climb the tree and kill the young owls shortly before they were ready to leave the nest. He then cut off their legs and received a reward when he turned the legs in to the local conservation officer. In the 1950s great horned owls were considered varmints and of no value. They were blamed by farmers for killing chickens and by hunters for killing small game animals. I sometimes thought, "I can't wait until I'm old enough to kill some owls." Fortunately, I never did.

Some years later a researcher pieced together the relationship between great horned owls and skunks. Skunks are the number one carrier of rabies in North America and they have only one natural predator—the great horned owl. Since most birds do not have a sense of smell and great horned owls are powerful enough to kill the much larger skunk, the skunk is the perfect prey for the owl. With that discovery the owl went from being on the varmint list to being protected.

One morning I went to work before the sun came up so I could set my mist nets to catch the earliest feeder birds. This day I wasn't the first person there. Parked in the parking lot was a milk delivery truck. Out stepped someone I knew from West Liberty.

"Kenny," I said, "what brings you out so early?"

He replied, "This isn't early for me. The cows determine when I get up and when I go to bed. Com'on back here. I have something for you."

He pounded on the back doors of the truck and there was an awful ruckus of bumping and bottles clanking.

Kenny said, "Go ahead open it up."

Inside was a great horned owl attempting to fly toward us right out of the truck but something was holding it back.

"Found it like this at one of my stops this morning. Thought you would like to have it," Kenny said.

Both legs of the owl were in a leg trap which was attached to a chain fastened to a pole.

When I approached the owl I thought, "This is going to be more difficult than I expected."

The owl stunk. It had been recently sprayed by a skunk. I got a cage, took a deep breath and, as quickly as I could, I grabbed the owl by the legs, opened the jaws of the trap, slid the legs out and put the owl in the cage.

"I knew you would want that owl. I got to go. I've already been here way too long," he said.

"Thanks Kenny!" I said and the milk truck sped off.

Besides some bruising on the legs, the owl was uninjured. Due to the skunk smell I put the cage on the back porch. Later that same day I banded it and released it near where it was found.

For years I usually had one or more birds in the process of healing. Later the Zoo took over the rehabilitation of birds as well as mammals and that was a weight off of my shoulders. The Zoo had more than adequate facilities and their staff was more qualified and better trained for taking care of all animals. They also had a veterinarian available any time they needed him.

I often used the rehab or live animal exhibit birds from the zoo in my teaching at the Nature Center. One day I received a call from a teacher in Steubenville, OH. She wanted me to visit her classroom and do a program about owls.

The Zoo had a great horned owl being rehabilitated so I made plans to borrow it. On the day before my owl program, I put a cage and my owl gloves in the back of my car and drove to the Zoo. The owl was alert and showed no signs of its previous injuries. It was healthy and seemed to have even more of an "attitude" than most great horned owls. I put on the gloves, grabbed the owl's legs and transferred it into my cage.

The young lady helping me asked, "Where did you get your gloves?"

"These were specially made. I bought them locally, had them reinforced with heavier leather and added the arm extensions myself. I only use them with the great horned owls," I told her.

"Do you think I could borrow them?" she asked. "They would make my job so much easier with some of the animals we have to deal with today."

"You can use them, but I have to have them back before the end of the day. I have to work with this owl at a school tomorrow morning," I answered.

She was very appreciative and promised to return them at day's end.

At 4:00 when the Zoo closed, I began wondering about the gloves, but thought she still might deliver them before we closed at 5:00.

At 4:30 I phoned the Zoo but there was no answer. I even drove over, only to find the doors locked and no one there.

Before I had those owl gloves, I had used shorter, heavy-duty leather work gloves and I still had several pairs, so I wasn't too worried about not getting the owl gloves back.

When I arrived home that evening I showed my kids the owl in its cage. They gawked and watched the owl huffing and puffing, while bobbing and slowly moving from side-to-side. My son, Josh, reached to touch the cage and the owl lunged toward him grabbing the thick screening on front. All three kids fell backwards and looked up at me with wide-eyed stares.

After my children went back to playing I thought, "This owl could be a handful tomorrow at the school. I better make sure I can handle it with the shorter gloves."

Years before I had had a great horned owl hold so tightly to my hand that I couldn't get if off. After a while the bird perched on my hand seemed heavier and heavier and my arm had dropped lower and lower. As my arm dropped, the owl slowly walked onto my wrist, up my arm and onto my shoulder. Since that owl was used to being held and the trail of puncture wounds up my arm had been shallow, I hadn't panicked. I was at the Nature Center at the time so I had finally been able to get help removing the owl.

I thought, "Tomorrow I will be in front of a group of school children. If the same thing were to happen then, it wouldn't be good at all."

I put on the gloves. I was reminded of information that I regularly taught in my owl programs—that owls have 200 to

300 hundred pounds per square inch of crushing power in their talons. An average adult human male has about 60 pounds per square inch in his hands. These gloves looked so scanty compared to the gloves I had become accustomed to using.

"I think I'm getting spoiled," I thought.

When I opened the top of the cage to reach in, the owl was on its back with outreached legs and sharply taloned toes wide open reaching for me. It was prepared to defend itself. Wanting to avoid the time it takes to unwrap those talons from around the gloves, I reached quickly for the legs. Something went terribly wrong—this time I was too slow. And worse yet, the gloves were not thick enough.

One of the talons went through the glove and deep into my hand. Even without being able to see the damage, I could tell I was in trouble. Trying to keep the owl from moving, I only disturbed it more and it squeezed tighter sending even more pain through my hand.

"There is no easy way out of this," I thought. "Great! Now what?"

At that same moment, from around the back corner of the house, came Richard, a photographer friend.

I said, "Richard, I need help! I have a talon in my hand."

By that time I had the owl out of the cage and lying against the ground.

Richard smiled and answered, "Okay, but let me take a few pictures first."

And he did take pictures...many pictures.

Finally Richard asked, "Now, what do you want me to do?"

Pointing, I said, "Put those gloves on. Now take hold of the owl's legs and hold tight."

I took the glove from my good hand so I could feel my way through what I was about to do.

"Squeeze the owl's legs as tight as you can," I directed.

With my thumb and pointer finger I grabbed the talon and thought, "There is really no easy way to do this." I took a deep breath.

The talon was almost two inches long and curved, making it very difficult to pull straight out. Pulling as hard as I could on the talon, it scrapped the inside of my hand its entire length, but I got it out. I took the glove off. The talon had gone all the way through my hand. It had entered between my middle and ring finger on my right hand and came through between the knuckles.

"Richard, I can't believe you showed up when you did," I said. "I wouldn't have known what to do."

Richard responded, "It was perfect timing. I think I got some great photos!"

Even though the wound went all the way through my hand there was little bleeding. I washed my hand and added two band aids.

When I awoke the next morning my wound didn't look so bad and there was hardly any pain so I went to the school with the owl. This time I didn't want to take any chances so I wore two pair of thick leather gloves. The program was a huge success even though the owl was quite rambunctious. Bobbing its head and looking at the kids as he refocused his eyes, I could see the kids were in a state of wonderment. That afternoon I delivered the owl back to the Zoo and retrieved my gloves. The young lady who had borrowed the gloves hadn't remembered to deliver them to me and was very apologetic. I didn't tell her what had happened.

Back at the Nature Center I told Dot about my bad owl experience.

She asked me, "Did you go to the doctor?"

"No," I replied, "I'm fine now."

Growing up, my grandmother was always the one who took care of all kinds of medical conditions that, for some folks, might require a doctor, including delivering an occasional baby. The only time I had gone to a doctor was for broken bones and for a nail through my foot. My present injury seemed fine now. When Dot went to Oglebay Institute's Administrative Offices to get the mail that afternoon she talked to others about my run-in with the owl. Shortly after she returned I received a call from the head of the Institute.

"I want you to go to the hospital…now," he said, "If you don't go today and there are any future complications they will not be covered under workman's comp."

At the emergency room I told the nurse about the owl putting a talon through my hand. She furrowed her brow and asked, "An owl? You did say an owl didn't you?"

She was even more shocked when she asked, "Who is your insurance carrier," and I answered, "It's covered under workman's comp."

"You're serious aren't you?" she remarked.

"Yes I am."

Soon a doctor came in, looked at the chart and then went back out. I could hear him say, "You aren't going to believe this. I got a guy in here who says he has a puncture wound all the way through his hand from an owl."

I thought, "It's not as if I were in gun battle on the street or had crowbar through my skull. It's a little hole through my hand and hardly noticeable."

Then I heard the doctor say, "And it's covered under workman's comp," which caused an even bigger commotion.

Someone said, "We should call that guy at the Nature Center to see if an owl could even do that."

In a raised voice I said, "**I am <u>that</u> guy.**"

BIRDING SEASONS

Significant aspects of my life were changing. I had always heard, and sometimes listened to the sounds of civilization: people speaking, cars speeding by, ticking clocks and distant airplanes. Now I heard other voices, from beyond civilization, coming from everywhere.

In winter I heard the frozen snow crunching beneath my feet no matter where I went. In the beech woods the dried dead leaves continued to hold on to their birthplace and, with the slightest breeze, rustled. Birds stingily saved their spring songs and only sparingly gave their music to the bare woods.

Spring brought additional voices. The melting snow and year's first rains joined as whispering rivulets that eventually merged to become streams. The solitary bird songs of winter became multitudes of beautiful choruses. I was becoming more conscious.

Summer brings the beginning of the end for most nesting birds. Early on the songs of many fulfilled males echoed the woodlands and meadows announcing successful nests. However, as time marched on the songs became fewer and fewer. Becoming aware also brought a kind of dejection—I was missing something in summer that for most of my life I never knew existed.

As fall approached there were male cicadas, katydids, grasshoppers, and crickets vying for nearby females with their songs. During the fall, until the first frost, I became accustomed to sleeping near an open window. Some nights I was captivated by the insect sounds—separating and identifying as many as I could. It was a long time before I fell asleep.

My activities with birds changed as the seasons changed. There were things about birds that were predictable. Fall migration, while not as exciting as in spring, gave me a chance to see northern breeders on their way south. In fall and winter, birds can easily be attracted to feeders and, for me that meant mist netting and banding. There were also occasional bird "hunts" like the Christmas Bird Count. Spring meant migration: new birds to see, identify and hopefully add to my life list. Many would be around only for a few short days before they moved on to their northern nesting grounds. Those that stayed to nest here were wonderful to see again at their most colorful. Late spring through high summer was breeding and nesting season—time to get to know the "locals" again.

There was a birder in the BBC who was so passionate about birds that he had set a life goal of seeing 700 species in North America. He and I had different approaches to birding. I was as intense as he was, but our focus was different. He focused on chasing rare birds that would add to his list and draw him closer to that magical 700 number. My focus was to learn as much as I could about the birds I saw all the time, year after year. I wanted to be able to hear a Tennessee warbler one year and recognize its song the next year and every time afterwards.

All the additions to my life list were exciting, but I didn't chase after them--mine were incidental. Besides, I taught about birds often and people expected me to know detailed information about each common, local and migrating species.

One day my 700-friend called the Nature Center, "Hi Bill. Did you hear what they did to the juncos?"

Not knowing anything about the juncos I answered, "No, I haven't heard."

"They grouped them!" he said. "There used to be four species…now there's only one. I lost three birds!"

Another time he called about the Ross' gull that appeared in 1975 along the Massachusetts' coast. Thousands of birders from all over the world went to see the bird. This gull breeds in the high arctic far north in North America and northeast Siberia and only migrates short distances to the south.

"Bill, do you want to go?" he asked. His plan was to drive to Massachusetts that same day, see the gull and drive back the next day. That didn't appeal to me so I declined. If we would have had several days I might have gone. He did the 36-hour trip and was excited.

My Special Problem's bird survey areas were still places I went regularly during all seasons of the year to see birds and, well, everything else. My forays into wild places took longer for me than they would for most other people. Other nature enthusiasts I knew had one primary nature interest and, unlike me, they had more common jobs not in nature-related fields. I was fortunate to have the best of both worlds. I could afford to take the time to observe everything.

While birding the field one spring where I had first seen the eastern bluebirds feeding on the sumac berries, I noticed some orange hawkweed flowers. They are one of my favorite flowers so instead of chasing birds I began to think about the plants of the area. I decided to visit the field at a later date and identify all the trees and other plants in this habitat. I noticed that the field was changing. Years earlier it had been a well-defined meadow, but now there were some invading trees that were not there when I did my surveys.

Two weeks later I left home with my *Flora of West Virginia* and a hand lens but no binoculars or bird book. I had decided my focus this day would be plants. In the survey field I began recording the names of all the trees along the edge and those that were invading. Then I began to record the herbaceous plants. Some I didn't know. I was excited to find two different yellow hawkweeds. Although their flowers looked identical, there were noticeable differences elsewhere on the plants. One had few flowers and the entire plant below the flowers was smooth or with very few hairs. The other was heavily flowered and the entire plant was quite hairy. These obvious differences made it easy to find them in the *Flora*, the smooth one was *H. venosum*, rattlesnake-weed, and the hairy one was *H. pretense*, field hawkweed.

The day was warm and sunny with a few big fluffy white clouds. I was in shirtsleeves sitting comfortably on the ground. As I was enjoying the plants I also relaxed and listened to the bird songs. Sometimes an indigo bunting sang, as would a cardinal, yellow-breasted chat or blue-winged warbler. Each time I heard a song I closed my eyes and visualized the bird in my mind. I realized that, since I knew the bird songs, I didn't need my binoculars or bird book to see the birds—they were all right there in my mind.

The blue-winged warbler sang again not far away. Compared to other warbler songs I was learning, this one was easy: two long buzzy notes—"BEE-BUZZZZZ!" It sang often. It was a most welcome sound. In my mind I saw this bright yellow bird with a dull-bluish back and wings. I pictured a narrow black eye line with two white bars on each wing. Through binoculars I had seen blue-winged warblers dozens of times. Suddenly, I heard the blue-winged song practically right on top of me. This time I looked up and saw—well, I wasn't sure what I saw. I had no idea what kind of bird I was looking at. Then it tilted its head back and sang, "BEE-BUZZZZZ!" I was totally confused!

I thought, "That's not a blue-winged warbler but it just sang a blue-winged song." As I watched it, again I saw and heard it sing, "BEE-BUZZZZZ!" Then it hit me. "Hybrids! Hybrids!"

There are hybrids between the blue-winged and golden-winged warblers. This had to be a hybrid. I had no idea what to call it. Not having my bird book with me, I ran all the way home.

My *Birds of North America* field guide confirmed I had discovered a Brewster's warbler, a cross between the golden-winged warbler and the blue-winged warbler. The drawing in the book looked exactly like the bird I found.

Right away I went back to the meadow, binoculars and field guide in hand. This time I approached the field as if I were tracking some dangerous adversarial prey. There was no sign of the Brewster's warbler. So I sat down and waited. Before long I was rewarded with, "BEE-BUZZZZZ!" And there it was, high atop a tree at the edge of the meadow. I watched it for several minutes until it flew to another location and began to sing again.

I thought, "Today is Saturday. I can check it out again tomorrow, and when I get to work on Monday, I can tell Dot. Boy, will she be surprised!"

On Monday I immediately told Dot. I also called several BBCers about my Brewster's warbler and many of them

wanted to know when I could take them to see the bird. I
decided on Tuesday after work. Among the 14 callers who
wanted to see the Brewsters was my friend who was chasing
after the magical 700 species.

Tuesday started as a beautiful morning but the forecast
was for rain most of the day. It began raining shortly before
noon and continued steadily the rest of the day. No one called
on Tuesday about my hybrid. My "Brewsters day" seemed
to be ruined. I left work that day shortly after 5:00 in a steady
rain, thinking, "Surely nobody's going to want to see the
Brewsters today." Still I glanced over at the restaurant as I
drove by—there were more cars there than I had ever seen
before.

At the top of the hill I turned around and drove back to the
restaurant. Almost everyone who had called was there. All
were well prepared with proper rain gear, ready to follow me
to the Brewsters field. As we were ready to get started, another
car pulled in—it was my 700-friend.

He was in a tailored suit with fancy leather dress shoes.
He had no rain gear or even an umbrella. I told him, "We are
going to be out away from the cars, tramping through weedy
areas. There will be briars and a barbed wire fence to deal
with."

He responded, "That's fine with me. I didn't have time
to go home for rain gear but I didn't want to miss this
opportunity!"

My 700 friend wasn't fazed the least little bit. His suit
was ruined: the pants were torn and the coat had what are,
ironically, referred to as "bird's nests" in several places. His
once-combed hair was soaked and hanging down toward
his eyes. When we arrived at the meadow it was still raining.
We waited a long time, even splitting up at one point to try

to flush the bird, but to no avail. My hybrid did not make
an appearance. I was very apologetic to everyone but, being
birders, they understood.

Even my 700-friend was fine with the trip saying, "Now I
know where to come. I will return in better weather." He did
and he was rewarded by seeing the Brewsters warbler.

Each time I visited the college arboretum that spring I
checked on my Brewsters. My friends all eventually would
see it, as would many others. The Brewster's warbler did not
return the next year.

Being out that spring, exploring, discovering, even when I
didn't find a hybrid warbler, kept my nature-appetite satisfied.
Migration had ended and late spring and early summer
brought nesting time. Although I had always considered
myself good at finding birds' nests, the birds were far better at
hiding them.

One clue about when a bird was going to its nest was that
it held food in its beak for a long time but didn't eat it. That
meant the food was for its babies. Baby birds require huge
amounts of food and the parents are busy all day feeding
them. When I first saw a parent bird with food I would follow
the bird with binoculars until it escaped my view. I would
move to where I last saw the bird. There I would wait until
the bird reappeared with food and I would follow it again.
I repeated the process of finding the parent and following,
finding and following, until I was near the nest. I was always
surprised at how many birds built their nests on or near the
ground.

Hiking through the arboretum one early summer day I was
listening to the loud, "Teacher, teacher, teacher, **teacher, teacher**,"
song of an ovenbird. Many warbler songs are more musical

and subdued and what I was hearing seemed impossible for such a tiny bird. Each time the ovenbird tilted its head and opened its beak, "Teacher, teacher, teacher, **teacher, teacher**," would boom out. It was as if the bird had swallowed a tiny megaphone that amplified its voice to impossible levels. Ovenbirds are more often heard than seen. They nest on the ground in deciduous woods with low sparse undergrowth. The tops of the nests are slightly arched with a cover of leaves, reminiscent of an old-time oven. This makes an ovenbird's nest nearly invisible against the leaf-littered forest floor.

Although ovenbirds are one of the larger warblers, they are difficult to observe. Hearing the song is easy but as soon as a person gets close, the bird stops singing. Their colors are not bright and the orange-crowned head is difficult to see from a distance. This particular ovenbird suddenly appeared with food in its mouth so I decided to find the nest. It didn't fly far. I went to that spot to wait. But instead of going to find food for its young, one of the parents began to chip loudly, indicating I was being scolded.

I thought, "I must already be too close to the nest."

I decided to move away from the area and observe through my binoculars. As I watched I noticed one of the birds always landed in front of a low barberry bush, stood for a few moments looking around and hopped into the bush. Knowing the nest probably wasn't in the bush, I moved to a vantage point where I could see the other side of the barberry. I was right. The ovenbird came through the bush, walked to the side of another low bush and disappeared from view. Again I moved to a better vantage point. Finally, I found the nest. It was truly invisible. The only way I could see the nest was that when a parent returned, beak full of foodstuff, four tiny hungry bird beaks would protrude from under the nest's roof begging for food.

Years later I was walking with a friend on his property one evening talking about birds and listening to the few birds that were singing.

LeJay asked, "Have you ever heard the ovenbird's skylark song?"

Not only had I not heard it, I had never even heard of it.

He said, "Follow me." Not too far along the trail we stopped. Then, as if LeJay had it all planned, I heard a song I had never heard before. It was a sweet, burbling, airy, gentle song from a bird I had thought only sang the loud and bold, "Teacher, teacher, teacher, teacher, teacher." Although we did not see the accompanying flight, John Burroughs (from *The Art of Seeing Things Essays,* by John Burroughs and Charlotte Zoe Walker) described it as:

"Surely it is an ordinary common place bird. But wait till the inspiration of its flight-song is upon it. What a change! Up it goes through the branches of the trees, leaping from limb to limb, faster and faster, till it shoots from the treetops 50 or more feet into the air above them, and bursts into an ecstasy of song, rapid, ringing, lyrical; no more like its habitual performance than a match is like a rocket; brief but thrilling; emphatic but musical. Having reached its climax of flight and song, the bird closes its wings and drops perpendicularly downward like the skylark. If its song were more prolonged, it would rival the song of that famous bird."

Mid-July through mid-August has always represented to me the only weeks of the year that are somewhat calm. Nesting is over for most birds, but fall migration hasn't yet begun. And many of the common yard birds find refuge in forests away from people.

One exception is the American goldfinch that is strictly a summer nesting species. That is because its nesting cycle is tied to the seeds forming on thistle plants.

The well-loved poem, *The Night Before Christmas*, has the line, "And away they all flew like the down of a thistle." All birders and nature enthusiasts have noticed the blow-away seed heads of the dandelion, milkweed and thistle. Blow-aways was the name I had always called the parachute-like floating seeds I sometimes noticed on breezy summer days while growing up in the Projects.

The seedpods of the milkweed were always referred to as "fishes". To us they were shaped like a fish, but seemed to have their scales on the inside.

Then there were the blow-aways we fondly referred to as "Santa Clauses." Nothing could match the pristine ballet-like flight of the Santa Clauses. They looked as if they had been constructed of a tiny seed surrounded by dozens of fine white hairs from Santa's beard.

Years later in my high school Algebra II class a Santa Claus floated in through an open window. As far as I was concerned Algebra was over for the day, or at least until the Santa Claus descended to the floor or was drawn out another window.

The American goldfinch also has an attraction to the Santa Claus seeds of the thistles, as they line their nests with "the down of a thistle." Being the expert nest builders they are, the goldfinch's soft layered nest lining is so tightly constructed that, if the parents don't protect the young during a rain, the nest fills up with water and the babies will drown. Unlike other insect-eating birds, American goldfinches feed their babies plant materials consisting mostly of thistle seeds.

One hot August day I was on the meadow plateau behind my home. Goldfinches were singing a wide variety of songs including their familiar, "Potato-chip, potato-chip, potato-chip," flight song. Some busy goldfinch activity in a smooth arrow-wood shrub caught my attention, so I moved closer. About eye level was a goldfinch nest and I backed away to observe. There were five well-developed young in the nest. The nest location and ease of observation made this ideal for photography so I decided to return early the next morning with my bird blind.

Near sunrise the next morning I began towards the meadow with my blind, tripod, binoculars, camera, camera bag and several magazines. The equipment was heavy, but I had grown used to it. We were in the midst of a heat wave, but the early morning hike was refreshing. My homemade blind, consisting of a framework of PVC pipe and a camouflaged covering, was easy and fast to set up. The parent birds had showed some concern as I set up close to the nest, but before long I was in the blind and, to the birds, it was as if I wasn't there at all.

The parent birds had already begun the day-long routine of feeding their young. Goldfinch habits are different from those of other birds. I recalled one time I had photographed willow flycatchers. About every thirty seconds a parent bird had returned to the nest with a damselfly or small dragonfly. Each time a parent visited, I shot several pictures. After one and one-half hours I was finished, took the blind down and left. Today was going to be a much longer day.

The goldfinches were visiting their nest with food about every 45 minutes. When a parent returned I heard the babies' dainty light voices that signaled me to get ready. In the four-foot square area inside the blind I sat on a milk crate. Moments later a parent flew to an arrow-wood stem above the nest while all the babies reached and begged for food. The parent had a gullet filled with plant material that was slowly regurgitated into the mouth of each baby. Their transparent skin allowed me to see the whole process in detail. "Click, click, click, click," the hum of my camera's shutter with film whirling through didn't bother the birds a bit, nor did the rapid firing of my speed-light flash. Then it was time to get back to waiting.

Again, after approximately 45 minutes, the babies began to clamor at the return of their parents. "FEED ME, FEED ME, FEED ME," they demanded in the loudest voices they could muster. By the time the morning had passed and the 95 degree afternoon heat was upon us my clothes were soaked. At times I lifted the bottom backside of the blind and sucked some of the cool outside air into my lungs.

Every 45 minutes there were calls from the baby goldfinches, a flurry of noise from my camera and then more sitting and waiting. By the time I had been in the blind eight hours, the parents had visited the nest ten times and I had shot almost 50 photos—not enough, I thought, to be assured a few great American goldfinch photos. In those days I could go for long periods of time without food, but I began to regret not bringing any water. I was tired of sitting, tired of standing, tired of reading and getting tired of goldfinches.

Looking around the four foot square area inside the blind I thought if I moved the milk crate outside there might be enough room to lie down under the tripod's legs. There was just enough room if I bent my legs with the backs of my feet against my rear end. I also discovered I could get some of that cool 95 degree air from time to time by lifting the back edge of the blind. All of a sudden I was awakened by the baby goldfinches calling and begging for food. I had fallen asleep.

As I tried to get up quickly to get to the camera for a few more pictures, I discovered my legs and feet had fallen asleep. I grabbed a leg of the tripod to help keep my balance and pull me up. As I stood, my legs were still tingling and weak so I leaned against the tripod, the tripod leaned against the blind and, before I knew it, the tripod, the blind and I were all on the ground. The parent goldfinches were having a fit, so I scampered out of the blind and hurried to the shade of a nearby dogwood tree.

Two weeks later I received the slides and was relieved to find several exceptional photos.

Years later I began working at the Allegheny Front Migration Observatory each September. The addition of this fall activity brought my birding year full circle. From winter bird-banding to spring migration to summer calm (and Goldfinches) to fall migration, I was able to chase birds year round with a wide ranging and varied assortment of activities.

T. A.

Soon after becoming the Interpretive Naturalist for Oglebay Institute's Brooks Nature Center I became aware of just how geographically far reaching the educational aspect really was of what I would be required to do. Oglebay Institute owned 18 acres of land, a peninsula projecting into Lake Terra Alta, one-half mile high in the West Virginia Mountains. From mid-June to early July the Terra Alta Mountain Nature Camp was held there. It is an adult nature studies camp. Founded by A.B. Brooks in 1929, it was, and still is, the longest, continuous running adult nature camp in the United States.

John Christie wanted me to be at the camp for part of the summer. I was to attend and help out where I could during Mountain Nature Camp and then stay and help with High School Ecology Camp. Dr. Greg Eddy was co-director of the camps along with Dr. Jay Buckelew from Bethany College.

As soon as I arrived at TA (Terra Alta), Greg introduced me to the staff: Jay Buckelew; Libby Bartholomew, retired botanist from the Botany Department at West Virginia University; Forest Buchannan, retired principal from Ohio; and Nellie, the camp cook. The first activity was a campfire Sunday evening at dusk. Everyone sat on the ground or on logs that circled the campfire. No flashlights were allowed and the campfire was yet to be lit. We all sat quietly as darkness began overtaking the light. All of a sudden a song exploded from the woodland not far away. I recognized it as a thrush, but didn't know what kind.

I thought, "Here I am, at my job, in the West Virginia Mountains, listening to one of the most beautiful sounds on the entire planet." I couldn't help but smile.

Over and over it sang. Then another joined in from a different direction and then another. So many times previously I had been alone in wild places experiencing life in its purest forms. Listening to these birds, although I was among 30 people, I felt so joined to the songs, it was as if only the birds and I existed. For those moments I was alone, tightly bonded to each bird as it sang its ethereal music.

After a time, one person arose, approached the fire pit, lit a match, carefully laid it against the tinder and then returned to his seat. We all watched as the fire grew. The thrushes continued to sing, the fire began to crackle and hiss and sizzle, and then, without instruction, almost everyone began singing:

> "Each campfire lights anew,
> the flame of friendship true.
> The joy we've had in knowing you,
> will last our whole life through."

After those words, everyone continued humming the melody through again and then immediately continued with the Rhododendron Song:

"I want to wake up in the morning,
Where the Rhododendron grow,
Where the sun comes a'peepin'
Into where I'm a sleepin'
And the song birds say, "Hello!"
I want to wander thru the wildwood
Where the fragrant breezes blow
And drift back to the mountains
Where the Rhododendron grow.

The order in which everything progressed was tradition at TA. Greg stood up and introduced the staff and me. Then all the campers introduced themselves.

One of the campers asked, "What was that wonderful bird that was singing?"

By the nods and affirmations from many of the campers and me, the question was on many of our minds.

Greg answered, "That's our camp bird, the veery. It's a thrush and the song is unforgettable. The veeries entertain us each evening before and during campfire. Their singing is our signal for lighting the fire."

He was right about the song being unforgettable. I needed to hear most bird songs repeatedly before I owned them. But this song was one I knew I would remember from that first time. It was that special, that beautiful. Later someone would remark, "It reminds me of a flutist playing a series of descending notes into a hollow log." And it does.

Walking back to my tent after campfire, I looked up and saw more stars than I had ever seen before. I stared into the vastness of the universe and, as had happened many times before, everything became a blank. There was no aspect of comprehension in my being. I was looking and I was seeing, but I couldn't fathom the enormity of it all. A chill went down my spine, partly from trying to understand and partly from the cool night air. I fell asleep thinking about the veeries, the stars and this wonderful place, so affectionately referred to as…TA.

Early the next morning I heard a loud metallic ringing: it was the triangle bell that alerted everyone that they had one-half hour before the bird walk. One-by-one we assembled in front of the dining hall.

So many birds were singing around us that we could have done the entire bird walk right in front of the dining hall, but after a while we began our walk down the camp lane. The lane, an old gravel/dirt road, was well compacted but also rutted. Leafy branches from the adjacent trees reached out and over, forming a tunnel all the way to the end. At the end of the lane we could see the sun hitting a large grassy meadow.

Early morning mountain air is cooler and damper than I was used to, and this morning had me wishing to move on, quickly, to the warming sun. The tree canopy above appeared to be grudgingly keeping the sunlight from us. Looking up through the tree canopy above, I could see the sunlight. Some of it filtered through the leaves toward us, but only rare bits would touch someone's arm or face, so softly, so gently, so briefly that no warmth could be felt. If it had not been for the birds, I think we all might have dashed for the meadow to share its obvious warmth.

Each time I was with a group of birders, I obeyed the unspoken rules: be quiet, be still, look and listen. But at TA the rules seemed more like suggestions. Not all the campers were birders but still they loved the bird walks. And I realized from the campfire the night before that some had been to TA many times previously so they had new things to tell and

old things to reminisce about with the friends they had made
at Mountain Nature Camp in years past. Listening to the
birds I felt comfortable at times, and uncomfortable at other
times, but mostly uncomfortable. At the campfire I had been
introduced as: "The Interpretive Naturalist from Oglebay who
is here to help with birds, wildflowers and other things." At my
introduction I had felt important and accomplished. Here, on
the bird walk, I felt very inadequate.

Many of the birds at TA were new to me. Some I had seen
migrating through at home, but their songs were foreign to
me. My mind was a jumble of conflicting thoughts, "Am I
supposed to teach these people? How can I teach what I don't
know myself?"

Wanting so much to learn these new bird songs, I was
finding it difficult to concentrate on their music instead of the
worries in my head. One warbler that sang often as we walked
the lane was the black-throated green warbler. Its, "ZEE-ZEE-
zee-zu-ZEE" song was repeated often, as were the songs of
other black-throated green warblers.

I thought about Greg and Glen telling me the importance
of learning the songs: "When the trees are all leafed out, often
times all we have are the songs."

And that was true at this time of year at TA. I only got
fleeting glimpses of the black-throated greens, but their songs
were constant on every bird walk and at many places on field
trips away from the camp. Almost to the end of the lane, closer
to the sunlight, Greg and Jay stopped suddenly. We all stood
silently and listened. A beautiful song was emanating from the
forest. The song was thin but musical. The music reminded me
of a slight waterfall, almost silently falling into a small pool
below, heard only by those ears intent on listening to every
perceivable sound, no matter how soft. To my list of favorite

bird songs, I added this one. However, I still had no idea what the bird was and neither Greg nor Jay seemed eager to tell us.

Finally, someone whispered, "What is it?"

Greg answered, "I have no idea. I was hoping Jay knew. I don't think I have ever heard this song before."

Jay didn't know either. But just from our descriptions and chatter, even though his ears couldn't hear the bird anymore, Forest knew. He had heard the bird and learned its song many years earlier. Now at 67 years old he had lost the ability to hear certain ranges of sound.

With a great smile on his face, he said, "It's a brown creeper and I didn't even see or hear the bird!"

Some campers pulled bird guides from their pockets and satchels to show others what a brown creeper looks like. I already knew the bird to see it, but now I began to become familiar with the song.

Finally, we reached the paved Terra Alta Lake Road that ran perpendicular to the camp lane. Just about everybody gravitated toward the warm areas of sunlight. The open field in front of us had meadow plants along the road edge and the rest was a large, yet to be cut, hay field. Across the field on the right ran a long set of electrical wires atop high goalpost-like poles.

Someone said, "Birds on the wire."

We all put our binoculars to our faces and saw four eastern meadowlarks warming in the sunlight. A meadowlark has always reminded me of Superman, but instead of the large red S surrounded by blue on his chest, a meadowlark has a black V surrounded by mostly yellow on its breast. "Spring-of-the-year, Spring-of-the-year," are the words many put to the song of the eastern meadowlark.

Over the meadow we could see the vapors rising as a mist above the grasses and other plants, some with colorful flowers.

Red-winged blackbirds, brightened by the sun, whirled back and forth through the mist. The males with their bright red epaulets and familiar call of, "Konk-la-ree," announced to other red-wings to stay away.

This being my first time at TA, I wasn't aware of another "camp bird" of sorts. When someone said, "Listen!" what we heard was a song that was quite different from any I had heard before. Although new to me past campers had big smiles on their faces.

One lady said, "I love that bubbly song. I was hoping they would come back."

"There's one…at two o'clock…it's a male," someone else said.

I quickly looked only to get a glimpse of the bird as it disappeared into the tall grass. Eventually a male appeared long enough for everyone to see it: a bobolink, a new life bird for me. Bobolinks are made for fields filled with dandelions and other yellow flowers. When on the ground among the flowers, the yellow on the back of the head and neck allows them to blend very well.

After finding it in my field guide I noticed the voice was described as, "Loud, long and bubbling." Another person's field guide described it as, "Song, in hovering flight and quivering descent, ecstatic and bubbling, starting with low, reedy notes and rollicking upward." In a word, the song was FUN!

Eventually, I was told by Don Altemus, an accomplished birder, naturalist with the Cleveland Metroparks and later long-time Bird Leader at TA, that the words he tried to put to the bobolink's music were, "A glippity, glippity, onka- la-rusala, lossa-la-rue." Kids love that description and I have always been amazed at how many have remembered it.

Everybody arrived at the dining hall at the same time, including the breakfast setup group.

Nellie, the cook, was standing in the doorway asking, "Where was my setup crew?"

Someone responded, "We were on our way back when the bobolinks started singing...honest."

Nellie sternly answered, "How many times have I heard that excuse?"

One of the veteran TA campers leaned over to me and whispered, "Her bark's a lot worse than her bite."

Then Nellie smiled and welcomed everyone in. As she walked back toward the kitchen, we could hear Nellie grumbling, "What am I going to do with this bunch? It's all birds, birds, birds with them."

Well, she had it partly right. More importantly for some, it was also, "food, food, food." Food had never been a priority for me. Little did I know that was about to change.

At TA, oatmeal is a tradition.

"Yuck," I thought. As I was serving myself, I heard someone say, "I rarely eat oatmeal at home, but I love TA oatmeal."

To my surprise, I loved it too.

I was well into my second bowl when Nellie walked into the dining hall and announced, "Don't fill up on oatmeal. Save room for breakfast."

"Breakfast?" I thought, "Wasn't this breakfast?"

Soon each long dining table had platters filled with scrambled eggs, bacon and potatoes. And it all was delicious. Another long-standing TA tradition is plenty of tasty food. Every meal, the entire week, was delicious. Forty years later, even though there are different cooks in the TA kitchen, the food is still great.

When I tell people that I return year after year to TA for the food, it's the truth.

Following breakfast and chores, were the classes. 1972s classes were: Birds, led by Greg and Jay; Wildflowers led by Libby Bartholomew; and a Nature Walk led by Forest Buchanan.

I decided to do Wildflowers first. My wildflower knowledge was extensive, or so I thought, until I met Libby. She was short and heavy-set and walked with a cane. She and Dr. Core were close friends. When I discovered the Dr. Core connection, I felt as if I were among royalty. Dr. Core was one of the authors of *The Flora of West Virginia*, my 1000+ page textbook for Systematic Botany.

"This is where it all happens," she said. "Out here where the real plants are, not in some classroom with your nose in a textbook," she roared.

Libby was a keying machine, not that she needed keys to identify the flowers we were finding. But she knew we were novices and was eager for us to know and learn. We keyed out every flower we found. She was one of the happiest, most endearing people I would ever meet. She and I hit it off right away.

The hand lens I use today I got from Libby that first day in her wildflower class. Every time I use it I recall times such as at Cranesville Swamp, before the boardwalk was built, as she was walking along prodding the soggy clumps of vegetation with her cane. All of a sudden the cane went deep into the bog and Libby disappeared behind several high sphagnum moss hummocks. She rose back up as if nothing had happened and continued on, only to have it happen again later.

Libby was never embarrassed about her falls, and we, too, realized, "It's Libby. That's who and how she is."

More than once I saw her strike her cane against the ground and chastise a camper, "Don't you dare pick that flower! It's there for a purpose and the purpose is not to have us pick it."

She would then gently talk about the wildflowers and anyone could see she was sincere in her concern for the well-being of every creature, including us campers.

Following Monday morning's class there was a short time before lunch. New campers were becoming acquainted with the old-timers. A popular meeting place was the wooden benches in front of the dining hall.

One common camp bird that most of us already knew was the northern parula, a small warbler. It regularly sang most of the day from a stand of tall spruce trees to one side of the dining hall. Hearing the parula was one thing, but trying to see it was another. Before each meal at least one person would be trying to get a good look at the bird. The song is a buzzy trill-like crescendo with a single noted hiccup or sneeze at the end, "zeeeeeeee-up."

Often looking through binoculars until our arms were tired, we would stop for mealtime, only to return afterwards to try again. Some persisted and were rewarded with spectacular views, with the sun in the perfect position in the sky, allowing the colors to jump out like a blaze. Others might see the bird in the open, but with the sun behind so that all one saw would be a black silhouette. And still others would never see the parula at all. Every year, in the same stand of spruce trees, TA harbored a singing northern parula warbler.

During part of Forest Buchanan's tenure at TA, for the third topic he often taught a general botany class, sometimes tying in ecology, showing how everything was a small part of a bigger picture. Not being able to hear most birds any longer, he usually talked about plants, chiefly ferns, clubmosses, trees and woody shrubs. More than anyone I had ever met; Forest was the best-rounded naturalist when it came to taxonomy. In addition to the birds and wildflowers, he was an expert in trees, grasses and ferns as well. Forest was an accomplished nature photographer, taxidermist and big-game hunter.

Over the years I sometimes went on trips specifically searching for something he told me that he would like to photograph. Once I brought him a melanistic eastern garter snake. He and I searched through field guide after field guide trying to make it into something else, but there are only so many kinds of garter snakes. We even counted scale rows and finally came to the conclusion that it was just a common eastern garter snake, albeit a very black one.

On his walks Forest liked to call everything by its scientific name. It sounded a bit pretentious to those who hadn't met him before, but, with his gentle personality, he could get away with it and no one I know of ever thought less of him.

He would often hold up a plant he had already talked about and ask who remembered this fern, or tree, or plant?

If someone did, fine, but if no one volunteered an answer, he would pick someone and lead them on with hints and clues until they knew the answer. And then Forest would revel in their knowing the correct answer, even though he had practically given the answer away. There was never anyone who didn't eventually get the right answer. Forest always made sure of that.

Later that week, during a field trip to Cranesville Swamp, Forest, another camper and I were bringing up the rear. A prairie warbler began to sing.

"Forest," I said, "Do you hear that?"

He didn't hear it. The three of us stood there listening. Again it sang.

"Did you hear it?" I asked again, "It's a prairie warbler."

Then the other camper said, "There it is again. Did you hear it this time?" We both almost insisted that he must hear it.

Finally, Forest, as angry as Forest could ever be (which wasn't very) just said, "No, I can't hear it," and walked away.

On the drive back to camp, it finally hit me that of course he couldn't hear it. The prairie's song was now out of his hearing range. I felt embarrassed and foolish at how insistent I had been about him hearing the bird.

The TA Mountain Nature Camp has a long history of finding some of the rarest plants and animals in West Virginia and, on occasion, world records. On June 18, 1952 Forest had taken a group of campers from TA to a bog formed in the valley at the headwaters of White Oak Spring Run 4.5 miles northeast of the Mountain Nature Camp. As he was leading the group he flushed a bird from its nest containing three eggs. It was a white-throated sparrow, and the habitat, nest, and eggs were typical for the species.

The following day Forest took the campers back to the bog and found another white-throated sparrow nest with three eggs and the empty shell of another on the ground nearby. One of the eggs was that of a cowbird. The find was so significant that others came to confirm it, including experts from the Carnegie Museum of Natural History in Pittsburgh. That location became the southern-most place on the planet that this northern species of bird has been known to nest.

In 1974 we received a call from Roger Tory Peterson. He knew of the TA Mountain Nature Camp and wanted a favor. His son, Lee, was finishing up the *Field Guide to Edible Wild Plants* for the Peterson Field Guide series and he needed some photos for the book. Roger wanted to send Lee to TA. At camp

Greg told me that we were going to spend some time taking Lee Peterson to some special West Virginia places so he could get some needed photos.

One day a Volkswagon bus came down the camp's long lane and out got a tall lanky young man with red hair. It was Lee Peterson. Two of the photos he needed were of New Jersey tea and prickly pear cactus. Forest was the only one at camp who knew exactly where to go for the photos. Forest, Greg, Andy Hoffmann (a former Junior Nature camper from Wheeling) and I got into Greg's car and headed out with Lee following in his van.

Not long into the trip Greg looked into his rearview mirror and said, "I can't see Lee's van." We found the van parked and Lee high up on a rock outcropping. It seems he couldn't resist the temptation.

We informed him that he would be tempted a lot on today's trip in West Virginia, but we had a long day ahead of us and he needed to keep up with us.

We drove up and over the Dolly Sods mountain plateau where Lee photographed the New Jersey tea. Then we dropped off the Allegheny Front escarpment into the rain shadow lowlands to the east for the prickly pear cactus photos. Forest guided us to an expansive field that was part of a shale barrens where there were plenty of cacti.

The shale barrens and rain shadow areas have a flora very different due to the mountain ranges causing almost all rain to fall before it reached those areas. Most of the plants grew close to the ground with the only exceptions being a few short, shrubby hawthorn trees.

As Lee was looking around and setting up his camera equipment, Andy and I began exploring the barrens. Suddenly there was a loud, odd vibrating boom just above our heads. It was a common nighthawk flying almost straight up, high into the air. Then it dove straight down toward us. When it was about ten feet from us we heard that same sound again, just before it began another ascent. We both ducked and protected our heads. Forest and Greg came over to stand alongside us.

The bird continued the same aerial performance over and over. Soon we weren't ducking as it zoomed near and we could observe the entire flight and anticipate the sound. At the bottom of its dive the nighthawk quickly flexed its wings downward and as the air moved through the wing feathers it made the loud sound which had surprised us. Apparently we were too close to its eggs and we were being confronted. The whole performance reminded me of a tiny jet airplane buzzing onlookers on the ground. It was the first and only time I ever witnessed this display.

Our focus on the nighthawk was suddenly interrupted by an abrupt wind, dark black clouds and the heaviest rain imaginable. It was shocking. No one saw it coming and none of us were prepared. When we had arrived at the meadow, the sky had been sunny without a cloud in sight. Not only was the rainfall heavy but the water drops were huge and they hurt. I ran to one of the small hawthorns and hunkered down trying to escape the pain and to protect my binoculars from the rain. Moments later the sky cleared and it was sunny again. We were all drenched from head to toe and poor Lee's camera equipment was soaked. The last thing I remember after campfire that night was walking toward my tent and seeing Lee's lighted van with Lee still working on his wet camera equipment.

My first trip to TA Mountain Nature Camp had come to an end. Two weeks of chasing, learning, meeting people and making new friends were over. Now I had an entire day to myself before the students would begin arriving for the week-long High School Ecology Camp I was to lead.

I decided to explore an adjacent high point called Glover's Knob. Getting to the knob I flushed several bobolink. The meadows covering the top of the knob were home to nesting savannah and grasshopper sparrows under the watchful eye of a resident sparrow hawk. I sat for a long time just watching, listening and thinking.

For the entire two weeks at Mountain Nature Camp I hadn't done any work. Instead of being a leader or instructor as other staff members were, I had been more of a camper, being taught and being paid to learn. I wanted to do something productive to earn my keep.

On Sunday campers began arriving. The difference was they were high school students. Greg and Jay greeted each one along with their parents and introduced them to the camp's facilities. I, on the other hand, was doing nothing. Remembering how overgrown some parts of the woodland trails had become, I decided to cut some grass at the entry points and along the trails. Soon I had everything together. I pushed the mower to the nearest trail, started it and began mowing. Just moments later, as if out of nowhere, a hand grabbed my shoulder and pulled so hard, I fell to the ground.

The mower sputtered to a stop and I looked up at Greg who was admonishing me. "What do you think you are doing? You're a birder! You need to protect your ears!"

I haven't forgotten the lesson Greg taught me that day. Because I have protected my hearing from then on, I can still hear all the bird songs.

Much later I became the Program Director of the TA Mountain Nature Camp, in charge of recruiting instructors and trip leaders, as well as teaching many classes. TA will be with me for the rest of my life no matter where I am. I return to Mountain Nature Camp every chance I get.

FAMILY AND BIRDS

What a privilege it is to have children. Raising my children taught me about myself: shortcomings that were necessary to change and strengths that I continued to nourish. Children have ways of bringing out the best, and sometimes the worst, in us.

Often at least one of my children would accompany me on local forays birding. Barbed wire fences would find us sliding under on our backs. Everything in nature intrigued me, but Kelly would be interested if I could relate something special about a tree, a bird, or maybe a wildflower. Josh was younger and liked to beat on trees with sticks.

One of my most memorable times was a short outing with Josh. It was a beautiful day. The trees were at the peak of their fall color, and there wouldn't be many more beautiful days like this one. It was mushroom season and I decided to go mushrooming after work.

As I walked toward the house I could see Josh, then four-years-old, waiting excitedly at the door. No sooner than I entered the house Josh was pulling at my hand saying, "Com'on Dad let's go."

The shortest route to our destination was through a small

rural cemetery. Josh is fascinated with the smoothness and intricacies of the marble tombstones. He touches as many as he can as we pass by. I hear a red-breasted nuthatch calling from an old red cedar standing in the middle of the cemetery. Its tin whistle, "Yank-yank-yank," reminds me that cold weather will soon be upon us.

Josh asks, "What are you looking at?"

"A red-breasted nuthatch; I can hear it in that tree, but can't see it," I answer.

Then Josh asks the same question he always asks as we traverse the cemetery, "Where's Mildred?"

Josh never knew Mildred, but he has heard Bev and me speak of her. If West Liberty had a hall of heroes and heroines, Mildred would head the list. She had touched the lives of many people in town. One lady sings with the tongue of an angel thanks to voice lessons made possible by her. She provided piano lessons for many others, and countless bags of groceries for those who could not afford them. Josh likes "Mildred stories;" they are all good and happy stories.

As we sit near Mildred's grave, Josh sometimes asks about "going home." I am surprised at how much he pays attention to other conversations at home.

I think, "What do I tell my four-year-old about things I scarcely understand?"

He asks about heaven, to which I respond, "It will be a happy place, and a fun place."

Josh asks, "Will we play with cars?"

My answer to his simple, yet sincere questions is, "I don't know." Birds are far from my mind as I contemplate my son's questions about lofty, eternal matters. Josh and I sit and talk as long as he will listen which is usually not very long.

Having passed through the cemetery, my mind focuses

again on mushrooms. Walking toward the soccer field we can already see the white caps of some meadow mushrooms pushing their way up through the grass. A four-foot cyclone fence separates us from the field. At this point Josh usually stops short of the fence and looks up at me. Without saying a word, I know that he wants to be gently lifted to the other side of the fence. But this day is a monumental day in his life. Josh walks up to the fence and climbs over with very little difficulty.

"Wait till Mom finds out what you can do; she will be surprised."

Josh responds with a proud, "I know," and also adds, "I hurt my hand, but it didn't bleed."

One of the last things Josh would want to eat is a mushroom, but he likes to help gather them. He collects what he calls, "belly buttons." Running ahead, he finds several with broad white caps and chocolate-brown gills.

He tells me, "these are too old," and I agree.

"Here's a belly button," he yells.

We collect only the younger meadow mushrooms that appear as small white balls with pink gills barely visible.

A flock of killdeer is feeding in the field. As we draw closer they take flight, circle overhead, and land farther away. Josh continues his search for mushrooms as I watch the birds.

"Josh, look at all those birds."

He runs toward the flock; and when they again take flight and begin to circle, he stops to watch.

Josh turns to me and yells, "Dad, when are you going to teach me to fly?"

My heart and mind again soar as I think to myself, "I already am son, I already am."

EASTERN SCREECH-OWL SURVEYS

My eastern screech-owl (ESO) survey work began as a result of an article I read in a 1973 issue of *American Birds* concerning use of taped recordings to attract birds. Today that doesn't seem like a big deal but this was before such things such as iBird and BirdJam for one's iPod or iPhone. In 1973 cassette tape recorders were just coming onto the market for consumers and they were expensive, so we continued to use vocal imitations, using the whistling-through-a-ball-of-spit method to produce an ESO sound.

Andy Hoffmann, a young man I first met at the Oglebay Institute's Junior Nature Camp and later at the High School Ecology Camp at TA, became my screech-owling partner.

One evening in December 1973 Andy and I met at the Brooks Nature Center and we decided to make tape recordings of ESOs from vinyl records of bird songs from the Nature Center's library. Our early taped recordings were certainly not hi-fidelity.

That same evening we anxiously went out to test the recordings. Our results: five ESOs in Oglebay Park and another nine along the seven-mile road between Oglebay and West Liberty. We were shocked with the good results. I thought it amazing that this new technology had worked so well.

Previous surveys that Andy and I had done involved spending the hours from midnight to 6:00 a.m., whistling our night away along back roads. Now we could end our surveys without feeling like our lips were about to fall off.

The Christmas Bird Count (CBC) was less than two weeks away and we were eager to try our taped recordings again. Andy and I met at the Nature Center at midnight at the start of the count and did the same route as before. Our results: 17 ESOs. Before this there had never been an effort during the Wheeling CBC to count owls the way we did. Sure, there had been ESOs reported but they had been incidental.

Even though the results for the CBC had to be reported to a designated local coordinator, the count participants wouldn't know the resulting totals of species and total number of birds until the January BBC meeting. Andy and I were excited about being able to report our ESO survey results at the meeting. At the meeting when the list of birds was being announced and "17 ESOs," was revealed, everything became very quiet. Several people were curious about such a high number of screech-owls.

Someone jokingly said, "I bet your lips were tired."

When I explained that we didn't whistle but had used a tape recorder, several of the older BBC members were aghast at the idea.

One person questioned whether our use of a tape recorder was, "an honest and accurate means of determining the number of ESOs present in the CBC area."

Suddenly we went from being bird count heroes to being scrutinized for our methods. I cited our results from our survey of the same route taken just days before the actual CBC with similar results. Still, there were the doubters.

During the rest of that winter I experimented with short jaunts into woodlands calling owls. Sometimes I used whistles, sometimes a tape recorder. Regardless of how I called the owls the results were similar.

For the CBC of 1974 I recruited volunteers for the CBC owl count because I had to be out of town that weekend. My volunteers were Greg Eddy and Andy Hoffmann. Greg and Andy's results were 33 ESOs with more than half called in without the aid of the tape recorder. Instead of surveying the park and seven miles between the park and West Liberty, they decided to go wherever they wanted in the 15-mile diameter CBC area. This large number of ESOs encountered was at the time uncommon since owls were so rarely seen. These results challenged their long-held ideas.

The 1975 CBC was the "icing" on the cake and many of our doubters became believers. We had icy roads, and several inches of fresh snow. We thought about calling off the count, but since it was already 11:30 and everyone had already shown up, we decided to go ahead. This year was the first time we had two survey groups. Greg and two others would run one survey and Andy and I would do the other. We divided the count circle in half. Just after 6:00 we met back at the Nature Center to discuss the results. Greg's survey area had produced 36 ESOs using a tape recorder and Andy and I located 35 ESOs using only vocal imitations. The results confirmed to the doubters two things I already knew: using a tape recorder produces valid results and there are a lot more ESOs out there than most birders had ever imagined.

Then I began to wonder just how many ESOs we could locate if we could cover the entire CBC count area.

By this time we were becoming thought of in the bird club

as experts in locating ESOs so when people began arriving at 7:30 in the morning for the daytime count, right away they would want to know how many owls we had found. For many years when the results of the Wheeling CBC were published in *American Birds* we had the highest number of ESOs in all of North America. It didn't necessarily mean that the Wheeling area had more ESOs than anywhere else; it meant we were one of the few CBCs earnestly looking for them.

Besides counting ESOs for the CBCs, Andy and I often did surveys at other times. The frequent close encounters we had with ESOs taught me a lot. I became curious about the color phases of the owl. Each time we stopped to call an ESO and had a response, we tried to find it to see its color: gray or red. When an ESO called back, we would continue to run the recorder or to whistle back. Eventually there would be a silent period when the owl didn't respond. We discovered that meant the owl was flying closer. Once it got close enough we could shine a light around, locate the orange eye shine and often determine the color phase.

Surprisingly, we discovered that some owls were attracted to the recordings but never responded vocally. We learned to watch the sky for an ESO silhouette flying overhead. One night we were along a roadway lighted with an occasional street light. We stopped at a pull-off directly under one of the lights and began playing our recording. Soon we had an ESO response. From the intermittent calls we could tell the owl was getting closer. Finally it got close enough that we could just barely see it on a tree branch across the road. We played the call again. The owl flew toward us, right above our heads, looking down at us as it went by, flew headfirst into the light pole and fell to the ground.

Andy ran over and said, "It's a red phase."

We both watched as the owl slowly regained its senses and eventually flew off.

Another thing we had been learning about ESOs was that even though they are terribly efficient predators, they are not very intelligent.

Another time Andy and I stopped along a roadway to call ESOs. We played the tape on and off trying to provoke a response but heard nothing.

I said, "Look over there, across the creek, right in front of us. There's an owl on that lowest branch."

We had left the flashlight inside the car.

Andy said, "That's not an owl. Otherwise it would have called or flown away. It's just a bump on the branch."

We argued until I started to yell, jump and clap my hands trying to get it to fly from the branch.

Finally Andy said, "Let's go to the next stop. We've been here long enough." I still insisted it was an owl and wasn't yet ready to leave.

Searching around for something to throw I found part of an old bucket and heaved it across the creek up into the tree. The bump became airborne and flew away. We learned that owls wouldn't always respond to our best efforts.

We were always trying to be more efficient in our surveys and to try new things and ideas. One day at the Nature Center I was reading a review of a researcher who was using a bal-chatri trap (also known as a noose trap) to trap and band sparrow hawks (American kestrels). The bal-chatri originated in East India as a trap developed and used by falconers.

Our traps were constructed of one-quarter inch mesh hardware cloth in the shape of a small rectangular cage with a door on the underside to put in the live bait. Monofilament fishing line was attached to the top in several places and tied into large slip knots forming three-to-four-inch diameter nooses.

Anxiously we decided to try one of the traps on an owl. I had live mice at the Nature Center for feeding the snakes in our exhibits. We hadn't yet attached the nooses to the traps but wanted to see if we could actually attract an ESO to the trap. That night we put a mouse in through the bottom of the trap and went to a nearby location inside the park where we regularly encountered an owl in our surveys.

Within a minute we had an ESO answering the tape. We took the trap and set it on the ground near the base of a tree. Before we could walk back to the car and turn around, the owl was on the trap. We just looked at each other, surprised and delighted. The owl was working feverishly trying to get to the mouse. Andy and I decided to approach the owl to see how close we could get before it flew away. As we approached, the owl stopped and looked at us. We stopped and then the owl continued trying to get the mouse. We continued toward the owl and it again stopped and looked at us. We played this cat-and-mouse game until we were almost on top of it before it flew away. When we walked back to the car the owl flew down to the trap again.

Andy and I were so excited at this success that we thought of a plan to try to catch the owl. We would move the car to face the owl, turn on the high beams temporarily blinding the owl with the bright light and run in from each side to throw our coats over it. After moving the car and turning on the lights, the owl was still on the trap busily after the mouse. We slowly approached from each side and then made a mad dash throwing our coats. The owl got away. We did this several times and finally came to the conclusion that, even though ESOs are not very intelligent animals, on this night, this owl was definitely smarter than the two knuckleheads trying to catch it by throwing their coats at it.

Andy eventually went to graduate school in Pullman, Washington, and then onto Alaska to work as a biologist with the Department of Fish and Game. He returned on rare occasions to visit his family and sometimes helped with later ESO surveys. He happened to be home the year *that turned out to be our highest survey numbers ever.*

By 1987 I had divided the CBC survey area into 12 sections. This way the entire count area could be covered if I had enough volunteers. One rule I had for safety was that a route had to be covered by at least two people. That year I had only enough people to cover three routes. On my route the numbers of owls was so high I thought that Andy and the others would never believe it. At the end of the night we met at my home.

I asked Andy, "How many did you get?"

"You tell me first," he answered.

I replied, "I asked you first."

It turned out that he was apprehensive for the same reason I was.

"Fifty-eight," he finally admitted.

"Thank goodness!" I exclaimed. "We got 56 and I was worried my number would be too high to be believable."

The other group had found 37.

Something Andy did that night has become an important part of the criteria I used in future ESO surveys. Andy and his brother timed how long it took an owl to respond at each stop…four and a half minutes was the longest time. Now when I do ESO surveys we spend no more than five minutes calling at each stop. If an owl hasn't responded by then, they aren't going to.

My son Josh was six years old at the time and after hearing me talk about the ESOs, he wanted to go out and find some owls too. About 7:00 that evening we walked down the street to behind the college property. At first he was a little worried about walking in the woods because it was so dark, but soon he was wandering short distances away as I played the tape. Snow covered the ground so I always knew exactly where he was. Sometimes Josh would try to sneak up on me from behind but the crunching snow easily gave away his location.

I would hear, "Crunch……………..crunch…………… crunch……………..crunch," as Josh tried to get closer and at the last moment, just before he got to me, I always turned to face him.

He asked, "How do you always know where I am?"

I said, "Let me try to sneak up on you."

Right away he understood and said, "I hear the snow crunching."

Then he wanted to see how far away he had to be so that I couldn't hear his footsteps. When he was a good distance away, a nearby whitetail snorted loudly. Immediately I heard, "Crunch, crunch, crunch, crunch, crunch, crunch, crunch, crunch, crunch," and then Josh was holding onto my leg for dear life. We also discovered three more owls than evening.

The ESO total for the 1987 CBC count was 154. It wasn't the highest count we ever had, but it did represent the highest counts ever for those routes the three teams were able to cover. If all the routes had been covered that night I believe we might have counted over 300 ESOs that night.

After years of doing the Wheeling CBC I began to notice a difference between my ESO counts and the daylight CBC. The day-time count was more of a casual, traditional event. My ESO early morning counts were more focused and scientific.

In the 1970s most of the counts I did had no more than four or five people and were not always done in association with the CBC. At one BBC meeting several members suggested I do a count each year to coincide with the CBC. Most members thought it would be great having Wheeling thought of as the ESO capital of the world by having the highest ESO totals published in *American Birds*. Beginning in 1980 when I divided the CBC circle into 12 distinct survey areas, most of my volunteers were current and former students of mine from Oglebay Camps and West Liberty State College. Since few BBC members were involved in the ESO surveys they didn't understand all the planning, recruiting and contacting of volunteers that I did. My volunteers, as it turned out, were much tougher and more reliable than even I thought.

The 1990 CBC count was quite memorable. The weather forecast was for a terrible winter storm the day before the count and that is exactly what happened. I wondered if anyone would show up for the ESO count at all. The roads were icy and it was minus five degrees. Eighteen people showed up.

I always covered the same route. All in all I probably did my route at least 100 times in the 28 years I ran ESO surveys. Fortunately, I had an old CJ5 Jeep that would go anywhere regardless of the road conditions. My wife, Bev, was going with me that night. She had accompanied me on a number of surveys and knew what to expect.

This night, however, was a little different. Near the end of our survey we were on a dirt road coming out of a heavily wooded hollow onto a high ridge surrounded by large expanses of open farmland. At the last stop the wind was so strong I decided that even if an owl heard the tape and answered, we would never hear him due to the wind. So I decided to skip that last stop and continue on home. Bev didn't mind at all in that temperature.

Suddenly I slammed on the brakes. About four feet in front of us was a huge snow drift. It was taller than the jeep on the left side of the road and about three feet high on the right.

"Now what?" Bev asked, "Are we going to have to turn around and go back?" Going back meant a large detour.

"No way!" I answered, "We're going right through it."

"This is great!" I was thinking. "I love testing the Jeep."

I backed the Jeep back down the hill about 30 yards. I revved the engine a couple of times and looked over at Bev.

"Are you sure this is a good idea?" she asked.

The wind was howling and snow was blowing everywhere. I floored it and headed for the drift.

Bev yelled, "**What are you doing?**" Instead of aiming for the three foot high part of the drift, I went at the six-foot high section. The Jeep smashed into the wall of snow, went up and…well, it went up, but not over. We came to a stop sitting on top of the compacted snow. All of the wheels were about two feet off the ground.

"Why didn't you go through the low part?" Bev asked.

"I wanted to see what the Jeep would do," I answered.

"Now you know," she said, not at all happy with the situation. "Now what are we going to do?"

I didn't have a shovel. The wind was blowing so strongly I didn't want to be out for very long. Pushing from the back I was able to tilt the Jeep a small amount but not enough to get a wheel on the ground. After I climbed back into the Jeep Bev and I tried rocking in unison to get it to move. It was working. Finally we had a tire in the snow. When I gave the engine some gas, the tire threw the snow and all four tires were in the air again, but they were closer to the ground. After about

20 minutes of rocking the Jeep and several tries when a wheel had traction we were able to get off the drift.

All my volunteers safely finished their routes that night and we had counted 137 ESOs. But the number never appeared in *American Birds*. The BBC cancelled their daytime count and rescheduled it due to the "bad" weather. Only eleven participants showed up for their day count. Someone suggested I run the ESO count again to coincide with the new date.

I declined, thinking, "You have no clue!"

On the day of Wheeling's 1991 CBC I had 29 volunteers, more than double the participants of the day count. That morning we had our highest ESO numbers ever for a CBC...170. Other ESO surveys I did at other times produced higher totals, but they were not run in conjunction with a CBC. What's interesting about this count is that three-fourths of those owls were counted before 3:00 a.m. A weather front moved in about that time, spitting some rain. I am sure we could have counted over 200 ESOs had it not been for the weather change.

What had started in 1973 with just two people, had grown so much that there were sometimes two cars going on the same survey route. Many people just wanted to see an owl. One year I had two cars with ten people on one route. At each stop we had to wait until everyone got out of the cars, call and listen for the owls and then get them all back into the cars again. This was fun in a social way but not conducive to my scientific goals. This time consuming process made it hard to finish a route before daybreak.

As a result, I initiated a rule that each route leader had to run the entire route, to record the required data and to recruit at least one other volunteer for that route. I also put a limit of one car per route.

There was always a lot to do the night of the count: we always had new people to train, we had to make sure the tape players worked properly, the leaders had to be sure of their routes, everyone had to be familiar with the ESO and other owl calls and we had to be sure that everyone had a place in a vehicle since occasionally an exuberant leader would invite a few too many volunteers. We all met at my home in West Liberty, the center of the Wheeling CBC, at eleven p.m. and I would do a 45 minute program.

There was a rumor that began after the 1989 ESO count and continued until I stopped organizing and running counts. It all started innocently enough when, about a month before the next survey, a young lady asked when the next survey was.

I answered, "Dec. 17. We meet at my home at eleven p.m. on the 16th. Let me know if you would like to tag along?"

After she left a co-worker came out of his office and began to quiz me about the young lady who had just left.

"Who is she? What's her name? Do you think she will go on the owl count? If she goes can you make sure she goes with me?" he asked.

"I'll see what I can do," I told him.

The night of the count they were paired together. A local Wheeling newspaper reporter had asked if she could go along to do a story about the count and I agreed. One of my other leaders had recruited a man who had been on a date with the reporter some time before. The reporter and the new volunteer decided they wanted to go together and do their own route, which I agreed to. Both of the couples began dating and were eventually married. Two years later my co-worker and the young lady came back and counted owls as Mr. and Mrs.

So the rumor began, "Be careful! If you volunteer to help

Bill with one of his ESO surveys, you could end up getting married to one of the other volunteers." And it seemed to be true since three other couples who were paired together eventually also got married.

On several occasions my survey groups encountered the law. One time I had an Ohio County Sheriff's Deputy stop to check on what we were doing. He thought we were having car trouble.

After I explained about the owl survey he asked, "Would you mind if I waited to see if you find any?"

"No problem," I said.

Within minutes we had a response. The owl flew low right over us. Each time I played the tape the owl would fly across and back as if it were on a pendulum.

On one of our early counts Andy and I were using a tape recorder. An ESO answered. As the tape was playing we saw the silhouette of the owl from across the roadway flying even with the treetops. Suddenly it dropped right at us. We both threw our hands up to protect ourselves and the owl pulled up and swooped just above our heads. Unfortunately the damage was already done. When Andy threw his hands up, the tape recorder flew out of his hand and smashed onto the road. We finished the rest of the survey using vocal imitations.

Another time a volunteer reported that an ESO, "Dove at me and pulled my toboggan right off my head."

Oglebay Park was home to one of my favorite ESOs. Rarely was I able to know an owl but this one was different than all the others. My first encounter with owl H, as I called it, was on a cold snowy night beside a golf course. I was playing the tape and an ESO flew into view and landed on a tree branch about 20 feet away. When it began to answer, it had an odd, loud

note at the end of its whinny call. I likened it to a hiccup. As I
stood there thinking about the odd sound, the owl continued
to call. I walked over to it and it remained where it was and
still called.

I thought the bird seemed very brave, so I decided to
test it. I did a **"Whooo who-who-who…who-who"** call of a
great horned owl several times. The ESO continued to call.
Eventually I danced, whooped and hollered. The owl wasn't
fazed in the least. When I left that stop the owl was still there
and still calling. Owl H was quite reliable. For years to come, I
would stop at that same spot and get an ESO response, always
with a hiccup after each whinny.

At times when we were at a stop we would hear another
kind of owl off in the distance. Most of the time it was a great
horned owl. They are common owls in our area but their
population is limited by their large territories. ESOs have such
large populations, in part, due to their small territories.

Chance meeting with barred owls and barn owls were rare,
but there was one we will never forget. Andy and I were at
Bethany. It was 4:30 in the morning. We were both sleepy and
had decided to stay in the car at this stop. With the windows
open, our heads hanging downward, eyes closed and half
asleep, we were whistling trying to get a response. Suddenly,
out of nowhere, we heard the most dreadful, loud, blood-
curdling scream imaginable. Abruptly we sat up and grabbed
for the door locks. Again, it screamed. It was a barn owl. The
sound reminds me of the Nazgul screams in the *Lord of the
Rings* movies. We were wide-awake for the rest of the night.

At the end of each ESO survey most of us returned to
our homes and went to bed. The problem with falling asleep
after a survey was what I called **"THE ESO SYNDROME"**.
After hearing ESO calls all night long, the sound becomes

imprinted in the mind for a time. Trying to fall asleep I would continue to hear screech-owls calling from right inside my bedroom: loudly at first, then softer, and then even softer as if the imagined owls seemed to move farther away... zzzzzzzzzzzzzzz.

EASTERN SCREECH-OWLS — SCIENCE FAIR

One of the primary goals of my ESO studies was to determine the size of the bird's territory. I thought if I were to begin an active trapping program of selected locations, I could gain some insight into being able to define the territorial boundaries.

Little did I know that the solution would come from my 15 year-old daughter, Julie. Both of my daughters were active in Science Fair. Kelly, our youngest daughter, did studies on "The Thermoregulation of Bats In Cold Weather", "Conditions Affecting Color Change In the Eastern Gray Tree Frog" and "Which Chickadee Is More Common In West Liberty, West Virginia In Winter – Black-capped or Carolina?"

The "Thermoregulation of Bats" project came about as a result of a male red bat I found on an October morning. At first glance the bat appeared to be a recently fallen, dried leaf hanging in a bush. I put the bat into one of the over-sized pockets of my camo pants until I got back to the Nature Center. That night I took the bat home and the large classroom/photo studio in our home became the "Bat Cave" for several months. Hanging from the ceiling, the bat seemed right at home. The room was very cold during the winter, so our bat actually hibernated and was eventually released in late March.

As the bat hibernated, Kelly periodically held a thermometer against the bat's body to get a body temperature reading. After that, the room was heated to allow the bat to warm and wake up. It began to fly around the room. After a short while of flying I caught it and Kelly again took the body temperature. Then I fed it a bat diet I concocted from some predatory bird diet available to me from the Good Zoo at Oglebay. Once the bat was well fed, the room would be allowed to cool down slowly until it was cold again. The bat hung from the ceiling and hibernated again. This experiment was repeated a number of times.

One night while the bat was flying around the Bat Cave I put a ladder and several chairs in different parts of the room. My wife, daughters, son, and I positioned ourselves at various places at different heights as the bat flew. Then I turned the lights out. Sometimes the bat flew so close we could feel the air as it went past and even hear the wing beats, but it never touched any of us.

When it came time to have her project judged at the Science Fair, one of the two ladies judging the category said, "We hate bats. I can't even look at your photos, but we will let you tell us about your project anyway."

Even as a sixth grader, Kelly knew the judges were acting unprofessionally and weren't qualified to be science fair judges.

Kelly's chickadee project was very easy for her. Since I regularly banded birds at home, any time I caught a chickadee, Kelly would remove it from the mist net, take a

wing-chord and tail measurement and record those numbers.
Then I would band the bird and she would release it. At the
end of winter, using guidelines from Merrill Wood's, *A Bird-
Bander's Guide To Determination of Age and Sex Of Selected
Species*, she determined which were black-capped and which
were Carolina by the wing and tail lengths. After adding up
how many of each had been trapped, she simply figured the
percentages.

My daughter, Julie, did two bird-related Science Fair
projects. In ninth grade her project was "Pigment and
Structural Colors in Bird Feathers". Most birds' feathers get
their color from the chemistry in the foods the birds eat. Those
foods provide different birds with different kinds of pigments.
These pigments show color by absorbing some of the colors of
the light spectrum and reflecting others that we then see.

Northern cardinals reflect red, therefore we see red;
American goldfinches reflect yellow, Baltimore orioles reflect
orange and so on. The color blue is different, however.
Bluebirds do not reflect blue, yet we see blue. There are truly
no blue colored birds. The blue is not reflective but refractive.
It's physics and light playing tricks with our eyes. Instead of
the light reflecting off the feathers and showing the color of
the pigment, the light enters the feather, bends (refracts) and
this refracted light is what we see.

To study this, Julie took feathers from different kinds
of dead birds we found along roadways. My Bird Banding
Permit allowed me to salvage dead birds and I already had
several in our freezer. With mortar and pestle Julie ground
the red feathers of a cardinal with the resulting powder
being a red color. After grinding the feathers of a goldfinch,
the powder was yellow and the resulting color of the oriole
feathers was orange. She destroyed the structure of the

feathers but their respective colors did not change showing that these birds received their color from pigments in the feathers.

When she ground the eastern bluebird feathers into a powder, the powder was black. This demonstrated that the bluebird received its color from the feather structure, not pigment...destroy the structure and the blue color disappears.

Julie entered her project in the physics category of the Science Fair and won first place.

As a sophomore in high school Julie decided she wanted to do something with ESOs. We decided upon a simple project that would also be helpful to my research. Up until that point all of my ESO surveys were done between midnight and 6:00 a.m.. Julie was going to run 12 nearby surveys: four each at 6 p.m., 11 p.m., and 3 a.m. After all the surveys were run she would determine which were the optimum times to call owls, based upon how many responses she got from taped recordings.

The two major hurdles for someone her age were that she needed someone who had a driver's license (that would be me) and someone to wake her in the wee hours of the morning (and that also was me).

As we began to notice other interesting results in Julie's data the scope of the project grew beyond just noticing the times the owls responded most frequently. Most notable to me was that while plotting the owl responses on a topo map it was easy to see how many pairs of ESOs there were. After examining the data, we determined that in several inaccessible areas of the survey region there were likely to be six more pairs of ESOs. Based on actual ESO responses to taped recordings and the six theoretical pairs, there were probably 30 pairs of ESOs in the 8.75 square mile survey area. I had been very interested in discovering the size of an ESO's territory. And now I knew, thanks to my 15-year-old daughter's science fair project.

Up until then the only real research to define the size of the ESO's territory had been done by John and Frank Craighead in Michigan, during the 1940s. Their results were published in 1956 in the definitive work *Hawks, Owls and Wildlife*.

We decided it would be nice to have some original photos of the owls...red and gray phases for Julie's project. But I thought that might not be possible since, according to my owl surveys, the red phase ESOs were quite scarce.

Our first attempt at using one of my noose traps yielded a gray phase owl. The next evening I vocally called an owl deep in the 14 acre woods behind our house but it wouldn't come. Two days later we went into the woods to where we thought the owl had been calling from and built a rough four-sided blind from logs and branches. That night we set a noose trap with a mouse inside a short distance from the blind, went into the blind and began playing the tape.

Within minutes the owl was calling back and came right to where we were. Next thing we knew it was on the trap trying to get the mouse. After a few minutes we approached the trap, the owl jumped into the air and immediately plopped right back to the ground with a thump.

"Dad we caught it!" Julie yelled excitedly.

"Yes we did," I said, "and best of all, it's a red phase!"

Due to a mistake in paperwork from her school, she was told she would be allowed to participate, but could not be considered for any awards at the regional Science Fair.

Julie was discouraged enough to consider not entering the State Science Fair at Glenville State College but finally decided she would. Julie, several other students and the science fair coordinator from her high school traveled together to

Glenville. Saturday evening we received a call from Julie after the fair had ended.

"I won! I won!" she yelled.

"What did you win?" I asked.

"I won the grand prize!"

When she arrived home Julie told us, "I didn't win and then I did!"

She explained that the judges didn't seem interested in her project at first but another judge in another category had changed their minds. He knew John and Frank Craighead personally and was familiar with their book. The Craighead's had determined the ESO territory to be somewhere between 2.5 – 2.9 square miles. Julie showed how it was, in reality, only .29 square miles.

Julie won a number of awards including one of four grand prizes which included a trip to the International Science Fair in Puerto Rico.

The following year Julie was invited to the University of Florida in Gainesville to present a paper on her ESO project. She also had her project published in the BBC's publication, *The Redstart*, which subsequently resulted in her receiving the Floyd Bartley Award.

An amusing sideline was that she received numerous requests for copies of the article from owl researchers, many addressed to Dr. Julie Beatty, not realizing she was a sophomore in high school.

My ESO work moved into phase two: trapping and banding. Armed with the knowledge of the relative size of the ESO's territory, I set out to learn more about these birds. Besides being described as cute, adorable, charming, and loveable by people I knew, owls are also fierce and efficient.

Watching an ESO go for a mouse in a trap demonstrates this.

Their efficiency is mind-boggling. ESOs can eat whatever is available…cold-blooded vertebrates, small mammals, insects or birds. They do not appear to have any preferences concerning prey. ESOs are a necessary control of other animal populations. Although I can't always respect their intellectual skills, I have a profound admiration for their survival skills.

ESOs have two distinct color phases: gray and red (actually orange). The general consensus was that the color they are born is the color they stay throughout life. I questioned that idea based on my trapping of an occasional intermediate color phase with a brown color. Also, in some old writings about screech-owls kept as pets, there were some indications that the color could change.

I had noticed that although these owls eat whatever is available, when food is plentiful, they do seem to have a preference. On several occasions I had watched captive ESOs swallow an entire mouse in one long jerking gulp, but in the wild it didn't always happen that way. Wild ESOs are known for preferring the head and especially the brain of small mammals they catch. Checking an ESO nesting box I once found seven short-tailed shrews all nestled comfortably in one corner. They appeared to be sleeping, except they had no heads or if they did have a head, the brain had been removed.

Thinking about the color phases and the food preferences brought to mind some new approaches to my research. Finally, I decided to send a request to the Bird Banding Laboratory with the following information:

> Since 1973 I have been trapping, banding and studying the ESO. I am to a point in my research where I need an additional permit to allow me to

keep a small number (three at the most) of ESOs in captivity for an unspecified period of time. All would be released at the end of my research.

Most theories of ESO color phases are that of genetic origin. But my studies, and observations by others, indicated a possible relationship to diet. Following winters with little or no snowfall (in the Ohio Valley) the red phase screech-owl population increases. During these winters small mammals are very easy prey for the ESO; so easy that often only the head (preferred body part of the ESO) is consumed and the body discarded. Many times the cranial cavity is opened and only the brain is eaten.

During winters when snow covers the ground ESOs have a more difficult time locating small mammals. These voles, mice and shrews are consumed entirely. Following winters with significant snowfall the gray phase predominates and often the red phase owls are almost non-existent. I believe the red phase may have a strong correlation to the eastern screech-owl's brain rich diet during the winters with very little snow.

As part of my continuing research on ESO color phases I need to keep several ESOs color phases captive for a period of time feeding them a brain rich diet in order to test the correlation of color phase and diet.

I would also like my daughter, Julie Beatty, listed as a subpermittee. She has been working closely with me on this research project.

Sincerely,

Permission was granted.

Shortly after I began trapping ESOs I discovered something quite amazing. The first few times I set a trap, I called until I heard a vocal response from an ESO and then I would walk to the edge of the road and put the trap in a visible spot off the road. Next I hid behind the car and continued calling. Soon the owl came closer and onto the trap.

All my careful hiding and making the owl think no one was there turned out to be unnecessary. Soon I just stood in the open and called the owl. We could easily see each other. Most times the owl watched from a tree branch as I set the trap just below it. Before I could get back to the car I would hear a "THUMP," as the owl hit the trap.

Sometimes I even had ESOs hit the trap while it was still in my hands. The first time it happened the shock seemed to stop my heart. It really was a scare to have an owl hit the trap while I was holding it.

Now my routine became: set the trap while the owl watched, walk back to the car, and watch as the owl fought the trap to get the mouse. After a short while I would walk toward the trap, the owl would jump to fly, and then fall since its feet were tangled in the nooses.

One of the problems with my new research into ESO color phases was that mouse brains were in short supply. I opted for more readily available pork brains, hoping they would be a suitable substitute.

The night I went to trap the owl for my study it was about 20 degrees, with four inches of snow on the ground. I turned on the tape recorder and soon a whinny from an ESO could be heard. I continued playing the call until the owl was on a branch about fifteen feet high on the other side of the road.

Shining my headlamp on the owl I could see it was a gray phase—just what I needed. We studied each other for a while before I walked over and laid the trap in full view. The owl quickly pounced on the trap.

That evening I settled the owl into its new home, a cage in my classroom/photo studio. The first thing I did was to feed it some pork brains, which, with one finger in its mouth and the fingertip down the throat, was easily accomplished. The portions I fed the owl were quite generous; by weight, more than it probably ate in the wild. Each evening before going to bed and each morning before leaving for work I weighed the owl. Unfortunately, it was losing weight.

The weight loss was negligible at first but, with no weight gain whatsoever, the small losses began adding up. After nine days I finally decided that this wasn't working and I would have to release the owl back into the wild. I decided to keep it an additional week to fatten it up on more traditional owl food before releasing it.

A week later I went to release the owl. Holding the owl and watching it as it looked up at me, I thought, "Sorry little bird, I hope I didn't distress you too much."

Slowly I opened my hands and it flew to a branch near where it had perched the night I caught it. Sitting in my Jeep I scribbled some notes about the color phase fiasco and the stress I caused this little owl.

I was reminded of a quote by Malcolm Forbes, "Failure is success if we learn from it." There was no doubt that I learned from this.

All of a sudden I heard splashing and a mournful cry that was new to me. Exiting the Jeep I immediately looked for the owl. It wasn't there. Still hearing the splashing I saw a gray phase ESO sitting at the top of the stream bank in a tangle of tree roots. When I reached the stream bank the owl flew. Looking down at the water I saw a red phase owl holding my gray phase owl underwater. Flapping its wings and thrashing about, my owl was trying to get its head above water. Whenever my owl's face would come out of the water it would scream. When I jumped into the stream the red owl flew away.

My recent experiment just stood there in the water, wet from head to toe, looking more like a tiny E.T. rather than a fatly feathered ESO. I picked it up and took it to the Jeep. Once the heater warmed up I set the owl on the floor in the stream of warm air. After it dried, I picked it up and checked for injuries. I couldn't find any.

Having the owl in captivity for just over two weeks had allowed another owl to come in and set up its territory in my owl's previous home.

"Poor little thing," I thought, "and I'm the cause of this."

I took my owl to another spot along the road where I often stopped to survey ESOs. I had not gotten a response in this location for some time. This time it flew deeper into the woods. Never again would I take an owl from its habitat.

I never had an owl land on the trap and then fly away without getting its feet tangled in the slip knots, except once. For several years I had been teaching a Recreational Camping/ Outdoor Leisure Pursuits class for West Liberty State College. Regardless of weather conditions we went out. My first class was always "How to Dress for the Weather." Some students still came improperly dressed and had to suffer through a cold two hours, praying I would end the class early.

One semester I had seven bio majors out of a class of 35. Two, Jon and Amanda, were dating. Both were exceptional students and qualified for the college's mentoring program.

After Jon had taken my two mentoring classes, Amanda requested I mentor her in a program about ESOs. One of the classes I set up was a night time session along a rural back road to catch an ESO. So Amanda, Jon and I set out to trap an owl.

I told them, "We should have an easy time tonight. There is a very reliable owl that always answers the calls. All we have to do is get it on the trap. Every owl I've had on a trap has been caught."

When we arrived at the stop I began playing the call and before long we had an owl answering.

Placing the trap on the roof of my Jeep, we continued to play the call. The three of us sat on the road, backs leaning against the Jeep talking about school and owls.

"Thump!" the owl was on the trap. Jon and Amanda were eager to see what was happening on the roof of the jeep. I assured them that the owl would remain in the trap and that we shouldn't disturb it right away.

"Let's stand up and catch this owl," I said.

We all stood at once, the owl looked at us and then jumped and flew away.

"I can't believe it!" I said, "This is the first owl that has gotten away."

We tried several more times. The owl always returned, then flew away each time. Finally we sat down on the road.

I looked at Jonathon and said, "I know you have to study for a test tonight. Maybe we should get you and Amanda back to campus."

"I can study anytime," he answered, "but this is an opportunity of a lifetime!"

EASTERN SCREECH-OWL
NEST BOXES + ARCHIE

1988 brought a significant change in my approach
to my ESO studies. The West Virginia Department of
Natural Resources—Wildlife Divisions Nongame Program
awarded me a grant which included monies to buy climbing
equipment, and the state constructed 30 ESO nesting/roosting
boxes per my specifications. West Liberty State College
granted me permission to mount boxes in their 154-acre
arboretum and in a wooded area on campus. I also placed
boxes in the 14 acres behind my house.

Also of importance was that I quit my job at the Brooks
Nature Center in March 1990. Leaving the nature center was
most difficult but I wanted to be in the field more.

After 17 years of surveying and trapping ESOs, I was
known by some as the Owl Man. For many years I had a
Federal Bird Rehabilitation Permit specifically for ESOs. It
allowed me to legally hold injured ESOs until the time they
could be released back into the wild. Most adult injuries were
car-related as owls seem to be attracted to small mammals
crossing roadways.

The adult owls were ferocious. To me, the worst injury was a talon under a fingernail or cuticle. The baby owls had an attitude, but they didn't have the strength or determination to back it up.

My children would sometimes argue over who would care for an owl. My son Josh was too young to care for an owl by himself, so he sometimes would help me. Julie and Kelly were old enough to be assigned the duties of feeding, exercising, and cleaning the cage of a particular owl.

One day I went into the owl room and the owl immediately jumped from its perch and hid in the bottom far corner of the cage. When Julie entered the room, the owl quickly flew to the front of the cage and clung to the bars. As I watched, its eyes followed her wherever she went. "That was odd," I thought.

As an experiment, I asked Julie to leave the room. Soon the owl returned to the far corner of the cage. Julie peered through the crack between the door and wall and said, "I don't see it."

I responded, "That's the point. Walk back in here and see what the owl does." When she entered the room again, the owl jumped to the front of the cage.

"It knows you," I said, "It recognizes you as its caregiver and associates you with food."

My ESO research provided me with great photo opportunities. Setting up photos of owls being rehabilitated might seem like an easy task; however, since owls are nocturnal, daytime photos often involved working with sleepy owls that would only look through tiny slits between their eyelids. On rare occasions there would be an ESO that would have bright, wide-open eyes during the day.

Owl behavior is not always predictable. After I presented a program for the BBC that included some owl photos, one of the members asked if she could take some pictures the next time I set up for owl photos. I agreed and said, "We'll have to wait until I have a wide-eyed owl."

The next time this occurred, I spent the morning setting up some different backgrounds. This owl was especially cooperative. It peered from tree cavities, peeked out from white pine boughs, and posed perfectly amidst berry-laden holly branches. In every instance, its large black, yellow-bordered pupils stood out in the photos.

That afternoon I called Pat and told her I had some nice set-ups with a very cooperative owl. As Pat walked in, the owl moved back into the recesses of the pine branches, hunkered down, and closed its eyes.

"Well, it wasn't acting like that this morning," I said and added, "Why don't you get set up and then we'll see what we can do."

While Pat was setting up her camera equipment, I was prodding and gently urging the owl to "come out and join the fun." If I hadn't known better I might have thought that someone had switched owls. Our best efforts only resulted in the owl sitting in the open with its eyes mostly closed. Today Pat and I still laugh about her great photos of the sleepiest ESO on the planet. Shortly after she left, the owl was all bright-eyed again, ready for another round of photos.

Although climbing 30 trees in a day to check owl boxes was strenuous work, it wasn't nearly as difficult as the walks between the boxes. Every time I checked boxes, I carried a five-gallon bucket with a hammer, nails, tree climbers, and banding equipment, as well as a climbing harness slung over my shoulder. Much of the time I also carried binoculars, a camera, and camera bag.

Upon opening a box, I never knew what might be inside.

Squirrels used the boxes, as well as mice and other birds. One box was out of commission for several years due to a honeybee hive inside. Another time I opened a box only to find a large black rat snake coiled, ready to strike. I took excellent photos of baby and adult squirrels, as well as mice nursing young, and of course, ESOs.

ESO boxes with nests are incredibly foul. The first time I found an ESO in a nest box, I was excited. Reaching in for the sleeping owl, I gently wrapped my hand around it, brought it out from the box, and held it in front of me looking at it. Without warning, it excitedly woke up and immediately defecated on me; all over my pants and shoes, and it stunk. That first day of checking boxes, three different owls GOT me. The slimy, wet excrement was hidden by my camouflaged pants, but the odor was not.

Subsequent visits to check owl boxes found me using a special technique. I would gently take hold of the sleeping owl and quickly pull it out and then reach out as far away from myself as possible. When the owl awoke, the goo would fall to the ground 20 feet below.

When I found owls in the boxes they were always asleep, except for one. After climbing a tree, I slid the side panel away and there was a wide-eyed ESO bobbing and weaving, all fluffed out, huffing and puffing and clacking its beak, as if saying, "You want a part of me big guy?"

All other times the owl would be facing a corner, head leaning against the 90-degree angle, apparently asleep. When there were babies in the box, the excrement just built up on the bottom of the box. Other researchers' studies stated that the boxes should be cleaned after nesting season, which I did. However, I was late one year and discovered that the invertebrate decomposers had done it for me. All the excrement and meat from left over animal parts was gone. From then on, I just let nature take its course.

The owls used the boxes for nesting and roosting. Part of my research involved collecting the regurgitated pellets and examining them for animal parts to determine what the owls were eating and if certain boxes were preferred based on availability of specific kinds of prey.

Almost immediately I accumulated a backlog of pellets that I could not examine in a timely fashion. That problem was solved thanks to a college professor friend. We both benefited by having his students examine the pellets. Yearly, they provided me with a detailed analysis of each group of pellets based on which box they were taken from. One of my conclusions about nesting sites based on specific food availability was that food wasn't as important as was a suitable nesting cavity.

The ESO ate anything and everything. If the nest box was near a stream, the pellets contained many crayfish parts and/or fish scales. Besides the pellets there might be crayfish pincers, a dried frog leg, fish fins, or even parts of a salamander in the box. During winter months there was a preponderance of small mammals, especially short-tailed shrews. And during the bird migrations, the boxes were littered with feathers. Some boxes appeared as if a bomb had exploded inside the bird, resulting in feathers stuck to the roof and all sides of the box. One box was decorated with blue jay feathers, another with cardinal feathers. Most often the owl would decorate using a variety of bird feathers.

When screech owls are on the nest they do not sit on the eggs like most other birds. Instead the mother lays on them sleeping face down on its stomach. The nest can contain three to five eggs, but about 90 percent of the nests I monitored had four eggs. Near the time the eggs were due to hatch I could hold an egg near my ear and hear the owlet peeping from inside and sometimes hear the egg tooth tapping on the interior shell wall. Sometimes I would see the first signs of cracks and a day or two later, the newly-born chick.

Once, I discovered an egg with several radiating cracks. With a pair of tweezers, I carefully removed the pieces of cracked shell. Because the cracking always begins where the egg tooth is tapping, I knew I would find the head and face just beneath the cracked areas of the shell. Once the face was exposed, I continued to expose other parts of the bird. A leg and taloned foot were folded from below, up and around the back of the head. Anyone with claustrophobia would feel very uncomfortable seeing how crowded a bird is just before hatching. I positioned the egg for some photos. The next day I returned for photos of the one-day-old owlet. These photos appeared in numerous publications including a special two-page spread in *Ranger Rick Magazine*, titled "Screecher Feature."

There were numerous other photo opportunities. Josh often accompanied me when I checked active nests. There was a nest that had five 10-day-old owlets ready to be banded. I wanted photos of all five babies at once, nicely posed, in a row. Josh and I headed out to the box. We took a five gallon bucket, some soft rags, and a rope. I climbed the tree with the rope attached to my belt and the other end attached to the bucket handle. I pulled the bucket up and set it in my lap.

Inside the box I found the mother owl prostrate on top of the babies, sound asleep. Gently, I lifted her from the nest and gradually, one-by-one lifted each baby onto the soft rags in the bucket. When I set the mother back down, she was still sound asleep. We took the babies home, and I spent about two hours posing them in different hollow logs and taking photos. Afterwards, we returned the babies to the nest, again gently lifting the mother and softly setting the babies back underneath her. She never woke up.

One day I received a call from a lady in Washington, PA. She had been walking in the early morning and saw something unusual that she described as, "A pure white pile of feathers that moved."

Upon closer examination she saw it was a baby bird, but unlike any she had ever seen.

"It's bigger, has tiny white feathers covering the body, and long claws on the toes," she said.

It was a baby ESO. Unlike most other baby birds, ESOs have feathers covering their tiny bodies. Attempts to stand the little owl upright caused it to wobble back and forth, then lean to one side, then fall over. I guessed it was two days old. My family just adored this tiny baby.

I was adamant that, "We do not name owls that we care for and will eventually be releasing." Secretly, the owl came to be called, "Archie." When I first heard the whispered references to "Archie," I scowled (a little) but said nothing. Soon it was all out in the open and Archie was a major topic of conversation. After school, I could usually find my children lying on the floor surrounding the tiny feather ball, just watching and laughing, gently touching his soft feathers.

Archie liked having the top of his head lightly scratched, but he didn't like our hands anywhere near his toes and feet. He would become wide-eyed, dance a bit, clack his beak, then backup, and then look as if to say, "I don't like that. You should know better."

Within 10 days of Archie's arrival, he could have easily been mistaken for any other ESO his age if it were not for his uncharacteristic behavior. His cage door was kept open and most times he would sit outside, on top. Soon it became commonplace to see Archie on Julie's shoulder being chauffeured around the house and yard. Archie was spending more time in Julie's bedroom than in or on his cage, and so was Kelly.

There were times I would see all three kids outside playing and Archie perched nearby, sometimes on a picnic table, on a low branch, or even on a bicycle handlebar. Archie followed their every move as they played and ran around the yard. One day, when we were all outside with Archie on the ground among us, a cat ran in and went right for Archie. All five of us went after the cat, but it escaped with only a reprimand.

We decided that Archie needed a safer place to stay while outside. I attached a roomy wood duck box to a porch support that faced out into the yard. The box was low enough to allow us to reach it, but high enough to keep cats and dogs at bay. The box had a flat roof so Archie could either sit in the entry hole or stand on the roof.

Archie was fed commercially formulated meals known as "predatory bird diet" for about 3 weeks. Then it was time to introduce him to live mice and time he learned to fly. We then discovered two shocking things about Archie. First, I placed him on the floor in the middle of the classroom and put a live mouse in front of him. Instead of intently watching the mouse, or occasionally clawing at it, or immediately pouncing on it like other owls did, Archie became wide-eyed, turned, and then ran to the nearest corner of the room. There he remained, cowering.

After supper that same day, we took Archie into the backyard for a flying lesson. Archie was gently tossed into the air, opened his wings, and in a panic, flew straight into the ground. After several more attempts, and several flights into the ground I thought, "Archie is afraid of heights. Now what?"

His vulnerability made this young owl all the more endearing. Another discovery that really surprised me was the range of foods he would eat. One evening during supper, Archie was perched on a nearby cage while we were busily eating. One of the kids accidentally dropped a piece of a beet on the floor. Archie jumped from the cage, ran over, picked up the beet, and swallowed it.

All of a sudden another small piece of beet was on the floor and Archie ate it. "That's enough," I reprimanded. "He may eat beets, but that doesn't mean they are good for him."

"Well, if beets aren't good for us, why do we have to eat them?" Josh asked.

It was a family rule that everyone ate anything we grew in the garden, but I answered Josh with, "Archie is not an us." Someone quickly rebuked me. "Archie is one of us."

This beet incident sparked a discussion which brought up a point that everyone needed to remember: Archie, like every other owl we have had, will one day be released back into the wild. That sobering truth calmed everyone and we resumed eating. Later we would also discover that Archie would eat green beans and watermelon. Archie's progress toward becoming releasable was negligible.

We were approaching the 90-day point at which time, according to my rehabilitation permit, "Any owl not rehabilitated within 90 days was to be destroyed."

I was sure Archie did not fit into this category. After all, Archie wasn't being rehabilitated from some kind of injury that prevented him from surviving in the wild. Also, I personally didn't believe in keeping owls as pets. Furthermore, I didn't want my children to view Archie as a pet and be emotionally crushed at the time of his release.

As time went on, Archie would eat a dead mouse if it was

offered in pieces. Eventually, he would tear a dead mouse apart himself, but he would still run away at the sight of a live mouse.

One morning I made a decision concerning Archie's hunting skills. Each morning, before work, I would place Archie outside in the wood duck box. Most days when I returned, he was just as I left him, comfortably sitting peering from the box.

This day would be different. One of my live traps had a short-tailed shrew. I put the shrew in the bottom of the box, pushed Archie inside, and nailed a square piece of paneling over the entrance. I told Bev what I had done and then left for work.

Upon returning home that evening I thought, "Today was the day Archie learned to kill and eat his own mouse." I put my ear near the box and even tapped the box several times. There was no sound. The instant I removed the cover, a feathered ball of orange shot from the box as if fired from a cannon; it was Archie. I picked him up and placed him in the entry hole, but he kept jumping to the ground.

I was certain he ate the shrew; but when I opened the front of the box, the shrew was running around inside, alive and well.

In a shocking moment of enlightenment I thought, "What have I done? I put this poor owl through eight hours of its worst nightmare."

Imagining myself locked in a darkened room for eight hours with a black mamba, I regretted what I had done. More than a week passed before Archie would go into the box again. He never cooperated in our attempted flight training exercises, but he did begin gliding from his box to the ground every day about dusk. And he didn't seem to mind when Bev scooped

him up and brought him inside for the night. However, he
began to leave his box and would be found on a nearby tree
branch. Bev called me at work one day and asked, "Archie's
on the neighbor's porch roof. What should I do?"

I replied, "Get a ladder and get him down or keep an eye
on him and I will get him when I come home."

Soon there came a time when I would regularly hear,
"Dad, Archie's up in the tree," or "Dad, Archie's on the roof."

Each time, I would retrieve him and place him back in the
box. Even though Archie frequently left the comfort of his box
for a nearby lofty perch, we never did see him fly.

One day when we were all home, Julie said, "Archie's out
of the box again."

We all went out to search for him. Finally, he was spotted
high up in an 80-foot Norway spruce.

Kelly asked, "How are we going to get him down from
there?"

"We aren't," I answered. "He's on his own. We are going to
have to say our goodbyes from here."

Josh reacted with crying; yelling in despair over losing his
companion. Another reaction was — he won't leave if I can
help it. Another — sad, but accepting, and Bev's reaction —
sad but joyful, knowing that he was fulfilling the purpose for
which he was created.

Archie had been with us now for two years. This was
the last we would see Archie, except for me. One day while
checking owl boxes in the 14-acre woods, I climbed a tree and
a red phase ESO popped its head out and looked at me.

I thought, "That's odd. That's never happened before."

All other owls remained inside the box never peering out.
As I climbed closer, the owl looked out at me again, then
nervously looked around and flew out. I was able to reassure

the family that Archie was alive and well, hunting and surviving on his own.

Although I couldn't be sure this owl was Archie, I thought, "Of course, it's Archie. He's always been different. He's his own owl."

My ESO nest box studies confirmed Julie's science fair project data concerning the size of an ESO's territory. After 28 years of ESO surveys, nine years of trapping, and 12 years of monitoring the nest boxes and having banded 100s of ESOs, I officially ended my research.

I removed all the nesting boxes, repaired some, scavenged parts from one to fix another, and took about 15 to a BBC meeting and said, "These are for anyone who would like to have one."

They were all taken. Now I leisurely do ESO surveys, monitor two nest boxes, and very rarely trap an owl. ESOs are my favorite bird.

BROOKS NATURE CENTER — BOB

John Christie came in one morning and told Dot and me, "I was offered a job in PA, near Philadelphia, and I am going to take it."

The Nature Committee offered me the job, and the Director of Oglebay Institute told me, "It would mean more money, and you could relax more and not have to be out all the time." Basically, that meant it was an office job, and I already knew that from working there, so I declined the offer.

Two more times during my 18 years at the Brooks Nature Center I would be offered that same job. Both times I would decline. In the meantime my title was Interim Director of Nature Education. Dot and I had briefly met with all who visited the nature center for interviews. After interviewing and narrowing the field of candidates, it was decided to offer the job to Bob Gingerich who had been working at a nature-related job in New Hampshire. The first day as Director, Bob dressed in a western-style shirt, cowboy hat, and turquoise Indian jewelry.

I thought, "He wasn't dressed that way for his interview."

Bob politely greeted Dot and me and then went into his office. A short time later he emerged carrying a bull whip.

The whip had hung on the back of the office door for many years. It had been confiscated from a boy who brought it to Junior Nature Camp. Bob walked out into the parking lot and began swinging and cracking the whip. Dot and I stared out the window, shocked and confused. Over and over again, he cracked it. When he stopped, he came inside and walked back into his office without saying a word.

Looking at the dismay on Dot's face I thought, "Maybe I should have taken the job."

When Bob became Director of the Nature Education Program I knew the job would be different. Soon I would discover that Bob was very creative; however, his creativity also had a downside. Near the end of each year he evaluated the work of Brooks Nature Center employees. But one year he gave the form to each staff member and requested, "I would like you to evaluate yourself based on what you feel your job performance was this year. Afterwards we will have a one-on-one meeting about it."

I didn't want to give myself low scores because I knew I had done a good job, but I felt uncomfortable giving the highest score even though I may have deserved it. The scale was one to five, so I compromised by giving myself threes for all categories.

When it was my turn, I walked in and sat down. Bob looked at the form and looked and me. He did this several times before he said, "I've disagreed with your self-evaluation in all categories, except one. You've done a fine job this year, like all years. But I cannot give you a high score in creativity."

I sat quietly.

He continued with, I know you're a creative person, but you haven't really come up with any new ideas this year."

I remained silent.

He asked, "Well, don't you have anything to say?"

"No, I'm okay with that," I said.

Bob smiled, and said, "I'm not okay with it. Where are your ideas?"

I sighed, "Bob, you have more ideas than the man in the moon. Some are crazy, and most are things we can't do for some reason. But there are a few that are great. And the great ones I have to do; not you. You have enough ideas to require two full-time naturalists; but I am only one person. I have barely enough time to implement yours, I'll be darned if I am going to tell you my ideas."

Bob looked at me and said, "Good answer...good answer," and then gave me a five.

Bob was a people person. He wanted me to do less winter bird banding and reading nature magazines and do more teaching. To increase my interaction with the public, I began offering adult workshops.

Even though Bob wanted less time spent banding, he still wanted to offer public bird banding days. I explained that according to the BBL (Bird Banding Laboratory) my main emphasis was to band the birds, and until the majority of birds visiting the feeders were banded, I would be too busy to interact with the public. He understood, and each year I set my nets until the majority of the birds were caught and banded. Later in the season, when banding was done for educational/entertainment purposes I had time to talk with people, show them the birds close-up, demonstrate how the nets worked and so on.

Bob came to me one day and said, "I have an idea, and I want to run it past you." Knowing Bob, that translated to, "I have an idea, and I want you to do it."

And I was fine with that, as long as there were enough hours in the day.

"I want to offset our bird seed costs with a new program called Adopt a Bird," he said.

Initially Bob wanted a list of popular birds which visit peoples' feeders and, most importantly, that we band regularly. My list included: Northern cardinal, Carolina chickadee, American goldfinch, downy woodpecker, slate-colored junco. I wrote bios on all five species with the most interesting, entertaining information I could find. These bios, which were then printed onto elaborately-decorated, heavy cardstock, were very attractive and suitable for framing. We advertised it as Adopt-A-Bird; for a fee of _ _ someone could adopt a bird with a bag of bird seed or a feeder.

This was one of Bob's great ideas. With each Adopt-A-Bird, a unique bird band number was printed on the adoptee's certificate. From time to time I was busy keeping track of which banded birds were spoken for and making sure the birds were getting banded. We sent out a lot of certificates. Particularly popular were the adoption of goldfinches as gifts for golden anniversaries. And, for the most part, this fundraiser covered most of our bird seed costs.

Then there were Bob's crazy ideas. His laugh and the glint in his eye were often indicative as to how off the wall an idea might be.

Even Bob laughed at his crazy ideas, knowing they were most likely, undoable; however, there were some that were borderline, and he would try to work around the roadblocks and recruit my help.

One example was not only crazy, but most likely illegal.

Bob wanted to have a lottery with the prize being one million dollars.

Right away I thought, "Whatever it is, we won't be doing it."
Bob said, "Hear me out before you say no."

His idea was for me to band a bird; and whoever saw and accurately reported it, would win the million dollars. To Bob's credit, he had all the details figured out.

Right away I asked, "How would anybody read the band? The bands are hardly noticeable as it is."

"They wouldn't have to read it," he answered, "The band would be gold instead of silver, and there would be two differently colored bands on the other leg. They would have to identify the kind of bird, the colors of the bands, and which legs they were on."

He then asked, "What's a good migratory bird to band, one that will fly a long way in the spring?"

I answered, "Maybe a white-throated sparrow or a junco."

I asked, "And just where are we going to get the million dollars?"

There was that smile again. Right away I knew he had an answer.

"Why, Lloyds of London, of course," he answered. "What's the chance of anyone seeing our bird or any banded bird?" he asked.

"Pretty slim," I answered.

Bob continued, "We wouldn't have to pay much up front with the odds so much in our favor, and we could bring in a lot of money. We can't lose."

It kind of made sense to me. It was like his idea to make an oversized coat of many colors, like Joseph's in the Bible. The inside of the coat would have large pockets containing feathers, skulls, snake skins, antlers, seeds, etc. and I would wear it and pull out visual aids while doing my programs or leading a nature walk. Finally I said, "And what makes you think the BBL would go along with this?"

"Couldn't you talk to them?" he asked.

I answered, "Just by asking I might lose my permits."

"What if you didn't do it?" he asked.

"Do what?" I asked.

"What if someone else banded the bird?"

"You have to have a federal permit," I said.

After talking about the legalities for a while, the lottery idea had run its course, at least for this day.

Bob and Greg Park, our Camping Specialist, were Indian enthusiasts. One day Bob came to Greg and me and said, "I have an idea for a program that we could do together."

He called it Winter Lodge. Basically, it would be a late-fall through winter program for fifth graders. The students would arrive in the morning, sleep in a teepee that night, and leave the next afternoon. Greg and I would share in the programming, and Bob would do storytelling in the teepee before the kids went to sleep. Winter Lodge became one of our most popular programs with a waiting list of schools that wanted to participate.

Bob eventually turned Winter Lodge over to Greg and me, but not before we knew some good Indian stories. Most of the stories I told were about birds. An Iroquois story, How the Birds Got Their Feathers, related how buzzard visited Creator in the Sun Place and petitioned Creator for suits of feathers for the birds. My favorite was a story about a dream by the Crow Indian, Chief Plenty Coups, when he was nine years old. In part, a great storm with terrible winds came from all four corners of the earth. These winds destroyed everything, save one tall tree which was home to a chickadee. In the dream, "A voice told Plenty Coup that the chickadee was the weakest in strength, but the strongest of mind. The chickadee was willing to work for wisdom, was a good listener, had sharp hearing, minded his own business, and learned from the successes and failures of others."

Due to this dream young Plenty Coups would become a great Crow chief and save his people from the wars and misery other tribes would suffer in the Indian wars with the U.S. Chief Plenty Coups wore a dried body of a chickadee behind his ear for the rest of his life as a symbol of the power and understanding the chickadee gifted to him in this vision.

I designed a naming ceremony where each student, teacher, and chaperone would receive a nature name for the time they were at Winter Lodge. Before the kids chose their names, I talked about actual Native Americans who had animals as part of their name such as Sitting Bull, Crazy Horse, Sacajawea (Bird Woman), Standing Bear, and Tecumseh (Panther in the Sky). How Indians received their names would be explained in some detail. For example, some say that near the time of Red Cloud's birth in 1822, the sky became red from a bright fireball that streaked across the sky in Nebraska and other states on September 20, probably resulting in a number of Indians receiving the name Red Cloud or perhaps Red Sky.

They would keep their first name and pick the name of some wild animal from anywhere in the world as the second part of their name. Someone named Ann could become Ann Ant, Ann Antelope, Ann Armadillo, Ann Avocet, or any wild animal with an A. The names were to be kept a secret until I asked a name using Indian signs that Greg had taught me. Slowly waving my hand, palm open, in front of someone meant…What? Next I would point at the person, and finally I would fold my outstretched fingers and thumb together, bring them toward my face, almost touching my lips and quickly pull them away, which meant…called.

Each time I would ask a name and when the animal was revealed, I would tell them special things about the animal they chose.

A name of Taylor Turkey might find me right away gobbling like a turkey, and then telling what an important food source this bird was for some Indian tribes or how the turkey was a member of the "two-leggeds," because some Indian tribes grouped all living creatures based on how many legs they had.

It was not uncommon for people to recognize me when I was out and about in town. One day while shopping, I noticed a boy staring at me from the other end of the aisle. As we drew closer he kept watching me from behind his Mom's shopping cart.

When we were side by side, I looked at him and asked, "Do you know me?"

He answered, "Yes, I was at Winter Lodge."

With hand signs I asked, "What's your name?"

His eyes got real big and he loudly said, "I don't remember!"

Then in a panic he looked up at his mother, and said, "I forgot my name."

The mom looked at me and sternly asked, "Who are you?"

I sheepishly answered, "I'm Mr. Beatty. I had your son for a Winter Lodge program at Oglebay.

"Oh," she said, "He talks about Winter Lodge all the time. Are you the Indian or the Bird Man?" she asked.

One particular Winter Lodge was more memorable than others. We had a group of students from Follansbee. It was my turn to stay overnight, and 30 students, teachers, and chaperones were situated in the teepee ready for bed. We were arranged like spokes in a wheel. Everyone except me had the option of moving to the Nature Center anytime during the night. We had a fire circle in the center of the teepee and a stack of firewood near the entry way.

I always announced, "We let the fire go out. We don't add more wood. If you get cold, go to the Nature Center."

This night was supposed to be very cold. My sleeping bag was an old down military mummy bag with a wool liner and a hood that could be pulled over my face. In the middle of the night I awoke sweating and smelled a foul odor. Pulling the hood from my face, I saw flames shooting up and out the top of the teepee. The fire screen had become so hot the feathers in the end of my sleeping bag were smoldering. Looking around, there were only four kids still in the teepee. With the fire poker I got the flames to die down.

Turning to the boys I reprimanded them with, "I told you not to add any more wood."

One boy whispered guiltily, "I was cold."

They decided to stay and we all went back to bed. When I woke up that morning I could hear one boy's teeth chattering.

I went to him and said, "Why don't you go up to the nature center?"

He answered, "Noooo…oooo…ooo."

Looking at my watch I said, "Why don't we all go to the nature center?"

It was later than I had thought. When we walked in, some kids were already awake. The four boys were heroes. It had been nine degrees, the lowest temperature we ever had at Winter Lodge.

After breakfast I presented my bird banding program. What I didn't know then was that the bird banding left a permanent mark on the lives of two of the boys.

Months later, I received a phone call from a lady who said, "Mr. Beatty, I am the mother of one of the children you had at Winter Lodge last winter. I wouldn't bother you, but my son was outside today, in a tall pine tree trying to look into a bird's nest. It was lightning and storming and I was calling to him, but he was defiant and ignored me. He wouldn't come down. Would you talk to him? His name is Harold."

I agreed to talk to Harold and I think he listened to me explaining how dangerous it is to be outside when it's lightning. When his mom got back on the phone she told me how Harold and a friend spent every waking moment chasing birds.

She said, "I don't know what you did, but my husband and I are certainly grateful."

Later that summer Harold and his mom came to the nature center for his birthday and asked me to help them choose a bird book as a gift from our small bookstore. They did the same thing at Christmas.

One winter Bob and I put together a Winter Outdoor Education weekend. Our target audience was other nature and outdoor educators. One of our guest speakers was an editor from *Bird Watcher's Digest*. Harold's mom called me and asked, "Do you think the boys could come to hear the speaker?"

I thought it was a wonderful idea.

Then she said, "There is one thing they insist on. They want to sit with you, on either side of you."

During a break in the workshop I asked, "What's the last bird thing you did?"

One boy looked at the other and Harold said, "Well....we were out the other day and saw a red-tailed hawk flying over a field. We slowly crawled on our bellies to the middle of the field and then rolled over so we could see the sky. Then we pulled grass and weeds out and covered our heads and bodies and waited for the hawk."

Then they just sat staring at me.

Looking at the other boy, I asked, "Did you see it? Did the hawk return?"

"Yeah," he said, "But it took a long time."

When I looked back at Harold he said, "We were excited," then asked, "Have you ever done anything like that?"

I answered, "Yeah, and I was excited too."

PHONE CALLS

Every day the nature center would receive phone calls. Queries ranged from the bizarre to the common. In the summer months the most common was, "I have a snake in my house…how do I get rid of it?" and in the winter months, "I have a bird at my feeder I can't identify…it's fat, gray, and flies real fast, do you know what it is?"

When a call came in, or if someone brought something to the center for identification, Dot would make a note of it and sometimes, for the rest of the day, or maybe only one half hour, I would be on the phone answering questions. I enjoyed being available and able to help people, but being on the phone for hours on end really tired me out.

The most common bird-related calls dealt with identification or feeding. Some required careful listening and a host of questions from me. Often my first question would be, "Is it bigger than a sparrow, or bigger than a robin, or pigeon, or crow?"

Once I knew the size I could begin to narrow it down. Calls about blue woodpeckers were actually white-breasted nuthatches. A flock of red-breasted flycatchers (a real bird native to Eurasia) were in reality, a flock of eastern bluebirds someone saw one morning while walking their dog. A turkey pecking on the side of a tree turned out to be a pileated woodpecker.

A common query was, "I hear this owl every morning and would like to know what kind it is."

Sometimes while the person was still talking, I would lay the phone on my desk, cup my hands against my mouth, and give a mourning dove call. Then I would hear the caller excitedly saying, "That's what I hear. That's it. That's what I hear."

The nature center didn't open until 9:00, but I often arrived early to set nets for banding or to set up chairs for a morning program. From experience, I knew not to answer the phone, and Dot would take care of calls when she arrived. Early on, more than once, I got bogged down with a call and was unable to tend to birds in a mist net or prepare for a school visit. One particular morning the phone rang, then stopped, began ringing again, stopped; the phone was ringing a lot.

After Dot arrived, the calls continued pouring in. Dot came downstairs where I was working and asked, "Did you watch last night's weather?"

Neither of us had, so we were both in the dark about the calls, but they originated because of something the weatherman said about hummingbirds.

Several callers were people from the BBC who said, "You should call him. He should know better."

That afternoon I called a BBCer who had called earlier.

"What's the problem with the weatherman and the hummingbirds?" I asked.

She related that during the weather forecast he had said, "Someone from Wellsburg called to remind everyone to take down their hummingbird feeders so the poor little fellas don't stay up north too long and freeze." It was mid-afternoon, and we were still receiving hummingbird calls. Some folks were questioning us about what to do with their feeders.

When I did finally call the weatherman, I barely said my name; and he interrupted and jokingly said, "I was wondering when you were going to call. What took you so long?"

"We have been getting a lot of calls today,"....

Again he interrupted, "You think you have been getting a lot of calls; our phones have been ringing off the hook."

"What did you say last night?"

"Evidently the wrong thing," he answered.

I discussed how important it was to leave the feeders up until the last of the northern hummingbirds had moved through our area, and how they know when it's the right time to leave. He was very appreciative of the information. That same night I watched the weather. He came on and said, "Some people, some time in their lives have to eat a little crow for misspoken words. Tonight some might say, 'I might need to eat some hummingbird.' I want to thank the folks at the Brooks Nature Center for letting me know how important it is to keep those hummingbird feeders up until you're sure all the hummingbirds have migrated south."

One day a call came in while I was working on a bulletin board near the front door.

After briefly speaking with the caller, Dot put her hand over the phone and said, "It's for you; something about eagles."

"I have some baby eagles I found in a field behind my house."

"How do you know they're eagles?"

"Well, any darn fool can see they're eagles."

"How can I help?"

"Well, I don't want them. Can I bring them to you?"

He also told me he was from near Cadiz, OH. As I began to explain the complexities of possessing and transporting wild birds across state lines, he interrupted me saying, "Do you want em or not? If you don't want the darn things I'll just take them back out into the field and kill em."

I responded, "If you don't mind bringing them here, I will take them."

I went downstairs to begin another project, and before long Dot yelled down, "I think the eagle man may be here." I ran upstairs, looked out the window and watched an older man walking toward the front door carrying a large cardboard box.

When I opened the door for him, I asked, "What do you have in the box?"

He looked at me and answered, "Eagles! I called you; told you I would bring 'em."

He set the box on the counter and opened it.

Looking inside, I looked around, looked at him, looked back at Dot, looked back at him and thought, "Am I on Candid Camera?"

Then I asked him, "What makes you think these are eagles?"

He answered the same as on the phone, "Well, any darn fool can see they're eagles."

Then he asked, "What do you think they are?"

I answered, "They're chickens."

"CHICKENS!" he yelled. "Well, hell, if knew I was bringing them to someone who doesn't know a chicken from an eagle, I wouldn't have wasted my time. Do you want these eagles or not," he demanded.

I answered, "But they are chickens."

To which he answered, "If you don't want these damn eagles I'm gonna just take 'em home and kill 'em."

Bob was listening to everything from inside his office. He came out, looked in the box, smiled, looked at me, looked at the man and said, "I'll tell you what you can do. Take these baby eagles over to the zoo. Ask for Penny Miller; she'll know what to do with them."

The man looked at me and said, "Finally, someone who knows what they're talking about." Then he left.

The next day Penny called. She said, "Thanks, I really appreciated the eagles." I responded with, "Thought you would. We wanted to share the moment."

Penny related, "The man said if you rub salt on a chicken's egg, it will hatch out as an eagle."

Early on in my job when someone might call wanting to bring me a 12 foot copperhead, I might dismiss the caller with, "Copperheads never get that long...or even close that size. I'm really not interested."

One caller asked, "You know how when you use melted snow water to wash your whites, they come out so much brighter?"

I told her, "I've never done that."

"Well," she said, "I found some seeds in the water and wondered if you could identify them for me. I think they are from outer space."

I responded, "If they are from outer space, I don't think I would know what they are."

She never brought me the seeds. Before long, I was encouraging people to bring me their 12-foot copperheads, seeds from other planets, Siamese toads, and the like. I was curious. Instead of dismissing the caller, I would stay with their idea just to see where the call was going.

One call put me in an embarrassing situation. Greg Eddy called me one July morning and wanted a favor. He was leaving town for a while and had heard pine siskins in his neighborhood. Being far north nesters, the siskins shouldn't be around this area at this time of the year. Greg's neighborhood had huge lots and the neighborhood was more like a forest with houses.

Knowing that siskins preferred evergreens, I decided to concentrate on areas with groups of pines and spruces. From behind a nearby house I heard, "Shreeeeeee,"of a pine siskin. From the sounds, I knew there was more than one bird. From the roadway I saw a large stand of Scotch pine trees in the middle of five houses, all with their backs to the pines. I went through a yard into the pines. The birds were still singing, "Shreeeeeee, Shreeeeeee, Shreeeeeee." They seemed to be right in front of me, but high in the trees. Without warning, a flock of tiny birds flew from the trees, right over my head.

I followed the flock into another pine woods behind another home which I could barely see through the trees. The siskins were hiding somewhere in the pines. I could still hear their, "Shreeeeeee, Shreeeeeee, Shreeeeeee," calls. To gain a better vantage point, I walked away from the pines and off to the side.

Every now and again I caught a glimpse of a siskin, but only for an instant. They took to the air again, and I followed them through my binoculars and found myself looking at a young lady standing on her back porch on the second floor of her house. She was quite attractive with long blond hair and a sparse bikini. As she stood there smiling at me, I stood there still looking at her through the binoculars. She waved. I lowered the binoculars and waved back. Feeling she needed an explanation as to why a strange man was behind her house watching her through binoculars I walked over.

Right away she said, "Come on up."

There were stairs leading to the porch.

On the porch I thought, "Here I am on this hot day in GI camo pants and a sweaty t-shirt and right in front of me is an attractive young lady in her bikini."

She said, "Please sit down. Would you like some lemonade?"

I responded, "Yes, that would be nice."

She went inside and soon came out with my drink. Although she never asked me what I was doing, I still needed to justify why I was staring at her through my binoculars. I said, "My name is Bill Beatty and I was checking on some unusual birds in the area. They happened to be in your backyard and when they flew, I followed them with the binoculars and then....there you were."

Right away she said, "I saw you looking at something in the trees. And I was a bit curious. And when those birds flew past me, I knew you were looking for them." She continued with, "I wanted to be outside on such a beautiful day. Tomorrow I am getting married."

"Really," I said, "Congratulations!"

She thanked me and we sat talking and drinking lemonade. We talked about her excitement and even about the pine siskins and why their presence there was so unusual. When I left she wished me luck with the siskins, and I wished her luck with her wedding. I returned to Greg's house thinking, "That's enough excitement for one day. I don't want to press my luck."

My most bizarre call resulted in my being subpoenaed and testifying in court. Just like so many other days, this day began with Dot answering the phone and telling me, "This is for you...someone has questions about bird feeding."

The call was very typical of so many I received, with two exceptions: I assumed the call referred to feeding hummingbirds since it was still summertime, and the caller asked questions about what I did concerning my bird feeding.

"Do you feed birds?"

"I do, here at the Nature Center and also at home."

The man continued, "Do you feed a lot of birds?"

Other questions he asked were, "Do any other animals eat at your feeders? How much seed do you use? Do you ever see any rats?"

Overall, the call was a little strange until he asked, "How many times a day do you brush your teeth?"

Now, the call was more than a little strange.

Wanting to know where this call was going, I answered honestly and said, "I brush twice a day, once in the morning and before bedtime."

He then said, "Some say you should brush three times a day."

As quickly as the conversation switched from bird feeding to my personal hygiene, it switched back again.

"How many people do you think feed birds?"

"I read of a study that suggests one in four households in the U.S. have a bird feeder," I answered.

"Are there any diseases that birds carry?"

"Do you mean diseases that people can catch?" I asked.

"Yes," he answered.

"Most are extremely rare, but there is one that is more common than all the others – histoplasmosis."

He became very curious and even anxious when I mentioned it was a fungus transmitted via bird droppings.

Then it got bizarre again when he asked, "Do you bathe every day?"

We talked a little more, he thanked me, and the call was over. The next morning we were still talking about the strange phone call.

Dot then answered the phone looked at me and said, "It's for you."

"Are you Mr. Beatty?" the caller asked.

"Yes I am. May I help you with something?"

"Yes, you can. It's come to my attention that you had a phone conversation with a gentleman yesterday involving birds and bird feeding. Do you remember the call?" he asked.

"Yes, I do."

"He is the plaintiff in a court case in which I am involved. He is suing my client concerning damage to his vehicle from bird droppings and trying to get a court order to stop her from feeding birds. He is claiming my client's property is a serious health risk to the community. I would like to have you testify in the case as an expert witness."

He then asked, "If possible, would you mind driving by my client's home so you would be familiar with her property and her bird feeders?"

A few days later I decided to visit the bird feeding property. All the houses were adjacent to the street except one. This house was inset, between two houses, well away from the street. I immediately eliminated the inset house since it was so well landscaped with rock walls and flower gardens; and the lawn and shrubbery were well maintained. It stood out from all the others because it was so neat and clean. In my mind, the place I was searching for must be unkempt since it was possibly a health risk to the community.

Driving along the street carefully checking each property, the only place with active feeders and birds was the inset house, the most unlikely looking property. I parked my car, walked over to take a closer look at the feeding area and gardens, and then noticed the number on a low post in the ground. This was the place.

When the day of my court appearance finally arrived, I was excited. When I arrived at the courthouse, I met the lawyer who had subpoenaed me, and he said, "Let me show you the room where you will wait until you are called to testify."

I asked, "I can't be in the courtroom to find out what this is all about?"

He answered, "Unfortunately, no. Witnesses are only allowed in the courtroom during their testimony."

There were three other people in the waiting room. Soon I discovered that I didn't need to be in the courtroom to learn what this was all about. Listening to the conversations of the other three, I discovered that these neighbors have been feuding for decades. At one time, they had been friendly until something concerning a death in one family turned their friendship into hatred. Also, they had been to court on several occasions with frivolous lawsuits.

While waiting to testify, I thought, "This really isn't about bird feeding; it's about someone's intent on making someone else's life miserable."

When I took the stand the first question was, "Mr. Beatty, did you have the opportunity to visit the defendant's home to see her bird feeders?"

"Yes, I did," I answered.

The next question was, "Could you describe what you found and how this property compares to others in the neighborhood?"

I said, "I had expected to find a rundown poorly-maintained property, but instead found the opposite, a clean, well-cared for area with flower gardens and a very attractive yard."

The questions asked of me were of a nature that had me describing an area that couldn't possibly be a health hazard. After the defense attorney was finished, the plaintiff's attorney began asking me about health hazards concerning birds. One specific question, "Do you believe this particular bird feeding area could possibly attract rats?" led to other rat-related questions and finally, "Do you ever have rats at your feeders at Oglebay?"

I answered honestly and said, "Yes, I have seen rats at our feeders."

I was somewhat uncomfortable with my response because of Oglebay's image of being the cleanest, most inviting, healthiest park in the east.

I did have the opportunity to elaborate about rats and how, even though they are around, their nocturnal nature prevents us from observing them much.

After my testimony I was free to leave, so I returned to the Nature Center to give an account of my day in court. In the end I never did discover the court's final decision, but I suspected, with my testimony, the bird feeding was allowed to continue. The phone call concerning my own personal hygiene was an attempt to determine whose side I might be on if I was summoned to testify. And he found out.

Although I didn't know it at the time, probably the best call I ever received involved a lady who wanted to donate a parrot to the Nature Center.

Years before, I had accepted a parakeet. A lady had called and asked if I wanted the bird. I was reluctant, but she was so insistent, I agreed to have her bring it by. The bird was a very large parakeet. She explained that the bird could be noisy, but all I would have to do was drape the cloth cover she had

made over the cage and the bird would quiet down. I did not
want the bird, but I did want the cage, so I decided to accept
it. The cage had a large, heavy base that supported a tall, solid
pole with a hook at the top, on which hung the most beautiful
ornate barred cage. Everything was brass.

The bird's name was Sassy. And, my goodness was this
bird sassy. Any time someone entered the building, the bird
would squawk and scream. Even when covered, it would
scream incessantly if the phone rang. I moved the bird
downstairs into the exhibit hall only to discover when visitors
were talking to each other, the bird had to join in with shrieks
and screeches of its own.

Most troublesome was the fact that Sassy's noises were
extreme to the point they could damage one's hearing. It got
to the point I dreaded going to work and listening to her. One
day a lady came into the Nature Center and just fell in love
with Sassy, noise and all. I was upfront and honest about the
bird but she took her home anyway. Thank goodness.

When the parrot call came, I immediately thought of Sassy
the parakeet. There was no way I wanted to get into a similar
situation again.

The lady asked, "Do you ever accept donations of
animals?"

I responded, "Rarely. Our space is limited and we lack the
facilities to care for certain kinds of animals. Did you consider
calling the zoo?"

"I could call the zoo but I wanted you all to have it," she
answered.

"What kind of animal do you have?" I asked.

"It's a parrot. My son at one time worked in Venezuela and
took an egg from a nest he found. He incubated the egg and
it hatched. I have been to the Nature Center many times and

your place would be the perfect home," she said.

I responded, "Sometimes I accept an animal and it doesn't work out like I expect and I have to find another place for it."

"If it doesn't work out, I will take him back. He is such a good bird and very easy to care for," she said.

She had the parrot in a cardboard box and I thought, "She doesn't even have a cage for the bird. Already, this isn't good."

Upon opening the box I noticed that the parrot was smaller than I expected, about nine inches tall from its feet to the top of its head. The lady reached into the box and the bird stepped onto her hand.

I asked, "Can it fly?"

She answered, "I expect he can, but I really do not know. He's always been kept inside." She said, "Just lay your hand gently near his feet and he will step onto your hand."

He stepped right onto my hand. The parrot had green wings, back and tail with a blue head and breast and some red on the under tail covert feathers.

The lady said, "Before I forget, there is something in the car I have to get." She came back with a four-foot tall wooden stand.

"He's never been caged. He has always stayed on this perch, or sat on my hand or shoulder. If he is put on the floor he will use his beak and feet to climb onto something higher," she told me.

After the lady left, I took the parrot downstairs and placed the stand in the back middle of the exhibit hall, and then put my hand next to the perch and the parrot stepped right onto the perch.

A college intern and I decided the parrot needed a name. Since it was from Venezuela and it was mostly green, the parrot's name became Verde. Unlike the Sassy parakeet, Verde was a quiet little parrot.

Verde became a permanent and popular exhibit at the Nature Center. A prominent sign warned visitors that Verde might give a painful bite if touched. Anytime a hand approached, Verde would slowly, but deliberately open his beak and reach for the nearest finger. He wouldn't bite unless the hand actually touched him. What bothered him most was having his feet or toes touched.

Verde never attempted to fly, but did sometimes like to walk. When I would be working on an exhibit, it was not unusual for him to climb down his stand to the floor. When climbing, his beak was like a third foot. After reaching the floor, Verde would walk over to me and using his beak, grab hold of my pant leg, pull himself up as high as he could, grab hold with his feet, then reach upward as far as he could reach, pull himself up again, and continue this process until he was on my shoulder. There he would sit. If I bent over, Verde would walk to the upper part of my back. I never had to worry about him falling off. He always knew what he had to do to keep his balance.

When school groups came for programs there was always about 15 to 20 minutes for the kids to look at the exhibits before I began the program. Verde was a hit with the kids. There might be as many as 80 children; and when they were seated, there was a wide aisle down the middle. While I would talk to the group I could see Verde in the back of the room slowly and quietly climbing down from his perch. He would then waddle toward me like a penguin, right down the middle of the aisle. As he walked past each row, the kids in that row would look at him and laugh.

Upon arriving at his destination, me, he would climb up

my pant leg and shirt until he reached my shoulder and I would teach the entire time with Verde attached to me. In the beginning, Verde was a distraction from my teaching, until I realized that if I initially talked about him and tied him into the topics I was relating, the kids would accept him as part of the program and not as a disruption. The call about Verde was the best call I ever had while at the Brooks Nature Center.

MY BIG DAY

Serious birders have big days, big weeks, big months, and yes, big years. As a new birder I kept an up-to-date life list; but at some point, my focus changed. My main interest became knowing as much as possible about behavior, identification by sight and song, habitat, and how to relate this information to others. For me, teaching was my job and I needed to know about birds, not just spot as many as I could.

On Century Day I kept a list. On this particular Century Day I would bird to the top of a high ridge not far from the Ohio County Airport. A week earlier I found a Brewster's warbler there, which would be a one-of-a-kind find for the Century Day list. Little did I know this would be my best warbler day ever.

I was out the door at 7:30 and immediately heard a high-pitched, thin song from the sour cherry trees in the side yard. It was one of two warblers, but I was unable to separate the songs. I had to see the bird to be certain. Spotting some movement, I saw it: yellow below with black streaks, large white wing bar, and the identifying field mark was the chestnut-colored cheeks (1).

Walking to the car I heard "weeta-weeta-wee-TEE-oh" (2)

from the woods behind my house. Into the car and on the road I hear, "Sweet-sweet-sweeter than sweet (3)." Moments later, I hear a buzzy ascending trill ending in a sharp, emphatic "zip" (4). Driving along, it is a bit chilly with the windows down, but I am listening. The tops of the ridges appear sunny and warm. As I draw near the end of my drive, I hear American robin, northern cardinal, indigo bunting, American goldfinch, red-winged blackbird, and many others.

Upon exiting the car I hear a loud, exploding song and my binoculars are drawn to a brown-backed bird with a brown-streaked white breast, bouncing as it walks, with a constantly bobbing tail (5).

Right away the song reminds me that I have to cross the stream and the water will be cold.

Most spring mornings, my feet and lower legs become soaking wet as I bird and botanize the ravines and hillsides. I must cross a stream; and the water can be bone-chilling, but my singular purpose allows me to fight back the cold and continue my journey. After crossing the stream, I begin my long ascent. The steep hill is covered in bluebells, Dutchman's breeches, squirrel corn, trout lilies, and countless white trilliums.

My captivation with the mature woods, blankets of wildflowers, and a myriad of bird songs keeps me coming back to this physically uncomfortable location. Scarlet tanager, rose-breasted grosbeak, wood thrush, Acadian flycatcher, eastern wood pewee, and others are added to my list. In a flurry of wing beats, a wood duck startles me as it leaves its tree cavity high above. Directly in front of me is what first appears as a tiny nuthatch searching the trunk and larger branches of a tulip poplar tree. As the bird circles the tree I hear its characteristic "weesee-weesee-weesee-weesee" song

(6). From the treetops I hear ""ZEE-ZEE-zee-zu-ZEE (7)," but only as a whisper. Like so many other birds migrating north, this warbler will not announce loudly, "This is my territory, stay the heck away," until it reaches its nesting place.-

Two nesting warblers announce their territories as I continue my climb. The first is a bird of concern in many locales. Its population has been steadily declining throughout all of its range. In former years it was expected to be found on ridges and in valleys of most mature deciduous woodlands. "Zray-zray-zray-zreeeee (8)" it sings from only the highest tree tops. I learned this bird's song long before I ever saw one. Locating the singer of the other song that is thin, high-pitched and penetrating, I see some movement. The end of the refrain ascends upward, beyond the range of human hearing. Standing in the shade of the thick tree canopy I see the fiery throat of this bright bird (9). I am somewhat envious of its ability to seek out and easily obtain the heat from the sun. Surprised at how long it took to encounter this next bird, I immediately notice the distinctive orange patches on the wings and tail (10). Orange defines it as a male. Yellow patches would indicate a female. From far below a bird screams out, "Teacher, teacher, teacher, teacher, teacher (11)." Too far away to see the bird, I continue my trek to the top.

The sun is now penetrating the tree canopy and reaching the forest floor. I find a sunny location and bask in its comfort. Then I notice movement a short distance away. The bright yellow rump patches give the birds away (12). A small flock is eating last year's remaining poison ivy berries. Field sparrow, gray catbird, brown thrasher, chipping sparrow, red-tailed hawk and others are added to my list as I stand in sight of the meadow.

I am about to enter a completely different habitat

containing a new set of birds. Walking over to where the Brewster's warbler might be, I lose the cold feeling from my wet clothing and feet. The sky is a beautiful blue and the sun is bright. Noticing the sun's angle, I decide to change my route so the sun is at my back as I cross the meadows. I hear, "BEE-BUZZZZZ," the song I had to have, especially today. But I have to see the bird to be sure. Most birders identify this bird without even looking at it. That may be acceptable for identifying most birds, but this bird can crossbreed and produce hybrids that sing the same song.

I spot the bird in front of me. The sun illuminates the bird perfectly. Instead of the bright glow expected from the golden yellow breast, there is a white breast with a small centered yellow patch. And instead of bluish wings, the wings are dull gray, but it does have the two white wing bars (13). From the far end of this long meadow I hear the same, "BEE-BUZZZZZ." I am far away from the bird but can see the golden yellow reflecting the sun's light (14). Immediately, I know what it is. All of a sudden, the surrounding meadow and tree lines are quiet. There is no movement. A Cooper's hawk hurriedly glides across the meadow and then disappears behind a thin row of invading trees. Thinking, "It will be a few minutes before the birds become active again," I decide to rest and eat breakfast: a banana and an apple.

Hearing a flock of blue jays and a cardinal, I know it's time to resume my search. Part way through the meadow I see movement in the low trees. The bird is easy to find. A bright yellow crown and chestnut-colored sides give it away (15). "Witchity-whitchity-whitchity-witch," sounds from across the meadow, immediately followed by another "Witchity-whitchity-whitchity-witch" from behind me (16).

Thin, long lines of invading trees divide the meadow into

a collection of smaller meadows increasing the edges and
populations of certain kinds of birds. A short distance away
I noticed a bird walking on the ground prowling for insects.
Much of the time it remained hidden and it was difficult to
locate. It flew to a thick barberry shrub. Finally, it ran into an
opening and stood on a rotting log. I nervously checked all the
field marks hoping my identification was correct. It would be
a life bird for me. Gray hood and throat, yellow belly, olive-
brown back, and complete white eye-ring…it is a life bird (17).
To be absolutely certain the bird was really the one I thought
it to be, I checked it against two others in my field guide. One
was too small; it did have a gray head and white eye-ring, but
the throat and breast were yellow and the eye-ring was not
as pronounced. The second bird had no eye-ring and hopped
instead of walking.

Now I had two birds on my list that no one else would
report today. The hybrid was exciting, but I had seen them
before. But this life bird is very difficult to find during
migration. It would be the only time I would find one. Years
later I would see them in the spring at Magee Marsh, and
take them from mist nets in the fall at the Allegheny Front
Migration Observatory, but I owned this one, I found it.

Beyond this tree line I heard the distinctive whistles,
calls, and croaks of a bird I would sometimes hear at night
as I drifted off to sleep. As impressive as its repertoire was, it
paled in comparison to its courtship flights (18). And today the
light was perfect to highlight its large, brilliant yellow breast.
Slowly sneaking through the brushy tree line, I stopped and
watched from behind a honeysuckle shrub. I could see the
throat expand and feathers fluff as it cawed, squawked, and
chirped. It stood out in glowing fashion from the greenery
surrounding it, but it didn't fly.

I was a little disappointed, but could imagine the entertaining flights I was fortunate to witness in days' past. And I already have two warblers that no one else was likely to report. This one too, might be unique to today's count. They weren't found along any roadways I knew and finding one required considerable effort to hike to a suitable nesting habitat.

Instead of walking through the next meadow, I chose to walk the perimeter hoping to be less conspicuous. My experience taught me that in the early morning the birds were more likely to ignore my intrusions, possibly due to hunger. As the day progressed, birds would become more cautious and their activity waned.

In a thicket in front of me was movement. The bird is small and I see some yellow, but it won't sit still. It flies off from the other side of a multiflora rose shrub. Watching as it gains more distance, I see it dart into another thicket. For an instant, I see a beautifully patterned black necklace against a bright yellow throat, breast, and belly (19). I felt accomplished.

Seeing the necklace on this bird for less than a second, I knew exactly what it was. A few years earlier I would have been leafing through the pages of my field guide desperately hoping to find something similar. Sometimes a glance at a bird as it flew would immediately identify it as a woodpecker or a brown thrasher. Songs and field marks I could teach; but I was entering the arena of intangibles, the things that only come with experience. I remembered something Glen had told me years earlier. He had identified several birds by their chips. They all sounded the same to me, but I wanted to know how he knew. His answer was, "I can't teach you that, but one day you will know and understand."

There was an old jeep road nearby that traversed many

sections of the meadows. Where it entered the woodland on the other side of the ridge was a vernal pool. There was movement on the road about 30 yards away. The bird was small with yellow on the body, obviously a warbler, and it constantly bobbed its tail, whether walking or standing still (20). Because of the behavior I immediately recognized it. Even so, I watched it and studied its field marks.

Approaching the pool I heard, "dadup-dadup-dadup-dadup-dadup." The song is emanating from within a younger woodland with conspicuous undergrowth. Another sings a slightly different song, but of the same pattern and quality, "churry, churry, churry, churry, churry." The songs remind me of the foot sounds of a galloping horse. Though difficult to find and see, the long black sideburns, yellow spectacles, and bright yellow underside from beak to tail make the bird unique from all others (21).

Leaving the meadows, my woodland trip back to the car is all downhill. Near the bottom of this part of the woods is a small but impressive stand of old hemlocks, the only evergreens I have seen since the start of my hike. They appear so out-of-place, I imagine them as a planting of some homestead from long ago. A new song rings out from the hemlock stand. The song is familiar, but I know several birds that have a very similar song so I must see the bird. My birding skills have not yet progressed to the point I am able to separate these songs. I spend a lot of time here searching for the bird. The many insignificant glimpses I get remind me of hide-and-seek games I played as a youngster. The rare times this bird is in the open, it is darting from one hidden recess to another. When it is still, it is only visible through multitudes of needle-covered hemlock branches.

Suddenly the bird was in front of me, still, and in perfect

light. It was what I had hoped for; one of my favorite birds to see. The contrast of and pattern of colors are overwhelming. Yellow throat, breast, and belly with heavy black streaking from the top of the breast to the underbelly; a white even flash pattern on either side of the tail; from top to bottom, the head is layered with light gray, white, black, then yellow; yellow rump patch; and a large white wing patch (22). I imagine it as the cedar waxwing of the warblers, a bird of refinement, with every feather and color groomed into its proper place.

At Oglebay I bird and talk, ending our walk at picnic site #1 where we eat and afterwards go over the bird list. I found five birds that no one else reported. Besides my best warbler day ever, which included a life bird and a hybrid, I felt more comfortable than ever before with the BBC.

1) Cape May warbler
2) Hooded warbler
3) Yellow warbler
4) Northern parula
5) Louisiana waterthrush
6) Black-and-white warbler
7) Black-throated green warbler
8) Cerulean warbler
9) Blackburnian warbler
10) American redstart
11) Ovenbird
12) Yellow-rumped warbler
13) Brewster's warbler
14) Blue-winged warbler
15) Chestnut-sided warbler
16) Common yellowthroat
17) Connecticut warbler

18) Yellow-breasted chat
19) Canada warbler
20) Palm warbler
21) Kentucky warbler
22) Magnolia warbler

WILDFLOWER PILGRIMAGE

Dot often urged me to go to the West Virginia Wildflower Pilgrimage. She was a faithful attendee for many years. Unfortunately, the Pilgrimage was held during May, one of my busiest times of the year. Greg Eddy, Glen Phillips, Jay Buckelew, Judge John Worley, Chuck Conrad and others were all bird leaders at the event. To be a bird leader membership in the BBC was required. In 1977, I received a phone call from Chuck Conrad, Executive Director and a founder of the BBC.

"Hi, Bill, did you hear that Judge Worley died?"

"Yes, I heard about it. That's too bad."

Chuck said, "How would you like to take his place at the Wildflower Pilgrimage as a bird leader?"

"I would love to, but I have to get it cleared here at the nature center."

Chuck related, "You know, someone has to die before someone gets to be a Pilgrimage leader."

Glen asked if I wanted to go with him to the Pilgrimage, which I did. He would pick me up early Thursday morning. With Glen it was all birds, all the time.

The Wildflower Pilgrimage was held at Blackwater Falls State Park in Davis. Thursday evening there would be a nature-related program and all the leaders would be introduced.

Although I had heard much about Blackwater Falls, it would be a new adventure for me. The long road into the park followed along the east and south rim of the Blackwater Canyon. Both sides of the road were lined with eastern hemlock, red spruce, and yellow and black birch trees. Even though the canyon was immediately off to my right, the dense tree line blocked the view most of the time. Without warning, Glen swerved off the road and came to a sudden stop.

"What's wrong?"

"Nothing's wrong. Do you hear that bird singing off to the left?"

"Yes, I hear it,"

"What is it?" he asked.

I answered, "I don't know."

"Get out of the car," he said, and continued with, "get your binoculars and field guide, and come around to my side. Now, go find it."

He drove away yelling, "I will be back in about an hour."

There I stood watching Glen's car disappear. The bird was still singing, so I chased the song. The tree canopy was so dense, only reflected light could permeate it. Ferns and mosses where almost everywhere, and it was damp. So damp, I could feel the weight of the water in every breath I took. The bird continued to sing. There was a small stream bed with a trickle of water that substituted as a path as I slowly, carefully, and quietly approached the bird song.

I thought, "If I try to go to the exact spot where the bird is singing, it might become quiet and then leave the area."

I stopped and looked for a dry spot to sit; but there was none, so I sat on a damp, moss-covered rock. Right away I noticed how soft the rock was, but moments later the wetness and coolness penetrated through my pants. From where I sat, the song was very loud. It would unexpectedly explode and overwhelm the forest; and the song was rapid and patterned, the same every time.

"This song should be easy to learn and remember," I thought.

While listening I looked around at the surrounding forest. The setting seemed primal, reminding me of, *The Land Unknown,* a movie childhood friends and I saw at the Frederick Theater in East Pittsburgh. The memory was most likely still with me due to the fact that, after we paid our quarter to get in, we could stay and watch the movie as many times as we wanted. I probably saw this movie twelve times in three different visits.

"Okay," I thought, "It's time to see this bird."

Creeping closer to the sound, I left the low stream bed to a higher vantage point with a wider range of view. Shortly I found the bird, and it wasn't very far away. "I know this bird," I thought. It's plain, unstriking appearance was familiar; and the tail bob and teetering movements with every step gave it away.

"This is a Louisiana Waterthrush, but where is this other bird?" I wondered. Leaving the waterthrush I began scanning the surrounding area through binoculars. Exploding noisily, the song brought my attention back to where I had been looking, and there was the waterthrush again.

"Where's that bird?"

While watching the waterthrush, it tipped its head back, and then screamed the song, but not the song of a Louisiana waterthrush, instead it was the song I had been chasing.

As if struck by a lightning bolt I remembered, "There are two waterthrushes."

Opening my field guide to the warblers, I quickly saw
it was a life bird for me, a northern waterthrush. Even
though they look and act alike, there were differences. Most
outstanding was the yellowish-beige under parts, which I
could easily see. And the song, well, it was totally different.
Both waterthrushes have loud, explosive songs, but they are
patterned very differently. I watched and studied the bird
as it sang repeatedly. During the chase and then finding and
watching the northern waterthrush, everything else escaped
my attention.

"Honk, honk, honk." It was Glen.

After I jumped into the car Glen asked, "What was the
bird?"

"Northern waterthrush," I answered, as we drove away.
Glen drove straight to the BBC cabin. Some years, as many
as nine bird leaders would share the three bedrooms and
one shower. At the cabin I met Ralph Bell, Clark Miller, Gene
Hutton (Doc to all who knew him well), and Leon Wilson. Not
only was I the youngest bird leader, I was the youngest of all
the pilgrimage leaders. Of the eight other bird leaders, five
were more than 40 years my senior.

The first event of the Fifteenth Annual West Virginia
Wildflower Pilgrimage was a meeting for all pilgrims and
leaders with opening remarks from VIPs followed by tour
descriptions, and then the evening program, "Switzerland,"
presented by Bill Beatty...me, and I had never been outside of
the United States, let alone to Switzerland.

In a panic I thought, "Is this some kind of initiation by fire?
If so, I don't think it's very funny."

The BBC had recently taken a trip to Switzerland, and Dot
had gone as well as several of the bird leaders sitting near me in
the cabin. Calming down a bit, I began to think more logically

hoping that it was simply a misprint, which it was. At the meeting that evening I was awestruck at the attendance. There were 300 people with barely enough room to hold them all.

Among the first introductions were Dr. Earl Core, Libby Bartholomew, Bill Wylie, and George Breiding. Dr. Core was a giant in his field, known worldwide for the *Flora of West Virginia*, the textbook used in my Plant Taxonomy class. I knew Libby from Terra Alta, and she also was a wonderful botanist. Bill Wylie was perhaps the best all-around birder I would ever meet. And George Breiding was a great naturalist and teacher. Thinking about all the legends in their respective fields, I was honored to be in their company.

Back at the cabin we all sat around talking about birds. Doc Hutton was the first to go to bed, but I stayed up, not wanting to pass up this opportunity to rub elbows with such a group of elite birders.

Ralph said, "Does anyone want me to wake them up? I have my alarm set for five."

The enormity of the Pilgrimage and my role there weighed heavy on my mind, and I had trouble falling asleep.

"Beep, beep, beep, beep," Ralph's alarm was going off. It was loud enough to wake the entire building.

I thought, "It can't be time to get up already. It feels like I just went to bed."

This Friday morning Bird Walk was my first official program as a leader. All the other bird leaders from the BBC cabin were present as well as Bill Wylie and George Breiding. There were three options for the people who showed up for the walk: drive to the campground with Bill Wylie, go on the Elakela Trail with Ralph Bell, or walk the road with Glen. The rest of the leaders split up and went with one of the three main leaders. I walked the road.

As soon as we left the parking lot, I knew I was in trouble. In the lot there were American robins and chipping sparrows. Beyond those two birds, which I knew well, there were songs I did not recognize. In West Virginia these were the high mountain birds. Some I would hear whispering each spring migration, and others I rarely heard at all. In West Virginia these were the high mountain birds which only nest at the highest elevations.

Like so many other bird walks, it's not so much a matter of seeing what birds are out there, it's mostly birding by ear. Many times, carrying my field guide and binoculars was a matter of exercise not necessity. Early morning bird walks at the pilgrimage were like that. The seasoned bird leaders would point out all birds encountered along their routes with a long line of people in tow. And I, and the other leaders, would be intermingled among the participants.

The pilgrimage bird walks confirmed what I had come to believe years before that, many bird walks are as much about social interactions among people as they are about birds.

Magnolia warblers were common singers on the walk, and I needed more experience to be able to identify them with certainty. Blue-headed and red-eyed vireos both sang along the roadway. Separating these two songs posed significant difficulty. At this time in my birding experience, when I would be out alone, it felt good to know the songs were from vireos; but here at the pilgrimage, separating the two was important. Even today, more than 30 years later, there are rare times when one of these two vireo songs can confuse me. I am glad it's not possible to know it all, all of the time. The challenge is essential for me.

Following the bird walk, there was time for breakfast and then the field trips would begin. My field trip assignment was

the Sinks of Gandy, a half-mile natural cave cut by Gandy
Creek in Randolph County. Alan Miller, an entomologist with
the West Virginia Department of Natural Resources, and I
were to take a group of 37 people through the Sinks, which
meant wading through water that was sometimes waist deep.
My secretary, her sister, her two teenage nieces, and two
teenage cousins were in our group. I knew them all quite well.
Midway through the Sinks, we stopped to take a head count.

Alan said, "Let's wait here a moment; I don't see the older
lady with the cane."

From among the group a gruff voice responded, "This
older lady with the cane might just hit you upside the head."

When I turned my back to the water to look at the lady,
one of the nieces and one cousin came charging at me, each
grabbing one of my arms. In an instant I was on my back
underwater in Gandy Creek. My headlamp was pushed down
over my face and put a gash across the bridge of my nose.

After my first experience as a leader, I was wet from head-
to-toe, exhausted, injured, and thinking, "These pilgrimage
people are a rough group."

That evening everyone who went through the Sinks was
presented a card with the following poem written by Billy Edd
Wheeler especially for the Wildflower Pilgrimage:

I have seen the Cliffs of Dover,
I have met a Potentate,
Swam the river Nile,
Climbed the Empire State.
I've piped the deadly cobra from urns
in old Ubandi;
But friends I never lived
until I conquered the Sinks of Gandy.

I have swung John Henry's Hammer
Bet on Mark Twain's toad,
Carried heavier worlds than Atlas,
Born a Comstock lode
But with all my trophies I was just an also Randi,
Till I wormed and squirmed and rushed and blushed,
And got flushed through the Sinks of Gandy.

By the time Friday's activities had come to an end, I was ready for bed. I fell asleep almost immediately. "Beep, beep, beep," sounded Ralph's alarm. I was sure Ralph had accidentally set the wrong time on the alarm, but no, it was time to get up. Each morning everybody seemed so wide awake, especially those who had stayed up the latest.

I thought, "I'm 27 years old and most of the others here are in their 60s and 70s, how can they do it?"

My morning bird walk began and about 30 yards down the road, a bird sang that triggered some odd looks from the leaders. I wasn't familiar with the song. There were three, long ascending notes. We heard it several times. Then, unexpectedly, to me, (but not the other leaders) the three ascending notes were followed by a series of descending, shorter notes. Slowly up, and then rapidly down.

Greg said, "This happens every year, and always along this stretch of road, not anywhere else. We are going to have to see this bird. It is either a golden-crowned kinglet or Blackburnian warbler."

"Wow," I thought, "The other leaders are not sure of this bird, even Glen."

The red spruce and eastern hemlock trees had thick canopies, making it next to impossible to find a bird. About 20 people were scanning the trees with binoculars.

Shortly, someone said, "It's a Blackburnian."

Every year for the next 35+ years this very same situation would present itself to me, "Three or four ascending notes eventually followed by a descending series of notes." I would finally correctly identify which bird was singing, but only if I could hear both the rising and descending series of notes.

I sat with Dot and her family at the banquet that night. An unexpected benefit was awaiting me at their table. There were four teenage girls who were picky about their food. I found myself with an abundance of turkey, stuffing, mashed potatoes and gravy, corn, and apple, cherry, and blueberry pie; more than I could have ever hoped to eat, but I tried my best to accommodate it all.

Banquets concluded with Catherine Knapp, the West Virginia Garden Clubs' Pilgrimage co-host, handing out personalized ceramic cups to each leader. In later years Catherine and I would become good friends. My second year as a leader on my first Dolly Sods tour, Catherine went along as a pilgrim. I found her intimidating, but in a delightful way…quick witted, and very creative. At one point in the tour she asked me what birds she was hearing.

Confused, I asked, "What birds?"

She said, "What do you mean 'What birds?' They are singing all around us."

I answered sheepishly, "Those are spring peepers."

"What kind of bird is that?" she asked.

I said, "They're frogs."

"Oh!" she said.

On Saturday night, after the banquet, there was always a traditional party in the BBC cabin. Beforehand, I excused myself to take a nap. I was exhausted. I remember having a dream about a fire only to wake up sweating, breathing heavily, and feeling claustrophobic. In a panic I tried to throw the covers off, only to find they were so heavy it took considerable effort. Taking a deep breath of fresh air I discovered that all the coats of the partiers were piled on top of me.

In the years that followed I would ride to the pilgrimage with Glen and Greg. When it was over, I was always exhausted and slept, sitting upright between them. Occasionally, Glen would pull off the road and the two of them would shake me awake to see a bird. Once they woke me to see a life bird for me, the upland sandpiper. I always appreciated how well Greg and Glen took care of me.

DOLLY SODS

One of my favorite places is the Dolly Sods scenic area. It comprises 32,000 acres, of which 24,200 acres are designated as Federal Wilderness. One of the best descriptions of this area is "a bit of Canada gone astray." Basically, the Dolly Sods is a high mountain plateau with ridges and valleys cut by small streams. The wide, wet valley flood plains attract beaver. Black bear are common. Many large and small bogs dot the landscape and are home to numerous round-leaved sundews, gentians, lady's tresses orchids, cottongrass, and cranberries. From mid-July through August the meadows are full of ripe blueberries and huckleberries.

In 1964, Congress designated 9.1 million acres in different parts of the U.S. as wilderness. Today over 106 million acres are federally designated wilderness. In the early 1970s, backpacking as a recreational pursuit was relatively new. *Backpacker Magazine* was founded in 1973. West Virginia's first wilderness areas, Dolly Sods and Otter Creek were officially designated in 1975. That same year, Oglebay Institute's Brooks Nature Center would begin offering backpacking trips into West Virginia wilderness areas.

My introduction to Dolly Sods began as a job requirement.

Several of us went to Dolly Sods in 1974 with topo maps
to map out the trails in approximately 25,000 acres of the
plateau. There were obvious trails, old railroad grades from
the timbering days and jeep roads used by hunters; however,
no trail maps existed. After a week of hiking and mapping,
we knew the trails pretty well, at least when we looked at our
reworked topo maps.

At the nature center I had been teaching backpacking
workshops for two years to packed audiences, sometimes
turning people away for lack of room. My first backpacking
trip to the Sods was in July, 1975. I led a group of thirteen
teenage boys and one college intern on one of the most
exciting adventures of their lives.

One oversight in the trip was how hungry teenage
boys could get. While cooking supper the first night, I was
surrounded by what some might describe as a flock of
vultures. When supper was over, there were complaints for
more food. I suggested we catch some crayfish and eat them.
They rejected that idea right away.

One boy said, "Oooh, I would never eat that."

Several days into the trip, a boy came to me as a
spokesman for the group and requested, "Remember those
crayfish you were talking about the other day; you said we
could eat them; do you think we could catch some today?"

That night after supper, we began heating a large pot of
water. After dark we went to Red Creek with flashlights in
hand. To my delight, crayfish were everywhere, and they were
big. In all, we caught 84 in an hour. The water was boiling as I
poured the crayfish into the pot.

"How do we do this?" someone asked.

"You only eat the meat inside the tail," I answered.

Immediately they began tearing crayfish apart as if they
had been lost for weeks without anything to eat.

I was shocked and thought, "Another day and they might have cooked me." Although they continued to be hungry after every meal, at least that night they seemed satisfied.

During the week we hiked 47 miles and saw only one other person. That week on Dolly Sods changed me. There was, and has remained, a part of me that yearns for the mountains and the wonderful diversity of wild creatures that are found in these Appalachian Highlands. The last morning of the trip I instructed my intern to keep an eye on the boys while they packed up for the short hike to the van. I wanted some time alone and would return in about an hour.

A short hike away I came upon a great rock on the bank of Red Creek. It was high and looked out over the small stream. From the top of the rock I watched birds fly from the tree tops to catch insects. At first these birds were no more than silhouettes. However, through my binoculars I could see flickers of red from their wings and flashes of yellow from the tails. They were cedar waxwings. Occasionally one would land below me and I could see every detail of the bird. With sharp pointed crests and black masks, the waxwings seemed like bandits robbing the earth of its winged insects and insect-like creatures. The red-tipped wings and banded yellow tails, stood out from the earth-tone browns of the body. Of all the birds I have ever seen, cedar waxwings have impressed me as very orderly in their appearance, with every feather in place, and their demeanor as one of majesty.

Mayflies were hatching and rising from the water only to have their short adult lives ended by the gluttonous waxwings. Some mayflies fell back to the water where native brook trout and large minnows anxiously waited. Watching and pondering these life and death struggles, I was inspired to write a poem. On the pages of my small notebook I wrote July 7, 1975:

Silhouettes of wax against the sky,
Insects fleeting lest they die.

Large rocks, small rocks, water of white,
Fleeting by unending, day and night.

Natives rising, catching flies,
Then darting back from unseen eyes.

Holding on to all it has,
Nature's realm at peace, at last.

It was the first poem I had ever written and was so unlike me. The warring factions of tough guy from the projects and marshmallow-hearted guy, tempered by new interests and experiences, were confusing to me. I was reluctant to let these new feelings surface, but there were times I could not suppress them.

In 2005, I led a group of campers from Oglebay Institute's Mountain Nature Camp on a 6.5 mile hike in Dolly Sods. Half way in, something special happened along Left Fork, a stream that flows through a wide, flat valley full of bogs, swamps, and similar wetlands. As we rested and talked about our day, fortunately one of us was also listening to other sounds nearby.

Michele, a good birder from near Cleveland, Ohio asked, "Did anyone else hear that?"

No one else heard anything.

She said, "I'm pretty sure it was a white-throated sparrow."

It didn't sing again. In the meantime I had to relieve myself and walked a good distance away. When I returned, there were smiles on every face. They had all heard the white-throat. The white-throated sparrow is an easy song to learn and remember. The distinctive, "Old, old, Sam Peabody-Peabody-Peabody," words fit this bird's music perfectly. This song is a favorite of many birders.

However, it was the middle of June in West Virginia and bird songs were an indication of nesting. The southernmost place where this sparrow has been known to nest is West Virginia, but the nests have been extremely rare. Eventually we heard one note, "Old," that came from a wetland on the other side of Left Fork. We waited and heard the first two notes, "Old, Old." Finally, I heard the entire song, "Old, old, Sam Peabody, Peabody, Peabody." It was a magical moment for all the birders in the group. I can still remember that moment as if it happened yesterday. I continue to take yearly hikes to that spot during bird breeding season, but have yet to hear the song again.

Dolly Sods is so special to me that in 1978 I took my then seven-year-old daughter Julie for a long weekend backpacking trip there. I wanted all my children to experience how I felt about the Sods. Julie and I hiked in about two miles and camped at a beautiful site along Red Creek. It was the first week of October, and the temperature was 67 degrees when we arrived. Hiking out three days later, it was 39 and spitting snow.

In July 2011, Jan and I took Julie's daughter, Haley, to Dolly Sods for eight days. Haley was the same age as Julie was when I first took her. Julie warned me, "Haley hasn't been raised the way you raised me. She's not used to hiking and other outdoor things."

Instead of a tent, we had a trailer. The first day the three of us hiked from the campground to a high overlook along the

Allegheny Front. We went from one view to another, climbed over and around huge boulders, and traversed in and out of cave-like passages. After lunch we did a shorter hike on the Northland Loop Trail. Haley did great. The next day, we ended up hiking all the way to Stack Rocks, miles away. I was thrilled to discover that Haley was a hiker and liked it.

We kept a bird list. One of the first birds on the list was the American Woodcock. As we sat at the picnic table at dusk, the woodcock whirled down from above to land just a few feet away. It timber-doodled its way along, walking and bowing as only a woodcock does, intermittently probing for insects with its long bill. We watched it on several occasions, but always at dusk.

At the campsite we discovered a nest of cedar waxwings and watched the parents feeding the babies. While at Stack Rocks we ate our lunch and watched turkey vultures roosting on rock outcroppings to the north. Haley, looking through binoculars, saw the color of their featherless heads and understood the turkey part of the vulture's name. Haley's bird list totaled 53 species for the week, quite respectable for a novice, and for July, when many of the birds are becoming silent.

We gave each other wilderness names. I had called Jan White Wolf for years, but not for any particular reason. Haley decided she wanted a "wolf" name. I jokingly suggested Crazy Wolf.

She laughed and said, "Pap, I don't want that name."

Haley picked my name which was very appropriate, Camo Wolf.

I always wear camo clothing, to the point if I don't wear it, someone often remarks, "Where's your camo?" or "Are you feeling okay today?"

Haley's name was very appropriate, Trail Wolf. She loved to lead and was good at it. Besides a great hiker, we had a budding birder as a granddaughter. I had come full circle, from 1978 with my daughter Julie, and 33 years later to the same places on Dolly Sods with granddaughter Haley.

One of my favorite birding destinations is the first mile of the Rohrbaugh Plains Trail. During springtime, Rohrbaugh is alive with a multitude of melodic bird songs. The forest is evergreen and the undergrowth is comprised of vast thickets of mountain laurel and rhododendron. Everywhere one looks is a verdant display pleasing to the eyes as well as comforting to the soul. Even the rocks are moss-covered, dotted with tiny evergreen seedlings forming what appears as a miniature forest struggling to compete against the surrounding evergreen giants. And the trail is bordered by numerous nurse-logs, which give new life through the sacrifice of their own.

Rohrbaugh attracts many hikers for its visual beauty. A worthwhile hike is to traverse the first mile and return via the same path. At the trail head along Forest Service Road 19, the ovenbirds and blue-headed vireos sing from both sides of the road. The early uphill portion of Rohrbaugh is through a beech woods with sparse undergrowth in places, perfect nesting habitat for the ovenbirds. Further along into the beech trees, the dainty bell-like chipping song of the juncos along with the "ZEE-ZEE-zee-zu-ZEE" greetings of the black-throated green warblers begin to be heard by attentive ears. A distant raven and sometimes a flock of raucous blue jays can be heard as they fly through like loud teenagers oblivious to all others around them.

Soon, at the sight of the first tall red spruce are three high, light, airy trills in succession, signaling the presence of golden-crowned kinglets. Kinglets are heard from several locations as they announce their presence to other potential kinglet intruders. The kinglet pronouncements may stop as quickly as they began, not to be heard again along the trail.

At the topmost point of Rohrbaugh, the dense evergreen woods present a different, but most welcoming passage. Looking around, it's as if straddling two opposite worlds. One, a place of wide open spaces that can be explored by diverging from the trail, and the other stunningly beautiful, but restrictive with dense laurels lining both sides of the path. From high in a fir comes high musical notes pulling one's ears upward trying to follow the song into heavenly places where perhaps only other Blackburnians can hear. Swinging binoculars to my face I hope to get a glimpse of this fire-throated warbler, but most often have to be content with only the music.

Zur-zur-zur-zREEEE," lazily, but loudly springs forth from a red spruce just above the tangles of rhododendron. To the eye, it's a spectacular wash of blue-gray back and wing edgings bordered by a contrasting jet black face, throat, and sides, fronted with a pure white breast and under-belly. To the ear, the song is coarse and lethargic, not at all comparable to what the eye sees. A favorite to see and watch, the black-throated blue warbler is a preferred visual find of many birders.

From the highest evergreens, a song relatively new to Dolly Sods catches my ears. Not as well-known as other warbler songs it is a high pitched trill that falls apart at the end. I learned the bird as a myrtle warbler, then it became the yellow-rumped warbler; and the rumor is that the American Ornithologists' Union (AOU) is considering backtracking to myrtle again. Whatever the name was, is, or will be, this bird can be expected along much of the Rohrbaugh.

One of my favorites to see is the magnolia warbler, often singing regularly along the evergreen stretch of the Rohrbaugh. Like all the other birds along this stretch of trail, the Maggie, as some fondly call it, is invisible to all but the keenest and most patient eyes. Here, their favorite haunts are the shorter trees, especially the hemlocks. To some this song is difficult to learn and remember, most likely due to its similarities to other warblers that sing "weetsa" kinds of songs. Fortunately the habitat eliminates those other imitators and the magnolia's "weetsa" can safely be the expected song.

Suddenly, but briefly, the tin horn, "ank, ank, ank," call of the red-breasted nuthatch comes and then leaves not to be heard again. Exploding from near a small water course hidden deep inside the masses of laurel, begins a combination of beautiful tinkling and trill-like notes that seem to go on forever, but eventually ends with a very high, graceful trill. To see the bird, someone might not imagine such a lengthy, delicate, yet powerful song to be capable of a bird as tiny as the winter wren.

Sitting along the Rohrbaugh waiting for "the feeling" to pierce my innermost being, I am reminded as three hikers zoom past, that not everyone is aware. Some hear nothing as they pass through, and still others do not see or hear. Life is an unending race from one destination to another. To some, stopping means "life will pass me by." And to a few others, stopping to look and listen is life. Soon the contemplation returns and I am overwhelmed by the vastness, the hidden wisdom that I can only understand in part, and then "the feeling" of nothingness, as if I am back in the womb, knowing and understanding nothing. A chill runs down my spine in this moment of awe.

On the best days, along the Rohrbaugh, I am charmed with

the highpoint of songs that defies depiction. Best described in F. Schuyler Mathews, *Field Book of Wild Birds and their Music,*

"The song of the Hermit Thrush is the grand climax of all bird music; it is unquestionably so far removed from all the rest of the wild-wood singers' accomplishments that vaunted comparisons are invidious and wholly out of place."

Hermit thrushes along with veerys sing their flute-like songs intermittently along the lush path to add to the magnificence of songs regularly being sung. This is my favorite place for bird songs. Many groups of people have followed me first up, and then down and around the winding Rohrbaugh, but the most inspirational moments are when I am there alone. About 2.5 miles into the trail is one of the most scenic overlooks in West Virginia. It overlooks the Red Creek Valley across to Rocky Point a.k.a. Lion's Head. Another place to relax, look, experience, and contemplate. West Virginia is full of places and creatures that convey "the feeling."

As I grow older I understand more about so many different things. I chuckle at how many young people want everything NOW, and I understand having been there one time myself. But being older, I understand that to be truly satisfied, I have to have challenges; and nature studies are the challenges I choose.

A great birding challenge can be found at the 16,000 acre Canaan Valley National Wildlife Refuge. There are vast areas of wetlands and grassland on the refuge that is home to nine species of nesting sparrows: chipping, song, field, savannah, grasshopper, swamp, vesper, Henslow's, and clay-colored. These sparrows do not occur at one localized place in the valley, so seeing them cannot happen NOW. It will be a challenge.

In early March 2004, I decided to go snowshoeing on Dolly Sods. The day before I arrived, 14 inches of new snow had fallen. Anyone visiting Dolly Sods is greeted by a sign at the bottom of Forest Service Road 19: "No Snow Removal Beyond This Point." I could see that no cars had driven through the new snow. I was excited to be the first. My off-road truck had no difficulty at all plowing its way up the mountain through the deep snow. Soon I was on top passing the Dolly Sods picnic area on level ground.

I thought, "It should be smooth sailing from here."

All of a sudden, the road disappeared. Five feet in front of me was a 10-foot snowdrift. This was the end of the road. Beyond the drift were three others as tall as or taller than the first.

I left the truck parked in the middle of the road, in front of the drift. Donning my snowshoes and proper clothing, I snowshoed to the beginning of Rohrbaugh Trail. I was eager to experience this trail in the winter. To some it might have seemed eerily quiet. There was no wind moving branches or bending and creaking trees. No cars or people sounds were to be heard. I loved it. The snow-covered branches and absolute solitude surrounded me. When I looked at the trail register, no one had signed it since early January, more than two months earlier.

Not too far into my hike I became disoriented and briefly lost the trail. The evergreen portion of the Rohrbaugh was still beautiful, but in a different way. It was overcast, and there was snow everywhere. Much of the green was masked by the rolling white. Birds were not entertaining me; instead there were rare calls from kinglets and chickadees.

I decided to hike with less stopping. Soon I was out of the evergreen woodlands and into the deciduous forest. Soon I was hopelessly off the trail. Stopping and looking around, I decided what direction I should go.

"The road is that way," I surmised.

Checking my compass, it instructed me to go in the opposite direction. Regardless of what my sense of direction was telling me, I knew to follow the compass. After reaching the top and rise of the mountain, I knew the road was a short distance below. I decided to do some cold-training. Soon I was snowshoeing wearing only my boots, overpants, toboggan, and sunglasses. I felt like William Wallace in the movie Braveheart, "FREEDOM!" I was running and having a great time; alone in the wilderness, seemingly one with nature, one with myself. Looking around all I saw was cold, but there was no sense of cold in my mind or body. I was liberated.

Back at my truck, I removed my showshoes and tromped through the deep snow to the picnic ground in my hiking boots. The spring was running and I was able to get a great drink of Dolly Sods water. There was some movement on a tree across the open picnic ground area. Looking through my binoculars I saw three yellow-bellied sapsuckers. Against the muted winter colors, they were exquisite. The yellows and reds appeared as bright as I had ever seen them. And the contrasting black and white stood out too. I watched for a long time. These woodpeckers appeared to be having the time of their lives, making one think they were playing an endless game of tag or hide-and-seek.

I rarely saw all three at once. From behind the tree one would suddenly appear and another would just as quickly disappear. They looked to be nodding their heads with approval as they played their games. The only sounds I heard from them were scrapes from their claws while chasing around the tree trunk. And I thought I was the only one excited to be in this wonderland of cold, snow, and silence.

One of the best days of my life happened on Dolly Sods.

Today Jan and I judge all days based on that one day in August 2004. We were getting a late start on a hike beginning on Blackbird Knob Trail. After parking the car we were walking back to the Red Creek Campground to take a shortcut to the *Rock*, the first place along the trail with a scenic view of much of the Dolly Sods south wilderness. As we walked, a car slowed as it passed us and came to a stop about 20 yards beyond us.

We continued walking until we heard, "Bill Beatty, Bill Beatty," an older man approached with about the biggest smile I'd ever seen.

"I know you from the Wildflower Pilgrimage. I have seen some of your programs and been on a few of your tours."

At first I thought, "Jan and I have to get going. We are already getting a late start."

He was so happy and excited I couldn't help but allow the moment to unfold. He introduced himself as Mr. Jordan. Inside the car were his daughter and son-in-law. Standing in the middle of the roadway, Mr. Jordan was raving about the Wildflower Pilgrimage and how wonderful the event was. His sincerity could easily be realized by the tears in his eyes.

Then he said, "And Mrs. Knapp, she is such a wonderful lady. She makes the whole thing work. I can't wait to see her next year. She is so dear to me," and then he asked, "Well, how is she doing anyhow?"

I walked closer, put my arms around him, and said, "Catherine died about a month ago."

A few tears ran down Mr. Jordan's cheeks. My eyes welled up.

He said, "She was such a wonderful person. I will miss her."

I answered, "I will miss her, too. She was one of my dearest friends."

Before too long Mr. Jordan said, "Today is my 80th birthday and I wanted to come to Dolly Sods. My daughter and son-and-law brought me. Will you and Jan join us for lunch?"

I said, "We really don't have much in the way of food with us; just some energy bars and dried fruit."

He said, "We have sandwiches and a birthday cake. We can all share."

At site #1 at the campground we all sat at a picnic table eating and laughing and getting to know one another. The food was delicious. Mr. Jordan and his family were delightful.

As we parted company, I said to Jan, "That was quite remarkable. Regardless of what else happens along the trail, this is already a very special day."

Jan agreed and said, "Everywhere we go someone knows you, but this was different. This was special."

Jan and I hiked 6.5 miles that afternoon, bushwhacking all the way to the Left Fork and back by way of Red Creek and Alder Run. On the way back, I was remarking about it being August and how quiet it was without the birds singing. We were almost back to the *Rock* when the most amazing thing happened. From deep inside a red spruce woods a hermit thrush began to sing. We slowly walked carefully toward the song. We stood and listened and then another hermit thrush began to compete with the first in song. We occasionally looked at each other and smiled. We didn't dare speak a word. The birds sang for a long time; one from one side of the woods, and then the other from the opposite side.

We stood in reverence of the moment and I thought, "Even if we were to speak at this moment, what could we say?"

Eventually the birds stopped singing and we continued in silence. Later we talked and discussed how blessed we were to have this Mr. Jordan day.

RALPH-EAL...

...the master in the art of birds and birding

"It takes a very special man to give another man his deodorant," Ralph said.

"And it takes an extraordinary man to accept it," I answered.

Ralph and I had both arrived at the 37th annual Wildflower Pilgrimage on Thursday. He had forgotten his deodorant and wasn't going home until Sunday afternoon. I was leaving after the Friday tours to attend my daughter's Saturday high school graduation. Ever since the day I offered Ralph my deodorant we have been best friends.

Ralph often surprised me with things he would say or do. One evening after a Wildflower Pilgrimage leaders' meeting he and I were invited to one of the lodge rooms to share homemade desserts. One of the women had made a delicious looking German chocolate cake and offered us each a piece.

I took a small piece and it was delicious, but Ralph declined politely.

Another woman from North Carolina had a cake she referred to as a "friendship cake" and it too looked quite tasty. When someone said to her, "You better tell everyone what's in your cake," she admitted to having dried earthworms as one of the ingredients.

I took a small piece of the "earthworm" cake, and Ralph said, "Thank you, I think I would like some of that."

That surprised me.

Driving to our cabin that night I asked, "Why did you eat the cake with the worms?"

Ralph laughed and said, "I don't know. But it seemed like the right thing to do at the time."

To me the best word that describes Ralph is unpretentious. When I tell him how special he is to me and many others, he always says, "Cut the stuff."

Honestly, when I think of Ralph I think, "What's not to like?"

I first met Ralph Bell in May of 1977 at the fifteenth annual West Virginia Wildflower Pilgrimage. His name was familiar to me. Other birders I knew held him in high esteem. There are many expert birders around and some are just as humble and polite as Ralph is, but few have his years of experience or unique abilities.

Ralph was 99 when he passed away, and chased birds from a young boy till shortly before dying. As a young boy, he used to collect bird eggs for a local oologist. At one time collecting birds' eggs was very popular and legal. Ralph knew of a barn owl's nest in the hollow of a large sycamore tree. To get an egg for the collector he climbed the tree and entered the hollow part. Trying to reach the egg, he slipped and found himself on the ground inside the tree. Every time he attempted to get out he slipped back to the ground where he started. Fortunately, he had a pocket knife and began to carve hand and footholds into the wood inside the tree. Many hours later Ralph was able to climb out with the barn owl egg.

Although collecting a cerulean warbler egg wasn't as harrowing, Ralph told me it had a profound effect on his life and he knew even at a young age he would always be involved with birds.

Ralph's interest in birds includes not only wild birds but domestic birds as well. He graduated from Penn State University with a degree in Poultry Husbandry and eventually ran an egg business with 7,000 chickens.

Ralph can identify any warbler in drab fall plumage by looking only at its head. I don't know anyone else who is able to do that. But Ralph has an advantage few other birders have: he is colorblind. He sees differently than the rest of us and, based on my conversations with Ralph, I think this is not a handicap when it comes to his identification abilities.

To date I have banded about 8,000 birds. When I mention that to some people, their jaw drops in amazement and they say something like, "My goodness, that's a lot." Ralph, on the other hand, is responsible for over 250,000 birds being banded and that makes my jaw drop.

In the early 1950s Ralph and others began going to Bear Rocks on Dolly Sods to count hawks as they migrate south in the late summer and early fall. He received his Master Federal Bird Banding permit in 1954 and in 1958 began banding birds at what was known then as the Red Creek cabin site (today the Red Creek Campground) on Dolly Sods. Ralph told me, "We would sleep on the ground under picnic tables with rain ponchos draped over the tables."

He noticed that, although large numbers of birds were flying over the mist nets toward the southwest, they weren't actually catching many birds. In 1962 Ralph followed a

series of deer trails to the eastern rim of Dolly Sods known
as the Allegheny Front. What he found surprised him. Great
flocks of migrating birds funneled up through a hollow in
the Front and continued up over the mountain plateau. The
following year they set some nets along the Front which
were so productive that by 1965 all the banding was done
along the Front where it continues today. The banding
station is officially known as the Allegheny Front Migration
Observatory (AFMO).

For many years Ralph would ask, "When are you coming
to Dolly Sods to help with the banding?"

When I was working at the Brooks Nature Center I had
to tell him, "I'm too busy. Getting away for the Wildflower
Pilgrimage is about all I can manage."

After leaving the nature center and working on my own,
my reply was the same, "I'm too busy."

And I was very busy. Besides all my teaching, I was writing
and selling nature-related photos. There were times when I was
on Dolly Sods at the same time as the banding was happening
and would stop at the AFMO to see Ralph. He would say,
"I hope you came to help," but I never could—I was there
to visit and then head into the wilderness for several days of
photography. Busy as I was, I really did want to help at the
AFMO, but more than that, I really wanted to be around Ralph.

In 2004 I began to have time to help at the AFMO, not as a
bird bander, but a net-tender. The banders stay inside a small
shed, identifying, weighing, aging, sexing and banding the
birds—some days as few as ten birds and other days many
100s were caught. Not being the kind to sit still, I would rather
take birds from the 30 nets and walk them back to the banders.
Checking every net requires a nice hike over considerable rock
fields; in other words, lots of exercise.

What keeps me, and others I am sure, returning to the AFMO each year is a combination of things. For one thing, the night sky is the most star-lit sky imaginable. It's like looking at the night sky out over the ocean or in the desert.

Several things make me different from most people: I enjoy the cold, I find comfort in darkness, and being alone suits me perfectly, as long as I am outside. At most places on cold, dark nights, being alone is almost guaranteed, but not at the AFMO. The volunteers are a hearty bunch of folks who also cannot resist these same kinds of situations. Going out early to the AFMO I sometimes find Fred and Carol sitting in the open-fronted banding shed staring at the Milky Way. I sit or sometimes lay down on the "phone booth," the only rock where most cell phones can get a signal. My eyes fix on the stars, identifying the few constellations I know and wondering if other stars had some ancient name and legend.

When enough people arrive we begin unfurling the mist nets. It is still dark, but the anxiety of the Swainsons' thrushes to get moving is evident by the calls down below the crest of the mountain. Most days Swainsons' thrushes comprise the first wave of birds to be caught. Mixed in are hermit and wood thrushes, veerys and rarely a gray-cheeked thrush. At this early hour we have to wear headlamps as aids in finding and safely extracting the birds.

On busy mornings I hardly notice the daylight slowly overtaking the night. It is just as easy for me to be absorbed by the miracle of holding a handful of warm, feathered, breathing bird, as it is to get lost in seeing the enormous starry sky.

If all this isn't enough, the sunrises are spectacular. By sunrise most AFMO volunteers have arrived and we all share in this every-day but astounding occurrence.

The sunrise photos I took in 2004 were the last I would

ever take. Over the years I saw dozens of sunrises at the AFMO most of which "could not be equaled". But the very next morning was another sunrise that "could not be equaled". I realized I could spend a lifetime capturing Dolly Sods sunrises, each seemingly more spectacular than the last. So I decided, since all the sunrises are spectacular, my 2004 photos would be enough.

By 2004 Ralph was only visiting the AFMO for an anniversary celebration honoring him. His daughter Joanie became co-leader in 2000. Now she coordinates the scheduling of volunteers, oversees the overall operation and stays there for most of the two months the station is open.

The busiest AFMO day I experienced was a mild September morning in 2007. From 8:30 till 10:30 there were wave after wave of warblers funneling up the hollow toward the nets. So many birds were getting caught in the nets that the net tenders soon realized that we would have to close some of the nets just so we could keep up with the work. Jan and I were working 10 nets north of the banding shed and 10 other net-tenders were clearing the 20 nets to the south. When a dense fog had settled in it was impossible for us to see what was happening at the other set of nets.

Each south net has its own set of poles and, as each net was cleared, the net was closed allowing the net tenders to move to other nets. Jan and I had a dilemma. Eight of our 10 nets used shared poles. One net couldn't be closed without also closing the one that shared its pole. But when we cleared one net, it couldn't be closed due to all the birds in the next net. And our empty net was soon full of more birds. We had birds hitting the net all around us, within inches of our heads as we worked to remove other birds. We caught almost every kind of eastern warbler imaginable and, although we didn't know it until later, we even caught one unimaginable warbler.

From the fog to the south I heard, "Wonder if Jan and Bill are as busy as we are," and, "This is unbelievable!"

One repeated comment made me envious: "Another net closed!"

After the south nets were emptied and closed, one of the net-tenders walked over to where Jan and I were working. When he saw the situation he yelled, "Holy s_ _t! **WE NEED HELP OVER HERE!**"

The north nets were still full and looked like we hadn't removed a single bird. We now had 10 additional helpers and it was finally possible to get all the birds out of the nets and close the nets.

As the backlog of birds was being banded, some of us were recording the data for the banders and the rest were relaxing and talking about the busy bird day. But when Joanie declared, "I don't know what this bird is!" everyone stopped what they were doing.

We had never heard her say that before. Fall warblers are difficult for most people. Only when you have handled and banded tens of thousands does their identification become second nature. Joanie was holding a bird that I had taken from the net. When I had bagged it I had marked the bag "MAWA", the alpha code for the magnolia warbler, since the tail had the standard broad white band of a magnolia warbler. But looking closer, the under-tail coverts indicated the bird was a black-and-white warbler. And still other markings signified that the bird was a Cape May warbler. It was a hybrid, our unimaginable warbler. We took many photos of our improbable bird and when I review the photos from that day I can still see MAWA x BAWW x CMWA.

We had caught 945 birds in about two hours. Most days the net-tending and banding are over by noon, but by the time the banders were finished on this day it was after 3:30.

That same week we had days of 300+, 400+ and 600+ birds caught. Although those days were busy, we could easily handle the numbers. Today the north nets no longer share poles and we now know that 1,000 birds a day is pushing us to our limit.

Besides knowing Ralph from the West Virginia Wildflower Pilgrimage and the AFMO on Dolly Sods, I knew him from what I call "The Ralph Bell Birding Extravaganza" held annually at his former farm in SW Pennsylvania. On a Saturday in mid-May as many as 100 people gather for a full day of birding.

Ralph first invited me to attend by saying, "So many people show up, I need help parking the cars."

And that's what I do.

This event is not a "let's get started at 5:30 in the morning so we can get the best birds," kind of day. Rather, it is a family-oriented activity that does not begin until 9:00. Birding moms and dads with their children are common sights at the farm. And the kids there aren't fussing or crying--they are really birding. Many other seasoned birders are there, too, who wanted to learn from Ralph, see some great birds and share their birding skills with the novices.

Some birders arrive early to watch the purple martins banter back and forth while flying in and out of the many hollow gourds in the front yard. Tree swallows and eastern bluebirds nest in boxes on the property and are also easy to observe. At the same time the songs of the bobolinks in the acres of open meadows welcome the many visitors.

The day officially begins with a walk down a long, slightly winding road. Some people stuck with Ralph while others soon become fascinated by a bird someone else has spotted and before long there are as many as a dozen large and small groups focusing on different birds. The rest of the walk is like that. Three key elements made this a great birding day: 1) Ralph shared his talents and knowledge with us, 2) the habitats are varied and 3) Ralph had a Federal Depredation Permit that enabled him to control the cowbird population and thus allows everyone else to see and hear a wider variety of great birds. Ralph's ceruleans, hoodeds, redstarts and other warbler species can flourish since they rarely have the parasitic cowbirds laying eggs in their nests.There is a significant difference between Ralph's old neighborhood and similar birding habitats elsewhere. Ralph's ceruleans, hoodeds, redstarts and other warbler species can flourish since they rarely have the parasitic cowbirds laying eggs in their nests.

Walking with Cindy and Mary (West Virginia Wildflower Pilgrimage Bird Leaders) at Ralph's one day, we were listening to and talking about the bird songs we heard along the way. We often use mnemonics to help us identify many of the songs. Along most of the way we were hearing, "Pizz-A," the mnemonic I use for the Acadian flycatcher's song.

I suggested we do things a bit differently. We should try to make up some new phrases to identify the songs, with the name of a food in each phrase.

Anyone familiar with bird mnemonics, if they stopped and thought about this would realize that foods are already associated with two very familiar songs: "DRINK-your-tee-ee-ee-ee," the territorial song of the eastern towhee, and, "Po-ta-to-CHIP," the flight song of the American goldfinch.

Because I've taught bird songs to groups for many years

and I play with these kinds of things regularly in my own head, this new challenge was easier for me. "DRINK-your-teeeeeee," became, "SA-lam-ee-ee-ee-ee," and "Po-ta-to-CHIP," was easily converted to, "So-ur-cream-DIP." What are potato chips without a good dip? The "weeta-weeta-wee-TEE-oh," the song of the hooded warbler became, "Wheaties-wheaties-cheer-I-os." For the white-throated sparrow, we discussed changing "Old, old, Sam, Peabody-Peabody-Peabody," to "Eat, eat, your, broccoli-broccoli-broccoli," or "Dark, dark, blue, blueberries-blueberries- blueberries," or "I, I, chew, juicyfruit-juicyfruit-juicyfruit," my favorite chewing gum as a kid. "Chick-a-dee-dee-dee," became, "Chicken-fric-a-ssee-ssee-ssee." We thought of changing the black-capped chickadee's two-noted, "Su-sie," song to "Su-shi."

With all this talk of food we remembered the upcoming picnic. We picked up our pace. Following the walk many spread blankets or sit in lawn chairs and have a picnic lunch. For some the best part of the day is following the picnic. If the timing of the American kestrel nesting cooperates, we all take a leisurely walk through the expansive grassy meadows to the highest point on the farm.

Nowadays us younger folks climb the ladder and take the baby kestrels from a nest box and band the birds. If the kestrels aren't the right age, then sometimes we band bluebird babies from a nesting box near the house. The reactions of those who have never experienced this moment before and may never experience it again remind us of how fortunate we are. One little girl expressed it perfectly when she said, "It's so soft and warm. I will remember this day the rest of my life." I will too.

The Ralph K. Bell Bird Walk is still held at Ralph's old farm each May and is still a wonderful event for serious birders and novices alike.

WRONG SONG

Birds do not make rules concerning their behavior. But they do seem to follow certain rules based on our interpretation of what we observe when we are birding. People turn their observations into rules for birds.

When I identified my first blue-winged warbler I was under the impression that all blue-winged warblers sang the same song all the time. Then I began to learn about what some call summer songs, alternate songs, or just, the other song. Through my own experiences I discovered what I call the backwards song. Two good examples are the tufted titmouse and the Carolina wren. The titmouse typically sings, "Peter-peter-peter," but it also commonly sings, "Terpete, terpete, terpete." The syllables are reversed as well as the emphasis on each syllable. Carolina wrens are known for singing, "Teakettle, teakettle, teakettle," but they, too, reverse the syllables and emphasis with, "Kettletea, kettletea, kettletea."

There are the whisper songs commonly sung by the north nesting birds as they migrate through my area during spring migration. These are the same songs sung by the birds while on territory, but they are sung during migration as if they have a secret to tell and do not want others to eavesdrop and hear it.

One spring Jan and I were walking through a neighborhood when we thought we heard a hermit thrush singing. It continued to sing and we isolated the song coming from a stand of about six, 20-foot eastern hemlock trees. We stood and listened for 20 minutes while the sun was going down. The bird sang continuously, but only in a whisper.

My explanation for the whisper songs is, "These male birds are so anxious due to both physical changes and hormonal changes that they can't help themselves." However, these same songs become much louder and forceful when they are on their breeding grounds ready to defend their territories. It's as if these birds, upon reaching their territories, breathe a sigh of relief and just let it out, as loud as they can.

There are some birds like northern cardinals that have a multitude of songs. Some suggest the cardinal may have a repertoire of as many as 87 songs and/or variations. And there are those birds that produce a great variety of sounds, sometimes song-like, at times single notes, and other times trills, zips, and whistles. Blue jays do this and I have also found the tufted titmouse can be confounding by all the different noises it can make.

The Brewster's warbler I found on my Special Problems study plot presents a different kind of dilemma. It is the offspring of two different species of birds that sing similar, but different, songs. And as might be expected, the offspring produced may sing either song or some combination thereof.

Where blue-winged and golden-winged warbler territories overlap, they sometimes crossbreed; and the resulting offspring are likely to be a Brewster's warbler, and rarely a Lawrence's warbler. However, this explanation does not account for the Brewsters' warblers I have found. All my Brewsters have been in blue-winged warbler territories, far from any golden-winged warblers, so there has to be an additional explanation. What I believe happens is that during spring migration some crossbreeding occurs, maybe the day before or days before the birds reach their breeding territory. Some birds can easily fly 100 miles a day as they migrate. These two warblers have similar songs, but their songs are very different from all the other warbler species. The song similarity is probably enough to confuse some birds into interbreeding. And those physical and chemical changes that occur as the days lengthen put them in a position where they just can't help themselves.

After finding my first Brewster's, every time I heard a blue-wing sing I would try to see it, just in case. Well, my just-in-cases paid off. Within one year I had discovered four more Brewster's warblers in my county. The end result was an article in the Brooks Bird Club's publication, *The Redstart*. If possible, I check every blue-winged or golden-winged warbler song I hear. Due to my experiences, there is a possibility that either of these two songs could be coming from a hybrid.

Most birds mate within their own species and do not cross the species boundary. However, on rare occasions we encounter birds that break the rules we have created.

My next significant experience with a bird ignoring the rules was another hybrid. I was at Tygart Lake State Park for several days to train West Virginia State Park naturalists. One morning on a bird walk we heard a northern parula singing. I remembered that two years before there had been quite a stir about a Sutton's Warbler discovered at a Brooks Bird Club foray. The song had been recorded and the bird had been mist netted, banded, and photographed. Birder friends who had been at that foray told me that the bird always sang a double parula song: two songs in rapid succession.

Trying to make the class easy and enjoyable I was careful not to overwhelm them with all the different birds that were actually singing. I concentrated on songs that are fun and easy: "DRINK-your-teeeeeee," of the eastern towhee; "Cheer-cheer-cheer," of the northern cardinal; and "See-see Sus-ie," and "Chick-a-dee-de-dee," of the Carolina chickadee. I was ignoring the more difficult songs.

Then I heard a bird song that couldn't be ignored, the double northern parula song. Oddly, the bird was sitting on an electrical wire. I have never seen a northern parula on a wire before or since. This bird was singing a double northern parula song, but it looked like a yellow-throated warbler. We had found another Sutton's warbler!

When I teach about bird songs, there are certain standard concepts I try to convey. One such rule is: with a few exceptions, only male birds sing the songs. Another rule is: songs are often musical to our ears but actually represent aggressive verbal encounters between birds of the same species.

They mean something like, "If you come one wing-beat closer, buddy, you will be wearing your beak on the other side of your head."

Of course that level of active hostility doesn't happen, at least I haven't seen it...YET! The rule that has proven challenging to me lately is: each kind of bird sings basically the same song, which is different from those of other species. Of course, another rule that I sometimes add is: there are always exceptions to the rules, such as the mimic thrushes (northern mockingbird, brown thrasher and gray catbird here in West Virginia).

After years of chasing birds, I came to realize that birds sometimes vary their songs a bit...call it a dialect, a hiccup, an added note, whatever. In different parts of the country there is a dialect difference in certain bird species: towhees in the Outer Banks of North Carolina sing the same song as those in West Virginia, but there is an accent that distinguishes the songs. An eastern screech-owl I encountered regularly for several years had an extra note at the end of its song; something I referred to as a hiccup.

It has been over 20 years since my encounters with the hybrid bird songs, which are understandably different; but in the past year and a half I have encountered bird song rules being broken in astounding ways.

During the spring semester at West Liberty University, I teach two courses for the Physical Education Department: Recreational Camping/Outdoor Leisure Pursuits for PE majors and Outdoor Activities for non-majors. The last class day for both courses is a two-hour bird walk. Near the end of a bird walk in 2008 I stopped because I heard an eastern towhee call note. My hope was that the bird would sing the whole song, "DRINK-your-teeeeeee," or, "I'm Tow-hee-e-e-e," probably the easiest to remember and the most fun to learn. After I gave my students the words for the song, the bird began to sing the whole series of notes. As it sang I whispered the words. Faces lit up as they "got it." Then from the other direction, a cardinal began singing.

"Wow!" I thought, "now I can talk about the cardinal song, too." I reiterated one of the rules: "each kind of bird sings its own song, different from other species."

No sooner were the words out of my mouth than, "the towhee flew to a perch in full view, about 20 feet from us, and sang, "pretty-pretty-pretty"—the cardinal's song! The towhee sang the cardinal song four times before it flew away. I was astounded.

My next "birds not playing by our rules" was not a personal one, yet it is quite exceptional. One of my birding friends sent me an email:

"Hi, Bill,

Listen to the bird sing in the video below & see what you think.

Odd!

E.T."

What the video showed was a yellow-throated warbler singing a black-throated green warbler song over and over again. The bird in question showed no indication of being a hybrid even though the well-documented Sutton's warbler mentioned above looks like a yellow-throated warbler. But even if it were a Sutton's, where did the black-throated green song come from?

After my own attempts to think through the question, I deferred to Ralph Bell who has more field experience than anybody I know. I have the utmost respect for my 97-year-old bird guru.

He put his idea this way, "The birds in question were hatched close to or in the same territory as the birds whose song they sing, sometimes learning both their own and the other bird's song, or sometimes learning only one of the songs."

That makes sense to me...I can live with that explanation. The rules may sometimes be broken, but there is a simple, yet understandable explanation."

My latest "wrong bird song" incident happened while leading a field trip for the Mountain Nature Camp. We were on an all-day field trip to the Nature Conservancy's Cranesville Swamp Preserve, and on the way back to the vans three of us were far behind the rest of the group. I heard a Canada warbler sing and we wanted to get a look at this elusive bird.

After about two minutes, my friend Greg said, "You've gotta see this."

We went to Greg's vantage point and he guided our view to a beautiful indigo bunting glowing in the sunlight. And, yes, it was singing a perfect Canada warbler song, over and over again. While we watched, the only song the indigo sang was that of the Canada warbler.

I enjoy the challenge of something defying the rules, but when it comes to teaching new birders, I would rather not make it sound more difficult than it already is. When I started, had I known about the rule-breakers, that learning would have seemed even more intimidating.

MAGEE MARSH — THE WARBLER CAPITOL OF THE WORLD

Each year the Brooks Bird Club offered a wide variety of field trips. Several were so popular they were offered each year. Unfortunately, the only trips I was able to take were local one-day bird outings.

BBC Administrator, Carl Slater often spoke about the annual trip to what was called "Crane Creek." This was an extended trip lasting all weekend. I never was able to join the BBC on this trip. In 2008, Ohio Parks and Recreation closed the Crane Creek State Park and transferred the land to the Ohio Division of Wildlife adding to the size of the Magee Marsh Wildlife Area. Now most people simply and fondly refer to the area as Magee Marsh or just Magee.

On the spur of the moment Jan and I would often decide to do a birding day. Our most exciting bird encounter was one winter when at the Lake Isaac end of the Lake to Lake trail, we found a life bird for Jan. An oddity I had noticed during the previous summer was a dense thicket of alder at one end of the lake. Among and bordering the thicket were tree–sized alder that were heavily laden with cone-like fruits.

This particular day the wind was blowing snow in our faces; and although it would bite at our skin, we wanted to experience the lives of the wild creatures around us. Black-capped chickadees, tufted titmice, white-breasted nuthatches, slate-colored juncos, and several woodpecker species were found every time we hiked this trail.

Occasionally we encountered eastern bluebirds just before the boardwalk and shelter. Knowing birds have brighter plumages just before and during breeding season didn't diminish how bright the bluebirds appeared. They were brilliant against the winterscape. Their calls and song parts announced their location making them easy to observe.

The trail edges beyond to the tunnel often hid white-throated and American tree sparrows. Their contrasting colors, caught our eyes, and we would watch them until we were so cold it was necessary to move on.

Just before the end of the boardwalk, where the alder were, was a loop trail which we walked and found the usual cardinals feeding on dogwood berries and blue jays sounding through the woodlands.

Back at the boardwalk, we heard calls we couldn't place. And because we couldn't identify the calls, we knew they were special. When we saw the birds we counted a flock of 17. The calls were sometimes rapid, other times a slow, "Chet-chet-chet-chet-chet;" it seemed to depend on which bird was calling. Most called at the same time producing a cacophony. After a few short flights they alighted into the alder trees. They were common redpolls. This was Jan's first look at redpolls. What was nice about this find was that the alder cones kept them in the area, and they could be expected in the same location throughout the winter.

In 2009, Jan suggested we go to Magee Marsh, one of the

top ten birding destinations in North America. Neither of
us had ever been there. As we neared Lake Erie we ran into
wetlands, small creeks, and inlets where we saw gulls and
other water birds.

On the way into Magee we were on a causeway with a
number of other slow-moving cars. We stopped at one of the
pull-offs and looked for birds in the marshes on either side of
the road. We immediately found tree swallows, great egrets,
great blue herons, coots, pied-billed grebes, Canada geese,
mallards, a bald eagle, and others.

On our way again, we arrived at the lake and I was
shocked to see how many cars there were. If we had come for
a quiet day of birding and solitude, we were definitely in the
wrong place. We even chose the middle of the week to come,
thinking the weekends would be overly crowded.

As we were parking the car a man walked our way and
asked, "Do you have a knife I could borrow? I have a package
that is just impossible to open."

He had a strong English accent, and when we began to
converse with him he told us he had come from Great Britain
to Magee Marsh to chase birds. He said, "For years people had
told me about Magee Marsh. What they said seemed too good
to be true. And you know, they were wrong," and with a big
smile he said, "It's even better than what they said."

Simply stated, what makes Magee so popular is: 1)
birds are plentiful and everywhere, 2) the birds are easy to
find, 3) the birds are close, 4) almost every eastern songbird
imaginable is there at some time during spring migration and
4) most people are helpful to each other in finding birds.

Jan and I gravitated near 20 people with cameras and
binoculars. There were two birds they were watching: a
male scarlet tanager so close at times it seemed to be tame,

and a Baltimore oriole feeding on a halved orange someone attached to a low tree branch. Their binoculars were almost constantly on one of the birds; and when one of the birds got close, the sounds of camera shutters filled he air. I had never experienced anything quite like it.

Jan and I began looking for movement in the trees. Northern parula, black-throated green, Blackburnian, black-and-white, magnolia, chestnut-sided, hooded, yellow; all warblers, and were easy to see. We had hardly moved and we had great views of birds we often heard, but rarely saw.

At the boardwalk it was the same. People everywhere, birds everywhere.

For me the highlight was being able to see many of the birds without the aid of binoculars. My binoculars are useless at any distance closer than 20 feet. Jan's newer binoculars can focus to about four feet away, so the birds seemed as if they were about to land on her nose.

As we moved along the boardwalk, the habitats were different on either side. There are wet woods, drier wooded areas, open woodlands, thickets, waterways, ponds, tall trees, shorter trees, dead trees, areas with lots of fallen trees and brush piles all in a matter of approximately one mile of boardwalk. Numbers are etched into the top rail of the boardwalk so birders can relay information to others about what birds can be found where.

What surprised me most was how close the warblers were. It's as if I had wished to see a bay-breasted warbler, my favorite bird, at arm's length; and now my wish was finally coming true, many times over.

I didn't see any birds here that were new to me, but I had never seen warblers in their spring plumages this close. Almost all of the spectacular warbler views I have witnessed were reproduced many times over in this one day visit to Magee.

Seeing several people intently looking toward one particular area we walked over and whispered, "What are you looking at?"

Someone answered, "There's a Lincoln's sparrow in the brush just to the left of the large tree stump."

After we saw the Lincoln's sparrow, we noticed another group patiently taking turns looking through a spotting scope.

We saw a group patiently taking turns looking through a spotting scope, so Jan asked, "What are you looking at?"

The man with the scope said, "There is a sleeping eastern screech-owl perched on an old dead snag."

With certain birds like the eastern screech-owl, it was hard for me to get too excited. For 28 years they had been part of my almost daily routine. As much as Jan and others enjoyed looking at the owl, I enjoyed watching people seeing an owl for the very first time. They were bird watching; I was people watching.

Farther along the boardwalk there was a watercourse bordered by a dike on the far side.

As I began searching the weedy edges a man said, "We just checked this area thoroughly and there's nothing there."

He and several others began walking away.

I asked, "Did you happen to see a black-crowned night heron?"

He laughed and said, "No."

"I'm looking at one right now," I said.

He and his friends came hustling back.

"Where is it?" someone asked. After pointing it out, they still didn't see it.

Then someone said, "I got it."

Another asked, "Where?"

"Right where he said it was," was their response.

One by one we heard, "I see it now," and, "There it is," and, "Oh, yeah."

They were all looking at the bird, now and had probably looked at it before we arrived; but the bird was so well camouflaged in such a thick, brushy area, it didn't appear to be anything more than stems and trunks of the plants in which it was standing. Jan and I continued to the end of the boardwalk, seeing American redstarts and hearing common yellowthroats all along the way. Walking back to the car, we passed lines and groups of people walking and standing along the road edge looking at even more birds. During spring migration Magee is a birders' paradise. As the sun began to set we headed home and were already making plans to visit next year. This was one of the best birding days either of us had ever experienced.

The next year we decided to begin with the boardwalk. We casually walked, stopped, listened, and looked. Warblers were everywhere.

At one point I said to Jan, "There's a palm warbler."

It was on the ground looking for insects wagging its tail with every step as it ran right under the boardwalk where we were standing.

A lady nearby asked, "Where's the palm?"

"It's right here," I said, pointing at my feet. "It just ran under the boardwalk."

Moments later it came out the other side, and Jan and the lady began watching it.

"Here's, a waterthrush; a northern," I said.

Almost immediately Jan and the lady returned to my side of the boardwalk and began watching the northern waterthrush. It, too, was on the ground like the palm warbler had been; and like the palm, it seemed oblivious to all the activity along the walkway. Also, like the palm, it was looking for food. Constantly bobbing its tail the waterthrush was turning over leaves with its bill and stabbing at fleeing insects and other invertebrates. My attention was drawn to each and every movement, and movements were everywhere.

Someone said, "There's a beautiful Blackburnian high in the tree to the right."

Another person said, "I see it. It's beautiful."

I looked up and saw it too. The sun was hitting it as if a spotlight was aimed at it, and it was beautiful. Something moved across my field of view and I followed it with my binoculars.

"There's a Canada over here," I said.

"Where is it?" several people asked as they came to where I was. They easily found the Canada warbler.

Then I said, "I have a Philadelphia vireo over here."

The next thing I knew, all the people watching the Canada were at my side looking at the Philadelphia.

Magee is as busy as anyone would want it to be. Or it can be as empty as one would want. Jan and I found a bench where we could sit and relax. For a short time we decided to allow ourselves to rest and prepare for our next round of chasing birds. Instead of looking at the birds all around us, we began a conversation with a couple sitting near us. They were from Tennessee, and this was their first trip to Magee.

Jan said, "After our first time here last year, we decided to visit every year, and here we are again."

The lady asked, "Did you see a lot last year?"

Jan answered, "We sure did. Just like today. Birds were everywhere."

We all birded together for a while. At one point Jan and I began discussing what we were going to do about lunch.

Chuck, the man we had just met, overheard us and said, "Last night we ate at a diner nearby, and the fish was delicious."

He gave us directions and when we all arrived at the end of the boardwalk, we parted company. The couple headed for the beach to the east to chase additional birds, and Jan and I went to the fish place for lunch. At lunch I had a perch dinner, and Jan had walleye; and it was delicious. We talked about how much fun we were having: counting birds on the drive up, outstanding birds at Magee, and meeting some very nice birders. We wondered how the day could get any better. We would soon discover a bird that would make all the others we had seen pale by comparison.

When we left the diner, we drove straight back to Magee and planned to walk the boardwalk again. We noticed an abundance of cars in a small parking lot overflowing into the large grassy fields that paralleled a trail leading to the Lake Erie shorefront to the east. We decided to stop and inquire why so many people were there. Some of the cars were leaving and when we began our walk on the trail, many people were coming out.

I asked a man, "What's going on; why all the people?"

"A Kirtland's warbler was out there. But that was about 45 minutes ago," he answered.

"Did you get to see it?" I asked.

"Yes. It was flitting around in the trees for a while and singing too," he said.

Jan and I hurried in, and even though many people had left, there was still a crowd of people looking and hoping. We, too, decided to look for a while. Instead of standing with the group we began checking other areas along the beach. There were towhees, killdeer, white-eyed vireos, blue jays, some warblers, but no Kirtland's. We joined the group for about 30 minutes then began our second trip around the boardwalk. Almost everyone by now had heard about the Kirtland's and oftentimes we would hear the word "Kirtland's" mentioned as we wove our way through the crowds along the way. Before long we were back in our groove; chasing birds and showing and being shown where certain birds were to be found. Much of the time Jan and I were close birding; staying adjacent to one another.

"Jan, there's a real nice black-throated blue to the left at about ten o'clock."

"I don't see it, but I see a beautiful male hooded about where you are looking," she said,

I responded with, "I see your hooded and raise you a Wilson's, about where the hooded is but to the right."

We bantered back and forth as bird after bird came into view while we worked our way along the path. The Tennessee couple we met in the morning were in front of us and the lady was waving to us to come their way.

When we caught up she said, "Did you hear?"

"Hear what?" I asked.

"About the Kirtland's," she said, and continued, "Just after you all left, we went over to the beach trail and Chuck found the Kirtland's."

"Really! You sent us off to eat and you find a Kirtland's. Somehow I don't think that was fair," I jokingly said. Then I asked, "How did you know it was a Kirtland's?"

Chuck said, "I didn't at first. I heard a song I didn't know and when I found the bird, I knew it was a bird that looked familiar, and Kirtland's even popped into my mind. Then when I thought how impossible it would be to find one, I checked the field guide, and sure enough, it was a Kirtland's warbler. We watched it for a long time, and before we knew it, lots of others were watching it too. It didn't take long for the word to get out."

We birded together some more and all the time we talked about the Kirtland's warbler. Again, after dozens of birds, we were near the end of the boardwalk. All of a sudden people were walking briskly past us. The Kirtland's warbler was discovered on the beach again. The four of us continued to the beach and were soon with a semi-circle of about 40 people.

When we inquired about the bird someone said, "It was here a short time ago. You just missed it."

That was definitely not what we wanted to hear. What I wanted someone to say was, "There it is…right there in front of us…in the open…singing…easy to see." But that wasn't to be. Still we remained there and waited. We didn't have to wait long. Soon I saw some movement in a dense shrub about 20 feet in front of us. Immediately everyone wanted to know, "Where?" Less than a minute later the bird appeared. It was the Kirtland's. There was one bare branch in the front spanning between two thick areas of the bush and the Kirtland's was there, in the best place possible. Not wanting to take my binoculars off the bird, I wanted to make sure Jan saw the bird and asked, "Jan, do you see it?"

"I see it," she answered.

The bird looked at us, looked away, turned as if to show off its front, then its back. If a bird ever was to walk the runway at a fashion show, this was it. Everybody there saw the bird well and for a long time.

When the Kirtland's finally did disappear into the shrubbery we all breathed a sigh of relief signaling, "We were victorious; we saw one of the rarest birds on the planet, an endangered species, and we could also take our binoculars from our eyes and relax."

I said to some people standing near to me, "Chuck here is the one who found the Kirtlands earlier today," which resulted in a round of clapping and thanks.

Jan and I were excited to see a life bird for both of us, especially this warbler. Others around us were just as excited or even more so.

One lady said, "This is the best day of my life."

Another said, "I'm so happy I could cry."

One couple was so excited, they held hands and danced in a circle in the sand while laughing and giggling and congratulating each other.

Sometime after our Magee trip, I saw a photo of the crowds that gathered over the next few days after the Kirtland's was sighted and thought, "I am sure glad we saw it when there was only a handful of people there."

Magee is a special birding place, but that day it was very special.

In 2011, we camped a few miles from Magee and were told about a marbled godwit in a wet field behind a nearby ice cream store. The moment we finished parking the trailer, we went to find the godwit.

When the ice cream store was in sight I thought, "No cars are there; the godwit is probably gone."

There had been no sightings of the godwit for several days.

And we were told by the owners of the store, "If it comes back, you'll know by all the cars in the back lot.

We not only chased birds at Magee, but also at the bordering Ottawa National Wildlife Refuge, where we saw blue-winged and golden-winged warblers. The spring was wet and many of the fields along the back roads still had large, shallow pockets of water where we saw dunlins, American pipits, black-bellied and semi-palmated plovers, horned larks, and spotted and least sandpipers.

Northeast of Ottawa we visited the Metzger Marsh Wildlife Area where I saw one of my favorite birds, the black tern. There are some birds I never tire of watching, and the black tern is one of them. Their behavior reminds me of a hybrid between a swift and kestrel. Expertly gliding over the water and swamp edges, they swoop and dive, and then stop and hover for a time occasionally plunging earthward for insects or fish.

With all the excitement and good birds elsewhere, Magee was still the place to be. Like previous years, warblers and other spring migrants were everywhere along the boardwalk. On Thursday we didn't get far on the boardwalk when we noticed a small group intently looking at a particular location on the ground. We stopped to see what the fuss was. A mourning warbler had been sighted. Soon our small group grew to a very large group making it difficult for those wanting to pass. We were at number five on the handrail and word was getting out, "The mourning warbler at number five."

People were squeezing in beside me and three rows deep behind me and sitting on the north handrail, all hoping to see the mourning. The views I got were fleeting as it sometimes rapidly hopped between hideaways. Being in the front and against the handrail, Jan and I had support and clear sight, but we still wanted to get a better, more extended view of the bird.

Excitedly someone said, "There's a Connecticut...20 feet to the right of the mourning."

All binoculars immediately shifted toward the Connecticut

warbler. I looked around and noticed that now no one was interested in the mourning warbler. What happened next was astounding. The mourning hopped out into the open as if it was jealous of all the attention the Connecticut was receiving and put on a show, turning its head from one side to the other, slowly turning the entire body; front view, side view, back view. Jan and I were absorbed at how brash it had suddenly become.

After the excellent views of the mourning, we turned our attention to the Connecticut. At first it was just as shy as the mourning had been, sometimes walking through the dense underbrush providing barely a glimpse of its eye ring or gray hood. Then it would disappear for a time making us wonder if it had moved on without being detected. I began looking at the mourning again, then there was the Connecticut.

We watched until I began to feel selfish, so I asked a lady behind me if she would like to have my place. She was delighted. Jan offered her spot to the lady's friend. We looked at each other and without speaking a word questioned, "How in the world are we going to get out of here?"

The crowd had grown to well over one hundred people and most were waiting for an opportunity to get close enough to see one or both of these difficult birds. The mourning and Connecticut warblers were two of the best birds for the week, and we were delighted at seeing them so well. We had held both species in our hands at the Allegheny Front Migration Observatory on Dolly Sods, but they were in their fall colors, not the spring plumages we had just seen. For Jan, they were life birds in the wild. For me, they were the best views I had ever seen of either bird and another life experience to treasure.

Our last day, we had planned to hook up the trailer and leave for home so we could get some rest before Saturday's big day of birding at Ralph's. However, we were having such a wonderful week of chasing birds and meeting new people, we decided to take a quick, early trip to the boardwalk before we left.

We saw warbler after warbler species close up and many others kinds of birds. At handrail marker number 14 we fell behind on our time schedule. Several people were focused on a woodcock that proved difficult to find even though it was standing still in the open. We were there for a while before moving onward.

Soon we were stopped again to see a winter wren. After seeing the wren, another nice find, we spotted a gray-cheeked thrush, almost in the same locale. Then there was a bobolink, and then a Louisiana waterthrush. Near handrail marker 27 a group was blocking the boardwalk. Spotting scopes were set up looking at two different birds: a common nighthawk and a whippoorwill. What birder wouldn't stop to see these birds, even if they were already late for an important appointment? Jan and I looked at each other and just smiled.

Finally, the end was in sight, and as we scrambled toward the exit we heard, "Hey…Bill. How are you?"

It was a group of friends from West Virginia and New York. They were at Magee for the day. We talked about it being our fifth and last day.

"How many species have you seen?" someone asked.

At that point we were not really sure because we had seen several new birds on this last, quick trip around the boardwalk.

Jan added our new birds to the list and announced, "One-hundred-thirty-three."

"How many warblers?" another person asked.

"Twenty-seven," Jan said.

As the sun began to set we headed home and were already making plans to visit next year. This was one of the best birding days either of us had ever experienced.

FAVORITE BIRDS

All birders have their favorites birds and places to bird. My favorite bird is the eastern screech-owl.

If I considered only my bird banding experiences for my favorite bird, and based solely on behavior, the tufted titmouse would get the honor. The colors are not striking; the song doesn't compete musically with many other expert songsters, but the tufted titmouse has attitude. When I recall the 100s of tufted titmice I have banded, there has not been even one that has not bitten, scratched, grabbed, and screamed at me. Holding one at eye level, it is easy to see that the bird does not appear to be genuinely frightened. Instead, it is fuming.

Titmice are cavity nesters and line their nests with fur, often from live animals. They are bold, brash birds as can be noted from their frequent scolding of potential harmful intruders into their territories: cats, hawks, snakes, raccoons, people, etc. Yes, they are one of my favorite birds, a defiant bird, afraid of nothing. They are the watchmen of the woodlands, sounding the first alarm of peril, alerting all the other birds of impending danger.

Color is an indicator of favorites. Everyone has a favorite

color. One spring at the Brooks Nature Center I offered a one-day workshop titled, "Light Bulb Birds." My plan was to take participants into the field to see an eastern bluebird, scarlet tanager, indigo bunting, Baltimore oriole, and rose-breasted grosbeaks, all with light bulb popping colors.

Mary was a birding friend who came to my classes, and she was a good birder. One special quality I admired in Mary was that she loved looking at all birds, all the time. Scarlet tanagers of course excited her more than looking at a starling; but unlike some who, after seeing a bird a dozen or so times lose their fire for repeatedly looking at the same species, she had more excitement for common yard birds than anyone I ever knew.

Everything was working out perfectly in my workshop. I knew where the nests of the eastern bluebird and Baltimore oriole were located, and the group got a good look at the birds for as long as they wanted to watch. I taught the group to always approach the territories with the sun at their backs, otherwise, they would only see a silhouette regardless how colorful the bird is.

I knew the nesting territories and the territorial songs of the indigo bunting and scarlet tanager, so they were also easy to locate and eventually observe. To see the rose-breasted grosbeak we went to the West Liberty University woodlands. The grosbeak was going to be the most difficult to see. After arriving at the right location, I could hear them, but couldn't get a glimpse of the singing males. The male seemed to be taunting us, singing from high in the tree canopy, but not allowing us even the slightest view.

The nature center had recently begun selling a device called "The Audible Audubon." First I showed the picture on the Audible Audubon card then slid it into the sound device.

After the song played about three times, I was facing a group with their mouths agape and eyes staring in amazement to a point behind me, just above my head. The taped song brought a male right to us, and it was the best look at any light bulb bird all day.

A word of caution here: Playing the songs during breeding and nesting times can confuse songbirds and cause them to abandon their territories. The recordings should be used for in home, in car use only, but never loud enough outdoors to disrupt the bird's chances of successful nesting. One person I know told me he had used a recording only one time at a particular Henslow's sparrow location. Then I learned of two others who had done the same thing at the same location, the same day, for the same bird at different times of the day. And there may have been others. These devices should only be used for study and learning purposes and not in the field to attract songbirds.

My favorite bird to look at is the bay-breasted warbler. Until I began going to Magee Marsh it might be years before I would see a bay-breasted in its spring plumage. A northern nester, it only passes through my area during migration. Contrasting earth tone colors are what excite me most. Other birds I like a lot are the chestnut-sided, magnolia, and black-throated blue warblers. I never seem to grow weary looking at the white-crowned sparrow. The bright white crown contrasting with the alternating black streaks and the rich mix of chocolate, cinnamon, and clay brown on the wings and body always garner my attention.

On Dolly Sods one day I was hiking the Rohrbaugh Plains trail with plans to eat lunch at the overlook. After lunch and near the time I planned to leave, a kettle of turkey vultures rose out of the canyon. In the kettle was a solitary black vulture. Watching from above, I was surprised how beautiful the black vulture was to me. Not highly colorful, the vultures are not that attractive to most birders. And there is the distinct possibility that other elements of my situation had an impact on the vulture's beauty. I was alone, which is always a plus for how I interpret my feelings; and I was in one of the most beautiful settings in West Virginia. My outlook at that moment, without seeing any birds, was one of peace and contentment. For me, being alone and the location are important criteria as to how I feel about a particular bird.

One of my favorite songs is that of the winter wren. The winter wren has the most fun song I know. To hear it and watch it sing is quite a challenge. Only once have I watched one sing. With mouth agape for a full seven seconds, more than 100 separate continuous notes flow out. Along the Rohrbaugh, at Blackwater, and the Maryland access to Cranesville Swamp are excellent places to hear the winter wren's song.

A birder friend and great teacher, Bill Wylie, once described the song to me as a "Barrel of music tumbling down the mountainside with notes bursting out with each bump." This tiny bird seems barely capable of having enough energy and size to burst forth with such a magnificent golden thread of music.

Who among all birders does not immediately fall in love with the song of a wood, hermit, or Swainson's thrush, or the veery? All are magnificent singers. Each spring one of the favorite events in my year is the first time I hear each one of these thrushes. From my backyard the wood thrush serenades me daily if I allow it. And allowing bird songs to penetrate not only our attentions, but also our very souls can change us for all time.

Upon hearing my first wood thrush, it instantly became my favorite song and persisted as so for a long time afterwards, at least until I sat at my first campfire at Mountain Nature Camp and heard my first veery. And the veery lasted until I heard my first hermit thrush at Blackwater Falls.

"It is," Walt Whitman once said about the hermit thrush, "the sweetest, solemnest of all our singing birds."

John K. Terres in *The Audubon Society Encyclopedia of North American Birds* describes the song as: "opens with a clear flutelike note, followed by ethereal, bell-like tones, ascending and descending in no fixed order, rising until reach(ing) dizzying vocal heights and notes fade away in (a) silvery tinkle."

However, no flutist has ever or will ever be able to reproduce the song of the hermit thrush as it is produced by a complex system of syringeal muscles able to create multiple notes at the same time. The music is haunting, reminding me of aloneness, as if the earth is calling me to be absorbed into its being as it has all other wild creatures, to not be a part of, but one with every other wild creature on the planet; reminiscent of the John Singer Sargent painting, "The Hermit."

In West Virginia the hermit thrush is an elusive bird, hiding among the undergrowth in mixed hardwood/evergreen and evergreen forests. It walks the forest floor from one secret spot to another, stopping to flip leaves with its bill, in search of food: insects, spiders, and other tiny invertebrates from the leaf litter.

A wonderful Mohawk Indian story, *Sacred Song of the Hermit Thrush*, relates how all birds received their songs. The hermit thrush entered the Land of Happy Spirits and received the most beautiful song of all. The hermit thrush "cannot restrain himself and he must sing his beautiful song," and

"When he does this, the other birds cease their singing."

Whatever favorite bird one has or for whatever reasons it was chosen, one thing is sure, we all glory in that particular bird when we are fortunate enough to find it and for "the feeling" at that moment.

TWO BINOCULARS

I was about 10 years old and, like all kids, excited about opening presents on Christmas morning. There were two wrapped gifts for me. The first present was a pair of binoculars. After the initial, short-lived excitement I moved on to the second gift. Wow, it was just what I wanted…a Lucas McCain, *The Rifleman* rifle. Well, not a real rifle, but a toy replica. To me, it was the opportunity to keep my imaginary "town" protected from the bad guys. Later in the day my father showed me how to use the binoculars. I wasn't very excited.

The back corner of my closet floor became the resting place for the binoculars. They would remain unused, in my closet for 10 years.

My college Special Problems class required me to have a pair of binoculars for a winter bird survey. Luckily my mom found them for me hidden away in my closet. The binoculars were 7x35s from Sears. They became my frequent companion for several years of chasing birds and studying distant hillsides for wildflowers and other plants. My first pileated woodpecker, eastern bluebird and many others were seen through these binoculars.

Later in the day my father showed me how to use the binoculars. I wasn't very excited. Then I looked through the larger end and saw how everything looked so far away.

The back corner of my closet floor became the resting place for the binoculars.The first year I went to the Mountain Nature Camp at Terra Alta I took my Sears binoculars. We chased birds in swamps (my first swamp sparrow), along streams and rivers (my first cliff swallows), on mountain tops (my first hermit thrush), and around the 18 acres at camp (my first veery). My first golden-winged warbler and ovenbird were also found during that week.

One morning we awoke to a torrential downpour. From between my tent flaps I could see that some poor soul had left his binoculars on a bench outside all night.

"They must be ruined," I thought. They were! They were my binoculars…full of water and much heavier than they had been the day before.

I ended up borrowing a pair that worked less than stellar, but were better than nothing. I began asking others about their binoculars and tried some of theirs. I became convinced that the Bausch and Lomb 7x50s were the binoculars for me. There was a local optical company that carried the 7x50s but they cost $350 (in 1972).

So I continued to use the old pair of borrowed binoculars for two years. They didn't prevent me from seeing birds, but they did prevent me from seeing birds well. And for me and many others, that's what it is all about: seeing the details and colors as well as possible for proper identification and being able to appreciate the striking beauty of birds. Fall warblers are difficult enough to distinguish under normal circumstances, but just about impossible with poorly functioning binoculars.

At the nature center we had a bulletin board where I posted all sorts of nature-related information about birds seen recently in the park, wildflowers to expect and where to go to find them. One day, I saw a 3x5 card that read, "FOR SALE: Two pair of Bausch and Lomb 7x50s binoculars." The lady who answered offered to bring the binoculars to the nature center the next day.

Arriving at work the next morning I was a bit anxious because I hadn't thought to ask her the price. She was older than her voice had sounded on the phone. She told me how she and her husband had faithfully chased birds everywhere they went for many, many years. Unfortunately now her husband had Parkinson's disease, and neither of them could get around easily.

Both pairs of binoculars looked like new. They obviously had been well taken care of. One was embossed with the words, "United States Navy 1943." They both came with cases, one leather and the other a heavy rubberized plastic. One pair had solar filters which could easily be flipped in or out and were permanently fixed on the binoculars. The price...$60 each. I excitedly bought both pairs. The lady was thrilled and her eyes welled up.

She said, "I am so happy you bought them. I know they will be well taken care of and will be used by someone who appreciates them and loves the birds. My husband will be delighted."

So many wonderful birds were viewed though my 7x50s. There was one event, however, which surpassed all others. My favorite bird to observe, the bay-breasted warbler...the rich cinnamon brown flanks and chocolate brown cap contrasting with the black, white, and light ivory-yellow are exquisite to me. In this locale, they are seen only on migration, and not every year. With my new binoculars I could truly savor the delicious colors on the rare occasions when I spotted a migrating bay-breasted.

Hiking one day soon thereafter, I began seeing blue-eyed Marys, my favorite flower. Upon further exploration, I found an area of uncommon white forms mixed in with the normal blue-and-white flowers. All of a sudden my attention was drawn from the flowers to the light, airy, high-pitched song of a bay-breasted warbler. My binoculars gave me a long, spectacular look at the beautiful warbler before it flew off. Then I realized: here I stand among my favorite wildflowers watching my favorite bird. For me, it was one of those "looking into the heavens at the Milky Way and trying to comprehend the vastness" kind of moments: "the feeling."

I lived in West Virginia for 45 years. When I moved to a relatively flat part of Ohio, I often longed for the hills and wanted to move back someday. Unexpectedly, the opportunity to return presented itself, and we began to go through our possessions separating them for our yard sale.

As I pulled my other pair of binoculars from the closet I told Jan, "I should sell these. I never use them."

She agreed, but in the process of separating so many things, they were omitted from the "for sale" pile.

The weather was ideal and many people came by. We sold books, vinyl records, a bicycle, a snow blower, and 100s of other items.

Late in the day as we were talking about closing the sale, a car pulled up and a man yelled, "Do you have any binoculars?"

"Maybe," I said.

He turned the car engine off and got out.

"What kind of binoculars do you have? I'm only interested

in something old, cheap, and with good optics...preferably German."

"Well, I think I might have what you want, if I can find them. The binoculars I have are old, cheap and made in New York, but the company was founded by two Germans... Bausch and Lomb."

"How much?" he demanded.

"I paid $60 about 30 years ago," I said, " and they were already 31 years old then...I have a pair almost identical to them that I use just about every day...I bought both pairs on the same day...I was thinking $40."

I was curious and asked, "Jan and I are avid birders. What are you going to use them for?"

"Oh they are not for me," he answered, "They're for my brother back in Ireland. He raises sheep and is getting too old to chase after them. With these, he can sit on the porch and keep watch over the sheep on the far hillsides. Maybe he'll become interested in birds, too."

A wonderful picture formed in my mind of the old sheepherder keeping watch on his flock with my exceptional "closet" binoculars. I imagined him scanning the hillsides and perhaps seeing his first brightly-colored bird and becoming as excited as I did when I saw my first.

Later that evening I recalled the day I had first been introduced to both pairs of binoculars and the varied activities each of them had been through. Both may have been used aboard World War II ships with the solar shields in place, looking toward the sun, scanning the sky for enemy aircraft. Then, after sharing many years of watching birds together, their paths diverged...for one, many more years of outdoor bird watching excitement and, for the other, waiting in a dark closet. But now, a new life in Ireland awaited the closet binoculars.

BARE HANDING BIRDS

One day, Ralph Bell and I were talking about birds, and I shared some stories about catching birds in my bare hands. He said, "I really haven't made an effort to do that. You have me beat in that category.

The consensus that day was that due to my life's work I spend much more time outdoors than most other people, as well as make myself more available to unusual nature opportunities.

He also said, "Most people wouldn't do what you do. Instead of snatching a bird right from a tree, they would be satisfied to simply look at it where it was." We both sat and laughed about it as we continued our conversation.

My first bare-handed capture was a brown creeper. One of my duties as a naturalist included occasional trail maintenance. Resetting steps along a trail one day, I stopped to appreciate a giant white oak tree. Just then a brown creeper flew to the oak and landed right in front of me. I grabbed at it and missed. It flew around the tree and again landed in front of me. This time I slowly removed one of my heavy work gloves, quickly reached out, and caught the bird. I took it to the nature center, showed it to Dot, banded it and released it.

I thought, "That will never happen again."

Over the years I observed how brown creepers would search for food while creeping up a tree probing the bark crevices with their long curved bill. After reaching the treetop they would fly near the bottom of a nearby tree and creep upward looking for more food. Several times I tried to guess which tree would be the creeper's next choice. Once I was correct and bare-handed another creeper.

The nature center had two large side-by-side picture windows. A short distance outside the windows was an assortment of bird feeders. One day I noticed a hairy woodpecker on the thin top of a recently-planted tree. It was nervously looking around and struggling violently, making the tip of the tree move rapidly back and forth. The actions of the bird and movements of the tree reminded me of some kind of carnival ride…for birds.

Upon closer examination, I noticed the hairy had its legs wrapped around the tree and each foot was holding the opposite leg. Gently grabbing the bird, I carefully slid it up over the treetop, released its feet from its legs, took the bird inside, banded and released it. That circumstance I have never encountered again.

The nature center had an inset feeder with one-way glass so that people could sit inside next to the feeder and watch the birds eat without their knowledge. A pileated woodpecker began visiting the feeder but never ate anything. Instead, it would peck at the wooden frame and gouge out large pieces of wood. I was repairing the feeder daily. One day, the moment the bird flew in and began pecking the wood; I carefully went out the side door and walked slowly and cautiously along the building almost to the feeder. As I suddenly jumped in front of the feeder, the pileated flew directly into my belly, startling both of us. Suddenly I had a pileated woodpecker in my hands.

My first instinct was to protect myself from the beak. Had I known how formidable the claws were I might have been even more careful. The wound to my cuticle was similar and just as painful as that inflicted by an eastern screech-owl. And I wasn't prepared for the pileated's constant screams. I held the beak shut so the bird couldn't peck or scratch, but the piercing screams continued. Even holding it somewhat under and against my shirt didn't help. My only recourse was to get it banded and released as quickly as possible.

Arriving home at dusk one day, I heard a lot of commotion from our many "feeder" birds. As I walked into the backyard, I noticed an eastern screech-owl perched on a low branch just above my main hopper feeder. Its back was facing me, so I slowly crept away and entered the house from the front. My oldest daughter had two girlfriends visiting. Soon my wife, and the girls were gawking at the owl from the kitchen window.

Someone asked, "Do you think it's one you have caught before?"

After watching the owl for a short time through binoculars and seeing no band, we surmised it was a "new" bird.

I had an idea. "Why don't you girls come with me into the front yard and get the owl's attention."

The four girls were stationed far enough away to distract the bird without frightening it. And they slowly and steadily walked back-and-forth where I had instructed them. When I reached the backyard, I stealthily walked up to the owl. The plan was to reach up and take it off the branch, while it concentrated on the girls. Standing behind and under the branch I realized it was higher than expected. The few seconds

I paused and thought about the awkward situation seemed like an eternity. In one smooth motion I jumped, raised my arms, put my hands around the owl, lifted up and back, and landed back on the ground, bird in hand. It was a "new" bird and I promptly banded it.

After quitting my job at the nature center, I began writing some nature-related articles for various magazines. Some of my stories were complimented with my photos, and occasionally I was asked to provide photos to illustrate others' stories. Thinking I might be able to become a good nature photographer, I entered *National Wildlife Magazine's* photography contest. My entry was a picture of my four-year-old son holding five baby black rat snakes. The expression on Josh's face was a classic expression of excitement. My entry was one of 21 winners from over 8,000 photos submitted.

The next year, my entry was an eastern screech-owl peering from a hollowed out dead tree showing half the face. It, too, was one of the winning photos. Due to these successes, I began submitting photos to the magazines of The National Wildlife Federation.

I thought perhaps *Wonderful West Virginia* might like my photos; so after receiving the writer and photographer guidelines, I called the magazine. After a lot of run around, I finally spoke to the editor and told her that I had been doing research for the United States Fish & Wildlife Service pertaining to the eastern screech-owl and I would like to submit a story about it.

About two weeks later I received the most wonderful letter stating how much the editor liked my photos and that if I can take quality photos like these all the time, the magazine could certainly work with me. Before long I was writing regularly and illustrating my stories with my own photos. The editor also sent a list of nature-related stories the magazine hoped to publish in the next several years and wanted me to take the photos. Of all the stories and photos I submitted, none were ever rejected.

After a while my writing subsided and photography became my goal. During the warm weather months I would spend 8-10 hours a day taking pictures. I would leave the house around six in the morning and return near three in the afternoon. Fortunately, I lived within walking distance of many beautiful natural areas. Most days I left home walking.

Many people have told me they would love to do what I do, but I don't really think they understand how dirty, sweaty, and tired I became every day. The first thing I did after returning home from a day of photography was change clothes, get into my hammock between two cherry trees, and relax and read and eat at least half a watermelon.

One morning I started out on what was supposed to be a very hot day. The sun was just coming up. I decided to stay in the open and take advantage of the soft early morning light. There was a large grassy field with some milkweed and other common meadow plants mixed in. The dew was heavy and my feet and legs were instantly wet.

Carefully and slowly I began searching the field for wet insects and spiders. There were butterflies, flies, bugs, and beetles hiding under leaves, as well as some on the tips of the tall grasses attempting to dry out with the sun's warmth. With my camera on the tripod I took photo after photo. Getting my setups right took a long time, but once I had the correct lenses with the proper settings and focus, the actual taking of the photos went quickly.

Then I would move on to another nearby photo opportunity. It was summer, past the nesting season of most birds, and void of the multitude of songs common to the spring. Still, there were some songsters infrequently singing. Meadowlarks would burst forth with their, "Spring-of-the-YEAR, spring-of-the-YEAR," melody. Part of their singing might have been due to my intrusion into their habitat. They often left the meadow to wires above the edge of the field and would eventually return when I left the area they claimed as home.

Near the edge of the meadow I was continually scolded with a rapid rattle of the common yellowthroat, "Tic-tic-tic-tic-tic-tic-tic-tic-tic-tic-tic, tic-tic-tic-tic-tic-tic-tic-tic-tic-tic-tic." The field was drying and some insects were flying.

One edge of the meadow had an old fence line. The fence posts were dried from decades in the weather. They made for a pleasing background for wildflower, insect, and spider photos. The posts stood as a reminder of the American chestnut trees that once graced the forests.

I crossed the fence line and began hiking toward the stream and wetlands far below. Unfamiliar bird sounds were coming from what seemed like the open wet meadows near the stream. Immediately I wanted to chase the noises, but then remembered the brown thrasher that defended that area.

"The sounds must be from the thrasher," I thought.

Soon I had forgotten about the bird and began looking for more photo opportunities. Tiny flowers of the Deptford pink were imprinted onto my film, as well as a long line of ants from a not too distant colony. As I photographed, I continued toward the bottom of the valley. At the stream I watched the emerald jewelwing damselflies flitting about.

Then, there was that thrasher again, making the strange sounds. This time it was close. When I looked all I saw was a large, whitish-colored bird. It wasn't a thrasher. Through my binoculars I could see it was a parrot and it had what looked like a chain link around its leg. As I slowly approached it, the bird became more panicky. Unexpectedly to me, it paced back and forth on the branch, nervously bobbing its head, and yelling and screaming. When I was within 10 feet, it suddenly flew toward me, landed on the ground, and ran under a thick multiflora rose bush.

I took pruners from my camera bag and began cutting away the rosebush. All the while the bird was lying on its back screaming. Finally I was able to grab its legs; but when I did, it grabbed my hand with its beak and squeezed. Oh my did that hurt.

I took off my T-shirt, wrapped it around my hand, and allowed the frightened parrot to bite, which helped. Like the pileated woodpecker I had caught bare handed, the parrot's constant screaming hurt my ears. I decided to take the bird home and put it in a cage. Leaving all my camera gear by the stream, I hurried home through the woods with the parrot screaming all the way.

I began to run, which turned out to be a mistake. With each jarring step the parrot's screams became louder. At home I placed it in one of the owl cages, then returned for my gear.

I decided to take the bird to the Association of Zoos and Aquariums (AZA) in Oglebay Park. When I entered the room where I had put the parrot, it immediately began to scream. Softly talking to the bird did not calm it. After putting the caged bird into the back of the station wagon, I threw a blanket over it. That did help somewhat. Now the only time it screamed was when I made a noise. Closing the car door brought a loud, "Squawk." On route, I was careful to drive the many sharp turns slowly so as not to alarm the parrot.

From out of nowhere I heard, "Glory be to the Father."

I thought, "What?"

Then again, "Glory be to the Father."

Although I believe God has spoken to me in many obvious ways in the things I have seen and experienced in wild places, I had never, ever, for one moment thought I had heard God's audible voice…until maybe now.

I thought, "It's got to be the parrot."

The bird was quiet the rest of the trip. At AZA I told them about the bird; the director came out to the car and quickly identified it as an African gray parrot.

I said, "It even talks."

The director asked, "What does it say?"

"Well, on the way here it said, "Glory be to the Father."

He looked at me quizzically. "Really?"

The whole way home I questioned whether the parrot had really talked. Once home, the phone rang. "Hello, hello, hello, hello," burst from the blanket-covered cage.

When I answered the phone, I was trying to grasp the idea of the parrot talking and still be able to carry on a coherent conversation.

To this day I do not remember who was on the phone, but I do remember saying something like, "Hello," and then hearing again from the cage, "Hello," and me saying, "There's a parrot talking to me. It answered the phone before I answered the phone. I think it's a Catholic."

Every time the phone rang, "Hello, hello, hello, hello," came from our feathered guest.

We were feeding the parrot bananas and other fruits. Quite suddenly, it said, "I want a peanut, I want a peanut."

And it loved eating peanuts. It no longer screamed, but when I tried to pick it up, the bird continued to bite hard. We discovered the parrot would step from the perch in the cage onto my gloved hand.

Confirmation of its religious affiliation came when it exclaimed, "Hail Mary, full of grace."

It was obviously someone's escaped pet and I told my children that we would have to find the owner and return it. Secretly I was hoping that we might be able to keep it. Two nights later a friend came by the house and I showed him the bird.

Right away he said, "There's a wanted poster attached to the ATM machine at the college with that bird's picture on it."

It read: Wanted: Lost bird; answers to the name Charity. Reward! Call.........

That evening I received a call about the parrot. Charity belonged to Father Mike, a priest living at the Catholic Center just down the street. She had flown away several days before I found her. The parrot's demeanor changed immediately when she saw Father Mike. He reached for Charity, and she immediately walked onto his hand, then onto his lower arm and snuggled against him and kept caressing Father Mike with her head and beak. There was definitely an obvious bond between the two.

Just before leaving Father Mike said, "You know, at Sunday's service I told the congregation how heartbroken I was about losing Charity. Afterwards a lady came to me and said, 'Father Mike, you should call Bill Beatty. If anybody is going to find Charity, it will be him.'"

NICE-OLD-LADIES DON'T
CHEW-CHEW-CHEW-CHEW

One day I was in the field with a friend who taught voice. She is probably the best birder by song I have ever met. When hearing a bird, she might say, "That is a whole octave higher than the last bird we heard." And I would think, "Wow, that's neat, but what's an octave?" Learning bird songs is not the same for everyone.

My very first attempt to learn bird songs was listening to the songs on vinyl records. Although helpful, I needed to be in the field watching the bird sing its song. Sometimes I would hear a song and know, "I own that song. It's mine."

Early on I was introduced to mnemonics: associations, words, and phrases that serve as aids in remembering bird songs. Learning is always easier when having fun, and mnemonics is the most fun way for me to learn the songs. Very simply, the birds make the music, and we provide the lyrics.

The first mnemonic I was introduced to was for the white-throated sparrow. When the white-throated sparrow sings, the words that are brought forth in my mind are "Old, old, Sam, Peabody- Peabody-Peabody." Canadians might substitute

"Oh, oh, sweet, Canada-Canada-Canada."

For teaching purposes, most bird songs can be grouped into four main categories: association, uniqueness, birds that say their own name, and words and phrases. In my bird song classes I always begin with association songs. The song of the chipping sparrow was described to me as the sound of a sewing machine "chip-chip-chip-chip-chip-chip-chip," and to my college students, I have likened it to a machine gun's "rat-tat-tat-tat-tat-tat-tat-tat." The key is to use whatever association that works for you. One of the gray catbird sounds is reminiscent of the sound of a cat, hence the name catbird. When I hear a Kentucky warbler, I always think of the Kentucky Derby race horses and I hear the words, "Giddyup-giddyup-giddyup-giddyup," or a rapid, "Dadup-dadup-dadup-dadup-dadup." Both "lyrics" sound like a galloping horse. A white-breasted nuthatch is a happy sound, very much like a person laughing.

The second category is "unique". These bird songs or sounds are so unusual-that even non-birders might recognize them. Most people recognize the "caw, caw, caw" of the common crow. Then there is drumming, a unique sound which most people recognize. As a young boy, I somehow knew a woodpecker's drumming. And the sound varies depending on what object is being drummed. When a woodpecker drums, it often has more to do with making a loud sound than finding food. They will find the objects in their territory that produce the loudest sound. And the object may be the side of a house or the gutter or downspout.

One day a man called with a dilemma. "There is a woodpecker that wakes me every morning with its drumming on the downspout, just outside my bedroom window. I have a job where I don't have to be at work until 9:00 and I like to sleep in. Is there anything I can do to discourage it?"

I suggested, "If your downspout is metal, changing it to plastic might help. Plastic does not resonate as much and the bird might go elsewhere to make a louder noise. You could also try bird Tanglefoot, a clear sticky coating that deters birds from roosting areas and in your case, perhaps the downspout."

I also explained that woodpeckers were protected by strict Federal laws and shouldn't be harmed.

Days later the same man called again and said, "I replaced the downspout with plastic, and then the bird moved to the gutter. There is too much gutter on the house to replace. I even tried the Tanglefoot and it works, but the bird keeps moving to where I didn't spread any."

We talked some more and I even asked, "Do you have a room on the other side of your house where you could sleep, at least until nesting time is over?" He really didn't like that idea.

The call ended after I responded to his question, "If I were to harm the bird, just what could happen to me if I were caught?"

There is a different kind of mechanical drumming that is unique to only one North American bird, the ruffed grouse. It is the only bird that can break the sound barrier, hence the booming vibration. To watch a grouse drum, you would surely think the bird was beating its breast to produce the drumming sound, but not so. The male bird proudly puffs out his chest, braces his tail against a log and ruffs out his neck feathers. Then he slowly begins beating his wings until the beating becomes a blur. Some, including myself, believe the drumming can not only be heard but also felt by the observer. It was originally thought the wing feathers hitting the breast made the thumping sound. Instead, the sounds are small sonic booms produced from the air rushing in to fill the vacuum created by the outward movement of the wings.

The wild turkey's "gobble-gobble-gobble-gobble-gobble" is another unique bird sound. When I approached the turkeys at the Good Zoo, I would say "Shhhhhh, let's see if the turkeys want to talk." In my best turkey voice I would gobble, and most of the time the Toms would throw their heads up and answer.

The third category is birds that "say their own name". "Pee-weeeee, pee-weeeee, weeeeeee," is the song of the eastern wood pewee. The song is fun and easy; it was one of the first bird songs my children learned.

Knowing birds songs well can be a blessing or sometimes, a curse. In 1977, the TV mini-series, *Roots* aired. After supper each evening I found myself eager to watch it. The night of the last episode Bev and I were both anxious to see the ending. The family returned to Africa to visit the tribe from where they had originated. There was a beautiful scene where a large boat was navigating a very wide African river; and then, "Pee-weeeee." "Did you hear that?" I asked.

"Hear what?" Bev asked.

"I swear I just heard an eastern wood pewee," I said.

"What are you talking about? Let's just watch the movie," Bev said.

"Pee-weeeee."

"There it is again," I said.

"Can we just watch the movie?" Bev again said.

I continued, "They aren't even in Africa. They are somewhere in the United States, east of the Mississippi," to which Bev responded,

"Would you be quiet and at least let me watch the movie!"

I later discovered the African scene was filmed in Cypress Gardens, Florida.

Another time we were watching a Star Wars movie at a theater and I said, "Did you hear that?"

Bev responded, "No, I didn't, and I don't care; and I am sure no one else in this theater cares, so let us all watch the movie in peace and quiet."

I said, "But I am sure there are no wood thrushes on Dagobah Three. They filmed this somewhere in North America."

This time all I got was "the look", and I knew it was time to be quiet.

The most fun bird song is that of the eastern towhee. The first mnemonic I learned for the towhee was, "DRINK-your-teeeeeee," but the easiest way to remember the bird is by using "I'm-Tow-heeeeeee." With young people, and even teachers, after hearing a towhee, I used to have a spelling bee using one word: towhee.

I would say, "In 1984 a thirteen-year-old boy won the Fifty-Seventh annual National Spelling Bee in part by correctly spelling the word, towhee, after the only other opponent left standing misspelled it. Who thinks they know how to spell it?"

Many may think that it is an easy word to spell, but if you have never seen the word before, it is a most difficult word, even though it is spelled exactly as it sounds. Tohe, toehe, towhe, toohe, toehee, were spellings I often received and many spelled what I pronounced, but they were still not correct. To spell towhee correctly the first try, one either has to have seen the word before or get lucky. Other mnemonics for the towhee are, "I-am-freeeeeee," or "LOOK-at-meeeeeee," or "ONE-two-threeeeeee," or "SPELL-ing-beeeeeee."

Other examples are the eastern "Phoe-be, phoe-be, phoe-be," and "whip-poor-will, whip-poor-will, whip-poor-will."

One I heard called over 50 times, then another 50 times, and again, again, and again. "Kill-deer, kill-deer, kill-deer, kill-deer." They do not kill deer, but it is the song they sing, especially when they are flying.

The "chick-a-dee-dee-dee, chick-a-dee-dee-dee, chick-a-dee-dee-dee," call of the chickadees is sung by both West Virginia species. The faster Carolina call can be distinguished from the slower black-capped call once it has been heard often enough.

And what birder and many non-birders do not know the well-known song of the northern bobwhite, a quail and popular game bird? It often precedes its song with several loud "bobs" before putting it all together, "Bob, bob, bob, bob-WHITE."

My fourth and last category of mnemonics is "words and phrases." Some of the phrases fit perfectly, but others require a little imagination. The white-throated sparrow mentioned earlier has phrases that fit perfectly. On the other hand, there are some amusing phrases that fit, but we can't say the words fast enough; however, we can think the words fast enough. My favorite is one my secretary, Dot, taught me.

"Does anyone know what a tongue twister is?"

The usual response is, "It's something that if you say it real fast it doesn't come out right, but if you speak it slowly, you can say it."

"Well, I know one you don't know, and I bet you cannot say it. It's the words I put to the music of a bird called a warbling vireo."

I pause for a moment and move my hand up and down as if I am following the music in my mind, then say, "If-I-see-him, I-will-seize-him, and-I-will-squeeze-him, till-he-SQUIRTS." The key here is not being able to say it, but having fun trying.

Another "I can think it, faster than I can say it" song is that of the Canada warbler. "You-got-to-be-slick, and-look-quick, to-see-me," is the mnemonics for the Canada's song.

My college classes are taught outdoors, and it is a challenge to get the students interested in birds. On the bird watching day I often walk up to the biggest guy in the class. When I am almost nose-to-nose with him, I begin yelling, "WHAT DO YOU THINK YOU ARE DOING? IF YOU DON'T LEAVE MY TERRITORY NOW, YOU'LL BE WEARING YOUR BEAK ON THE OTHER SIDE OF YOUR HEAD!"

It's effective, I have their attention, and they listen as I begin to relate bird songs, territories, and other bird-related topics.

With most groups I relate one of the northern cardinal's often-heard songs as "Cheer-cheer-cheer-cheer." With my college students, I use "Beer-beer-beer-beer."

Other phrases I use at opportune moments. If we're out and I hear the-"Wheep-wheep-wheep-wheep" mnemonic most often used to describe the great-crested flycatcher, I might look at the group, point out the song, and then say, "Listen, it's calling your name. Creep-creep-creep-creep."

I cannot do that often, but it happens; and when it does, they enjoy it, but not as much as I do.

With the white-eyed vireo some hear "Chick, cherry-up, chick." When I'm with a group of students, I relate "Chick, hurry-up, Chick."

Then I tell the young ladies in the group, "If you ever meet a young man who talks to you like that, you get rid of him. You deserve more respect than that. Find someone who appreciates you and treats you with respect."

The tufted titmouse sings a name, but not its own, "Peter-peter-peter-peter."

"Nice-old-ladies-don't, CHEW-CHEW-CHEW-CHEW" is the phrase I use for the northern waterthrush.

Another phrase that fits perfectly is for the barred owl. "I-cook-for-me, who-cooks-for-you, Alllll?" is the mnemonic many birders know and use.

The familiar "Sweet-sweet-sweeter-than sweet" tells of the yellow warbler. I have heard this warbler sing other similar songs, but I often hear a perfect rendition of "Sweet-sweet-sweeter-than sweet."

What I suggest to anyone wanting to use mnemonics is to focus on one particular song and make up words or a series of words for that song. Be creative. It doesn't matter what your words are. What matters is what words work for you. One early morning my wife woke me from a sound sleep, shaking me and saying, "I have words. I have words."

Still half asleep I asked, "What are you taking about?

She said, "I have words for that bird's song. What kind of bird is it?"

"It's a Baltimore oriole. What are your words?" I asked.

"Burn your furniture, burn your furniture," Bev said.

Lying in bed I listened as the oriole sang over and over again, "Burn-your-furn-i-ture, burn-your-furn-i-ture, burn-your-furn-i-ture," and it fit perfectly.

TURKEY VULTURES

I said to Jan, "I know a quiet, scenic, private place where we can eat lunch today. No one will be there."

This morning at the A.F.M.O. (Allegheny Front Migration Observatory) was slow. The early wave of birds was over, and less than 100 birds were caught. The day was considered slow because there were more net tenders than we needed; however if there had been 1000 birds, we would have been shorthanded. From day-to-day we never know how many birds will hit the nets. On the slow days much of our time is spent standing or sitting around chatting, and on these days I get antsy to go hiking. The lunch site I picked would require an easy hike about two miles round trip.

All of my Dolly Sods experiences had been in tents; that is, until I met Jan. She did some camping in tents but mostly in trailers and RVs. Years before she introduced me to camping in a trailer. I was resistant, but willing to try. On my hikes I wanted to be exhausted at the end of the day. I wanted meager meals, feeling hungry, but not starving. Going to bed on a full stomach at Dolly Sods just didn't seem right for me. All my life, in physical activities, I gave 100 percent. Here I was camping in a trailer and enjoying it.

On rainy days I would think, "It could be worse. I could be in a tent." Then I would think, "Perish the thought. What kind of sissy have I become?"

Most likely these thoughts were left over from my life in the Projects when being "tough" was part of surviving and not being picked on by other neighborhood kids.

Our trailer had a refrigerator, a luxury of luxuries when in a wilderness area. I liked it, but still, it somehow didn't feel right. Getting used to this lifestyle of abundance at least while in the Dolly Sods Wilderness, required some getting used to, and I was adapting.

We hiked the road northward from the Red Creek Campground. On top of the first rise was a stand of red pine trees probably planted by the Civilian Conservation Corps in the 1930s. A short trail led east toward the Allegheny Front. Once through the trees there were blueberry and huckleberry heaths and still quite a few berries to be had. We stopped often to snack on the berries. The rest of the way we crossed large rock and boulder fields and picked our way using my "path of least resistance" method of bushwhacking. We stopped often to take photos of the lichen mosaics growing on rocks, and sun-bleached branches and tree stumps that had remained exposed to the elements for decades. We were close to our destination, a large outcrop of flat rocks: I had relaxed and ate lunch here many times before but always alone. It seemed important to share this spot with Jan.

The rocks were the perfect vantage point to see the entire valley, north and south, and much of the length of North Fork Mountain to the east. But there was a problem. A reluctant turkey vulture occupied *my* spot. At first I thought, "It's rare to get this close to a TV." Instead of bursting on the scene, we watched from a distance, hoping it wouldn't fly. And it didn't.

When I thought it was time to reclaim my spot, we walked right toward the bird; and it still didn't fly. I likened it to an obstinate teenager who thinks they know all there is to know and won't give an inch. And it was a young bird, still having a gray head instead of the more familiar red –colored head of an adult.

I was reminded of a turkey vulture that used to live at the zoo at Oglebay. Part of its wing was missing, and it could not be released back into the wild. There was an indoor exhibit hall that had large glass doors at each end. Above one of the doors was a concrete overhang where the vulture would roost. When people would walk through the doorway, the vulture would drop to the floor about 15 feet away.

Hearing the thump, visitors would turn around to see this almost three-foot tall, heavy-bodied, bald red-headed bird sternly looking at them. As he began walking toward them, the sheer panic on some faces was priceless, at least to me. More than once I saw a wife jump behind her husband, pushing him forward while he pushed back trying to get away. And if there were children, the family would sometimes all be in a panic trying to escape.

The vulture always seemed to be attacking, but it wasn't. For those who would hold their ground, the bird would simply walk over and untie their shoes. Then it would walk away and return to its perch. Even though some people loved this turkey vulture, others were so afraid they adamantly complained until the bird was removed from the exhibit hall.

Anyway, Jan and I bravely walked right up to the young vulture, and it ran to the edge of the rock and stopped. With our next step, it jumped off and glided effortlessly out toward the valley until it hit a pocket of warm air that carried it high into the sky. We sat and marveled at the view. Through binoculars we could see the banding station far below to the south. There were people sitting in lawn chairs and on rocks as they counted hawks and other raptors and monarch butterflies. The monarch butterflies were streaming past us in what seemed like an endless number. Later we discovered that over 2,400 monarchs had been counted in two hours. It was just one of many special days.

OF MITES AND MEN

Josh came into the house shouting, "Dad, Dad, I want to show you something. It's outside. I found baby birds."

Josh led me into the neighbor's backyard, around to the other side of their house and said, "Look."

"Okay, where are the baby birds?"

"In there," he said, pointing to a hole in one of the concrete blocks.

"How do you know there are baby birds in there?"

"I touched them.

Josh was five and curious, especially about wild things.

Looking up at me he said, "I didn't know there were babies."

"Then why did you reach in?"

"A bird went in."

Josh related how when he ran to the hole and tried to look in, the bird flew out and its wing scraped his face.

Josh reached in and said, "Dad, I feel them. They're warm."

He kept feeling them and said, "I think there are four."

When he pulled his arm out, it was covered with masses of almost microscopic black mites. There were thousands.

Not wanting to frighten him I said, "You know I wouldn't

let anything hurt you, don't you?"

"Yeah."

"Well, there are some tiny animals on your arm, but they won't hurt you."

Looking down at his arm he screamed, "Get them off!"

Horrified, he frantically brushed the mites from his arm.

"It's okay. They won't hurt you," I reassured him. Taking his arm, I said, "Let me help."

Right away some of the mites got on me, and I showed them to Josh.

"What do they feel like?" he asked.

Pointing at his own arm I reminded him, "They're still on you, too. What do they feel like to you?"

"They don't feel like anything," Josh answered.

And he was right. Their tiny size allowed them to move about without being felt. After his initial panic, Josh became calm and curious, and we talked about why the mites were on the birds and why they couldn't harm us.

From a distance we watched a starling going in and out of the hole.

After a while Josh said, "I'm going to ride my big-wheel."

I said, "Whoa there. No big-wheel until you take a shower and wash all the mites off."

"But you said they won't hurt me."

"They won't hurt you, but it's still good to wash them off."

Later I asked him to tell his sisters about what happened to him.

Looking at me as if he had no idea what I was talking about, I reminded him saying, "You know, the bird's nest, the mites."

Josh said, "Oh yeah. I forgot."

BIRD HAWKS

Not all bird watchers like all birds. House (English)
sparrows, European starlings, house finches, and mourning
doves are sometimes considered undesirable because their
numbers will overwhelm a feeding area. When they take over,
chickadees, cardinals, titmice, nuthatches, and other birds
become scarce.

Bird hawks also cause great distress to some people as they
are also attracted to seed-filled feeders, but for the purpose of
eating the birds feeding there. Cooper's and sharp-shinned
hawks, and the American kestrel are considered bird hunters.
The American kestrel is a falcon, a beautiful bird which eats
birds, insects, and mouse-sized mammals. Greg Park and I
once watched a kestrel snatch a house finch from a feeder and
sit on the window ledge in front of us as it picked the finch
apart.

Once I saw a Cooper's hawk appear out of nowhere, snatch
a male cardinal off a feeder and disappear into the forest.
There were times when a Cooper's would dive full force into a
multiflora rose thicket chasing after its next meal.

Talking to people on the phone gave me insights about
how very important birds were to certain groups of people.

One time Bob Gingerich said to me, "Sometimes you spend way too much time on the phone with some callers." He thought my time could be better spent with other job requirements. I agreed, but I had a dilemma. There were some older people who fed birds and called to talk. Based on the conversations and length of the calls, I realized that many of these people had little outside contact with others and wanted someone to talk to. The birds were their entertainment and their company. Some people named the birds that came to their feeders, and others spoke of their birds as if they were their children. When I explained this to Bob, he understood.

Perhaps this was the first call I received of its kind, since I remember it so vividly, but a lady called who was panicked to the point of tears. As she looked on, a hawk had just taken her chickadee, Chrissy, from her feeder.

She pleaded, "Oh please, please, you have to do something."

She was crying uncontrollably. The hawk was in plain sight stripping Chrissy of her feathers, preparing her for a meal. I told the lady to walk away from the window and not watch. All I could do was sympathize with her and try to console her. The conversation ended with me offering to talk with her again if she needed to talk. She was still crying when she hung up.

Hawks and the like eating our beloved birds is how it is; how it must be. Witnessing these events brings different feelings. Sometimes a feeling of sorrow surfaces for the bird being killed, but the feeling is fleeting and ends with me thankful I am not that poor bird or grateful there's nothing out here hunting me for food. And there is the feeling of awe, taking into account the hawk's efficiency and abilities. There is a balance; and although we cannot divorce ourselves from feeling sorrow for certain kinds of creatures, the balance is necessary and we must be careful not to second-guess its purpose.

Another call I received of a similar nature was from a Sister at the Mount de Chantal Visitation Academy in Wheeling. She was British and spoke with a strong accent.

She demanded, "You must come here and trap a kestrel." At the time of the call, the American kestrel was still known as the sparrow hawk; however she was familiar with the European kestrel, and they do look very much alike.

I asked, "Why do I need to trap it?"

"The dreadful thing is killing my linnets."

"I do have a permit to trap birds for research and educational purposes, but your situation doesn't fit into those limitations."

"Let me speak to your superior," she demanded.

"Well, in this situation, I do believe, I am my superior."

She was defiant through the entire conversation, insisting at every opportunity that, "This brutish bird must be stopped," and how, "The linnets are a noble and respectable bird."

Trying to reason with her about the necessity of life and death struggles in nature, she interrupted "Oh, poppy-cock. Surely you do not believe such nonsense."

The conversation ended with neither of us giving ground. Based on the conversation, I deduced the "linnets" were English sparrows which she had fondly adored since her girlhood in England.

There was one occasion concerning a bird hawk and its prey that brought me to a point of simultaneous sorrow and awe. I was near the nature center on a loop trail in winter. A Cooper's hawk glided by overhead, quickly swooped into a tree, and came out carrying a bird. It lighted onto a nearby branch. Through my binoculars I saw it held a very much alive, struggling chickadee. The hawk looked around and then flew down right into the stream where it held the tiny bird underwater. The chickadee continued to struggle, but rarely got its head above water. Soon it was still. I focused on the hawk. It was looking directly at me with "that look."

Some of you, who have looked into the eyes of a Cooper's hawk, will understand when I say, I am reluctant to describe "the look" for fear you will think terrible, undeserved thoughts about this bird.

DURKEY

One of the hike days with my college students had a bird emphasis although I didn't plan it that way. I was walking alongside a student from Uganda, when a large shadow passed over in front of us. I noticed his eyes following it.

Right away I said, "Turkey vulture."

He said, "What?"

I answered, "That shadow that passed was from a turkey vulture."

Several other students overheard and one said, "Mr. Beatty, not that we don't trust you, but how could you know that; you didn't even look up?"

Some of my students have never been in the wild before. This particular day there were two such students, one from inner city D.C. and another from the Bronx. One of my rural West Virginia students asked if he could tell these young men about the durkey. I had no idea what he was referring to, but I said, "Yeah, go ahead."

He said, "You know what a deer is, don't you? They are pretty big and have antlers and are in these woods."

They acknowledged knowing what a deer was.

Then he asked, "Mr. Beatty, are there turkeys in these woods?"

"Yes, I've seen some large flocks out here."

He continued, "Sometimes a deer will breed with a turkey and you get this big bird with a deer head and antlers, and a fat bird body with turkey legs. It can run and it can fly and it doesn't like anything around where it lives. Durkeys will attack anything that moves, even people. And those antlers are sharp and can do some serious damage; that is, if it doesn't stomp you to death with those big turkey feet."

Turning around, I saw the incredulous look on some students' faces and realized that Shawn and Eddie were swallowing the durkey story hook, line, and sinker.

My West Virginia student added, "They strike when you least expect it, when you don't see it coming; and if you do see it coming, it's the last thing you ever do see."

Before long Shawn and Eddie knew it was all a big joke by the reactions of all the other students.

The only reason I let this continue as long as it did was because of the camaraderie between the physical education majors. Of all my students, they have the most fun together, they know each other better, and they are always joking around with each other. And to be honest, I wanted to see where the story was going and how far it would go.

PILEATED PROWESS

Fortunate is how I feel about having so many wonderful encounters with wild creatures. These encounters are now memories. And the best part of being a birder is that there are more great memories to be made. There are moments in time that define who we are. Some moments change us for all time. One of the birds that has changed me is the pileated woodpecker. Two of my significant moments have involved pileated woodpeckers.

The pileated woodpecker was one of the earliest birds I could recognize and it was greatly responsible for encouraging me to chase and discover for the rest of my life. Near my home was a deep wooded ravine that had a small stream running its length. Several forks ran up the steep hillsides allowing the stream to receive significant water. Often when I was exhausted, I found a comfortable place to rest, usually a soft spot at the base of a tree where I could lean back, watch, listen and think. One morning as I sat, relaxing, catching my breath, there was a sound—just the whisper of something scratching nearby. Then I heard a familiar but also whispered sound...cluck, cluck. I immediately thought "pileated" but the quietness of the sound made me think I was wrong. Then there was a movement. No more than 20 feet away half of a face was peering at me from behind a tree. It was a pileated!

I remained motionless. The bird's half face would slowly appear, stare intently at me, and then just as slowly disappear behind the tree. After repeating this peeking game several times the woodpecker must have decided I posed no threat and stretched its face, head and neck out from behind the tree. It bobbed its head cartoon-like, up-and-down and side-to-side.

Then it began to "talk" to me, at least that is what it seemed like. I heard sounds I had never heard before from a pileated. Not the strident calls this magnificent forest bird usually booms through the forest—these were whispered, they were soft, apparently directed to me...clucks, mews and whimpering sounds. When the bird decided to move away it did so gradually, to the nearest tree behind it, then to the next and with each new tree the sounds became louder and louder as it kept a watchful eye on me.

Finally it leaped and, with several powerful downward thrust of its wings, was soon far away, leaving its loud more familiar notes and calls echoing through the forest. This was a very personal encounter with the incredible pileated.

Jan and I are both bird banders. We average about two banding days each week. In 2015 we banded 1196 new birds on our property. In late May of that year we had banded five baby eastern bluebirds. It was a beautiful spring day. High above in nearby treetops we could occasionally hear migrating warblers on their way north. I decided to put a mist net up to see if we might catch and band something interesting.

We kept an eye on the mist net but had just come in to eat some lunch. All of a sudden, Jan heard me yell, **"If I tell you to...run as fast as you can out to the back net and hold**

the net around the bird until I get there!!" Her banding experience helped her read my mind. She took one look for the direction of my eyes and quickly but quietly slipped out the side door and started toward the backyard.

Out the back door I ran, screaming like a banshee toward the bird on the other side of the fence. The startled pileated woodpecker feeding on a nearby stump flew right into the net and was momentarily caught. I stopped short at the fence and held my breath to see if Jan could get there in time.

SIDEBAR: *The reason Jan had to run to the net was because she was dressed and ready to go; I, on the other hand, had already removed my dirty pants, shoes and socks. Taking a bird like this out of a mist net can be involved and the bird often causes quite a commotion. Even though our neighbors aren't all that close, in the past a screaming woodpecker has brought a neighbor to the net to see what we were doing. Net-tending in my skivvies probably wouldn't make for good neighbor relations.*

This was only the second pileated woodpecker I have ever banded and it was Jan's first. It took both of us to control the powerful bird for the banding process and photos afterwards. As we marveled at the bird Jan said, "Doesn't it just remind you of a tiny dinosaur?" The pileated has a remarkably long neck compared to other woodpeckers. Its regal head and crest, constantly-moving lengthy neck, long-clawed feet and piercing stare reminded me of a miniature, colorful Velociraptor of Jurassic Park fame. We studied the long chisel-like beak, and the stiff tail feathers…knowing how rare this encounter was. Everything about the pileated woodpecker is impressive.

Unlike the first loud pileated I had previously caught and banded which shrieked a constant series of sharp calls and screams, this bird was very quiet. Finally, photos accomplished, it was time to release the "tiny dinosaur". Jan coached me on how to use the video feature of her camera to record the occasion. I started recording and she opened her hands. Our new friend flew high on the trunk of the nearest black locust tree. The last we saw him, he was hopping his way around to the back side of the trunk. I just couldn't tell if he peeked back around the trunk to look at me.

"THE FEELING"

For several years during my tenure as naturalist at
the Brooks Nature Center I wrote a story for a quarterly
newsletter. My stories were mostly about encounters with
wild creatures; informative and personal since they were
based on my own experiences. We exchanged newsletters with
a number of other nature centers. A center in Maryland had a
quote that describes almost perfectly how I feel about nature;
it describes what I have written about as "the feeling." This is
how I feel about so many of my experiences in nature...

"You shall know the night—it's space, its light, its music
You shall see earth sink and darkness and the universe
    appear.
No roof shall shut you from the presence of the moon,
You shall see mountains rise in the transparent shade
    before dawn.
You shall see – and feel, first light, and hear a ripple in the
    stillness.
You shall enter the living shelter of the forest.
You shall walk where only the wind has walked before.
You shall know immensity, and see continuing the

primeval forces of the world. You shall know not
one small segment but the whole of life, strange,
miraculous, living, dying, changing....
You shall see storms arise, and, drenched and deafened,
shall exult in them.
You shall top a rise and behold creation.
And you shall need the tongues of angels to tell what you
have seen."

By Nancy Newell in "This is the American Earth" by Ansel
Adams

WHAT IT ALL MEANS TO ME

I have always told people, "If you want to see and experience wonderful nature moments you must make yourself available to the opportunities."

Being available means getting outside in wild places alone. Taking a companion means talking, and talking alerts other creatures to your presence, reducing opportunity. Much of what I relate in teaching or in story has happened to me within walking distance of my home.

The key is going outside and experiencing the seasons and the elements firsthand. My perception of nature is very different than that of most other people. Some have told me, "I know what you mean. I went out early one morning," or "My Dad's a hunter and he goes out a lot." Unfortunately, no, you don't. If you go out *one* morning *now and then* or spend your outdoor times *some* days during hunting season, you still limit your opportunities.

I don't expect to bump into many people who have seen and experienced what I have. How many people do you know who have had fulltime jobs all their adult life that require them to go out and chase birds, photograph wildflowers, fungi, insects, and the like without limits?

Early on I did take advantage of many wonderful people who taught me. I didn't ask; they offered. Find these kinds of people. You will know them; they are friendly and eager. And when you know what they know, pay it forward. Bring your life full circle by freely giving what you have received.

I put myself in these situations by being outside in wild places. Most of my life is past, but I do not feel old. Nature rejuvenates me physically and mentally. Chasing birds takes me to places I hadn't anticipated…down a steep hill, across a gully, over a fallen tree. I am more fit because of it. My mind races as it chases after a new song. Is it a warbler, maybe a vireo, perhaps a flycatcher? There is no boredom…only wonderful, fun challenges for body and mind. And my spirit soars to heavenly places as I sigh with feelings too deep for words. How can one not go outdoors? It completes a person, mind, body and soul.

With the wonder comes obligation. Kind, available people shared their lives with me. How can I not do likewise? Do I want my knowledge and experience to end with me? Of course not. The joy of chasing birds can be relived in the first scarlet tanager, indigo bunting or pileated woodpecker that someone else sees. I revel in their awe and am grateful for being the person who can guide them into experiences that can change their life forever. It's me…all over again. The eastern bluebirds on sumac berry clusters rush in again and again, each time I see that sparkle in an eye. How fortunate are we who have become birders. Life is good, especially outdoors!